The Great Explosion

'A subtle, human history of the early twentieth century . . . Explosions are a fruitful subject in Dillon's hands, one that enables him to reflect movingly on the instant between life and death, on the frailty of human endeavour, and on the readiness of nations to tear one another apart. *The Great Explosion* deftly covers a tumultuous period of history while centring on the tiniest moments – just punctuation marks in time' *Financial Times*

'[Dillon's] main interest lies in the discovery that these natural wastes are also littered with the often strangely inscrutable debris of various human projects. More like a derelict art installation than a conventional landscape, his marsh is a place where semi-wild horses graze among derelict remnants of brick and concrete, where the howling wind uses rusted wire as a gibbet on which to hang tattered fragments of plastic from the sea, and where you can walk on paths that have outlasted the buildings and jetties to which they once led. For some, these once-malarial wetlands may be no more than a vast brownfield site waiting for another round of development. Dillon, however, recognizes them as the true face of a nation "haunted" by its military-industrial past: a habitat not just of plants and wild creatures but of peopled "stories" that can never be pulled fully clear of the mud . . . A brilliant evocation of place grasped in its modernity' *Guardian*

'Instead of a piece of nature writing, *The Great Explosion* is an excavation – not of a landscape but of a kind of estuary modernism, an account of what Dillon calls the "unnatural history" of the Kent marshes and its associations with the manufacture of high explosives . . . The result is exhilarating . . . *The Great Explosion* is a barrage of impressions and narrative . . . and

'[Dillon's] account of the Faversham explosion is as bold as it is dramatic, while his descriptive passages about the marshlands of Kent are so evocative that you can practically feel the mud sticking at your feet' *Evening Standard*

'Dillon . . . has a W. G. Sebald-like gift for interrogating the landscape . . . A work of real elegiac seriousness that goes to the heart of a case of human loss and destruction in England's sinister pastures green' *Irish Times*

'What a fascinating, unclassifiable, brilliant book, confirming Brian Dillon's reputation as one of our most innovative and elegant non-fictioneers. No one else could have written it' Robert Macfarlane, author of *The Old Ways*, *Landmarks*, *The Wild Places* and *Mountains of the Mind*

'*The Great Explosion* is exhilarating and moving and lyrical. It is a quiet evisceration of a landscape through the discovery of a lost history of destructiveness, a meditation on Englishness, an autobiography, a mapping of absences. I loved it' Edmund de Waal, author of *The Hare with Amber Eyes*

'Forensic, fascinating, endlessly interesting, Brian Dillon's personal journey into explosive territory is a gripping account of disaster and ingenuity. His language is never less than brilliant: in a quiet, measured manner, he sums up apocalyptic scenes and human stories. With accustomed literary skill, marshalling intriguing facts and an acute historical sensitivity, *The Great Explosion* travels from the twenty-first century back to the Great War, turning industrial chaos and deathly hardware into something oddly, evanescently beautiful' Philip Hoare, author of *Leviathan* and *The Sea Inside*

ABOUT THE AUTHOR

Brian Dillon is the author of *In the Dark Room*, a memoir that won the Irish Book Award for Nonfiction, and *Tormented Hope: Nine Hypochondriac Lives*, which was shortlisted for the Wellcome Trust Book Prize. He teaches at the Royal College of Art.

The Great Explosion

Gunpowder, the Great War, and
a disaster on the Kent marshes

BRIAN DILLON

PENGUIN BOOKS

PENGUIN BOOKS

UK | USA | Canada | Ireland | Australia
India | New Zealand | South Africa

Penguin Books is part of the Penguin Random House group of companies
whose addresses can be found at global.penguinrandomhouse.com.

First published by Penguin Ireland 2015
Published in Penguin Books 2016

001

Copyright © Brian Dillon, 2015

The moral right of the author has been asserted

Set in 12.48/15.78 pt Perpetua
Typeset by Jouve (UK), Milton Keynes
Printed in Great Britain by Clays Ltd, St Ives plc

A CIP catalogue record for this book is available from the British Library

ISBN: 978-0-241-95676-2

www.greenpenguin.co.uk

For Madaleine, Isaac and Genevieve

I tried to breathe but my breath would not come and I felt myself rush bodily out of myself and out and out and out and all the time bodily in the wind.

Ernest Hemingway, *A Farewell to Arms* (1929)

Contents

I

The Gunpowder Archipelago

Overture

It begins at night, when the machines are idle and the weak sun has sunk into an estuarine horizon.

At first there is little or nothing to see or hear, no clues regarding energies soon to be unleashed on the landscape, on its low buildings and the bodies moving among them. There is a new moon tonight, almost invisible, but the darkness below is not complete, nor the silence. There are lamps behind the windows of some of the buildings, though heavy curtains have been pulled to conceal them, and flashlights regularly probe the more thoroughly blacked-out districts of the marsh. Within certain structures, fires must be kept burning till dawn. There is the sound of heavy boots on wooden boards, scraping on concrete, plashing into wet mud and grass. There are voices low and weary, others cheerful as they drift away towards the deeper darkness at the edge of the site. We may imagine that the voices keep up despite fatigue, if only to ward off other sounds in the night air, with their intimations of wildness and death close at hand – the strangely human cry of a she-fox, the barn owl's screech that is more like a hiss. In darkness, and without the clamour of work, the place substitutes other sights and other noises, as much of watchfulness and readiness as of the day's end.

It is a Saturday night in the second spring of the Great War. Here on the marshes, among the huts and houses that the new workers have learned to call 'danger buildings', each day is much like any other. Only nightfall brings rest from the tasks at hand: unloading liquids and powders and pulp from boats and trucks, mixing or purifying the noxious mass, draining and sifting and drying. Or, out at the western edge of the factory, pouring and pressing, shaping this poison till it will squeeze into its metal bed and sleep for a while among serried ranks of shells or bombs before being hefted back onto lorries and trams, or down to the jetty. The stuff, so the older workers say – and some of them have been here since before the war – will strip your hands raw, or turn your whole skin yellow in a matter of weeks; for this reason, the young women who have come to work at the factory in the past year, and at others like it, have become known as 'canary girls'. There is nothing to be done but pull the belts tighter on thick new uniforms and think of the danger money and the men at the front, for whom this redoubled effort, this acceleration of production, was begun last summer. And not think too hard about the fires and worse that locals remember, about rumours and reports from other factories.

When it starts, we may surmise, it is with the merest pop or crackle. Unheard, unseen – or, even if noticed, of no very pressing import to those workers who know the place well. Later, at least one witness will report hearing a fizzing sound as he passed by building number 833 in the morning, but by then the process would have been well under way. Tomorrow the small sounds now quickening infinitesimally in this corner of the landscape will grow louder, until at last they gather around them other sounds of voices and machinery and movement, shouts and fast-moving rumours, telephone bells and revving engines. A rush of air and flame and earth, of shredded metal and split timbers. And at length a noise – or several, subsumed into one – that not all of those present will have time to hear. A sound that is also a force: a solid wave rushing across a flat expanse, a sound that swells among the surrounding buildings, the nearby fields, the boats and jetties of the shoreline, stretches out towards towns and cities, military camps on distant coasts. A sound grown from the seed of this small agitation of the air, here in the dark.

Excursus

New Year's Day, and once again I am walking the marshes of north Kent, hoping to summon a few ghosts. It has become a tradition: for the past decade and a half my partner F and I have spent New Year's Eve with friends who live out here on the edge of the old gunpowder works – the site is now a nature reserve – and most years we have all four struck out late in the morning into this lattice of ditches and paths, among stock-still sheep, expensively equipped birdwatchers and certain low scattered ruins that long ago I promised our hosts I would research properly. Today, though, we are happily distracted from our occasional conjectures regarding the events that occurred, some way off to the north-west of our starting point, in April 1916. Our friends' three young children are with us, and there are scooters to be steadied on the unevenly gravelled footpath, splashing steps to be counted across the largest puddles and an unseasonable number of flowers to be collected where the path slopes grassily away to drainage ditches on either side. I'm amazed, midwinter, to find myself bending down so that the eldest, our goddaughter, aged six in a matter of days, can gleefully blow a dandelion clock in my face.

Our friends live in Uplees House, one of a pair of large detached houses built at the start of the second decade of the twentieth century. This part of the county was for centuries the site of a sizeable military-industrial complex, and for some years the houses were occupied by managers from two of the explosives companies whose buildings and infrastructure had by that time ramified from the nearby village of Oare towards the Swale – the body of water that separates the Kent coast from the Isle of Sheppey – then along the shore in the direction of the estuary of the Medway River. There was another, much older, works adjacent to Oare, and still another, in fact the oldest, in the local market town of Faversham. Before this landscape and its coastline become visible we have to walk along the narrow tree-lined road that separates the two big houses, past a couple of bungalows on the left and a decayed orchard on the right where in the spring, when the weather turns, a few dwarf sheep (curious, friendly creatures you might from a distance take for lambs) will graze among grey branches fallen from the tall, old-fashioned apple trees. The road narrows to an unfinished path and brings us to a small house surrounded by unruly hedges and several elaborate and run-down birdhouses: an odd agglomeration of mock-Tudor replicas, raised on wooden poles, of the cottage to which they belong. There is an old wrought-iron gate – it is always open, stuck in a wet tussock – and then a sturdy aluminium one that gives out onto the marsh. At this time of year you have to open it wide to skirt around the sucking mud by the gatepost.

Here, away from the trees, flat land extends in most directions. A hawk passes overhead, too small to be a buzzard, its

wings too wide for a sparrowhawk. Peregrine? Hobby? It has gone before we decide. To the right, that is to the east, lurk a few dilapidated buildings that are reputed to have belonged to a pottery or tile works; in the grass between there and the ditch lies the rusted ribcage of an obscure item of farm machinery. Before us, the marsh. There are the usual sheep — these full size and filthy: a surprise to find them out here at the start of the year — and the small concrete-and-brick huts in which we suppose they must sometimes huddle. On my early visits here, I excitedly took these modest structures for remains of the gunpowder works, but the actual ruins are much harder to see against the grass and reeds, the shining lengths and irregular expanses of inland water.

To the west, on the other side of the footpath, the land is firmer. Only a sparse tracery of ditches interrupts the hummocky ground, the sheep, their droppings, and the few ragged concrete stelae visible from here. I have sometimes wandered off the path and along a track that crosses the ditch, to poke around at these anonymous grey platforms and occasional clumps of rufous steel.

Today's is a slow progress towards the shore; the fat tyres of the buggy I am pushing bump constantly on the deeply pitted path and threaten to wake its cargo of well-wrapped one-year-old. There may soon be tears from the other two as the thrill of visitors at breakfast time turns to cold and fatigue on the marshes. We aim to make it at least as far as the next gate, at the end of this straight path perpendicular to the coast. Just beyond the gate there is a curious reservoir or sump whose black surface has been in retreat for several months, seeming to thicken with every inch of oily water lost so that now it looks even more sinister than usual, the sloping sides of the old pebbled concrete threatening to reveal God-knows-what. We have often joked that one Sunday afternoon in summer – because ordinarily only high summer would see the water at such a low level – we might pass through the gate, ascend the grass slope to a surrounding fence and discover a human skull or skeletal limb poking from the iridescent slime, or the rusted curves of an ancient automobile with a collection of bones still clutching the wheel. It seems more plausible than ever as we reach the edge and pause before allowing the children forward to gasp and 'Ewww!' at the slick rectangular map of algae and dark water below us.

The children's good humour is holding up, so we press on to the grass ridge that serves as sea wall and well-trodden route west for the numerous walkers and birdwatchers that the Oare marshes attract every weekend. It is hard to find oneself alone out here at any time; such is the flatness of the territory and the richness of avian life that there are almost always figures moving on the horizon, paused statue-still with binoculars by the water's edge or passing in and out of the several wooden hides built in recent decades. Some of the 'twitchers' are dressed like hunters in ex-military gear, and so heavily laden with high-powered optical equipment, cameras,

tripods and monopods that you would think they have been
stationed here as guards, or have launched an ill-concealed but
vigilantly crewed commando raid on the coast. Today, however, as we turn left along the shore we meet only anoraked
loners with modest paraphernalia, and cheerful New Year
family outings like our own. The wind hits us so strongly up on
the sea wall that we can hardly hear their greetings.

As we quicken our pace, aiming to turn when we reach
the remains of a wooden jetty a couple of hundred yards ahead,
we try to identify certain landmarks to the west: the road
bridge to Sheppey gleaming white; the crosshatching of twin
power stations in the distance, Kingsnorth and Grain. It is just
a couple of years since the environmentalist protests at Kingsnorth against plans for a further coal-fired station, and a
notorious police operation to contain them. In a bizarrely
heavy-handed response to the protest, officers were bussed in
from around the country, 1,500 of them, and many housed at
the University of Kent, in Canterbury, not far from the house
I share with F. As they set out on a Saturday morning for their
rendezvous with the protestors, police vans tore past our
house with speakers blaring 'I Predict a Riot', a song by the
Kaiser Chiefs that I already hated. When the inevitable clash
was over, it was revealed that police had confiscated toilet
rolls, board games and clown costumes. Twelve officers had
reported, and been treated for, injuries sustained at Kingsnorth.
Of these, three had succumbed to heat exhaustion, one had cut
himself climbing a fence, another while fixing his car, and six
were bitten or stung by insects including a 'possible wasp'.

Perhaps the Isle of Grain is wilder, more hostile than it
looks from here. (It is not, in any case, an island, but the tip of
a low tongue of land around which the Thames, to the north,

and the Medway, to the south, flow into the sea.) I have been inside the Grain station: a part-time facility now put into service only when a deficit threatens the National Grid; at such times, my guide told me, the station can run effectively with one member of staff to oversee the whole plant, as if piloting a ghost ship along the Medway shore. As we walk in its direction I wonder if this person is on duty today, and I recall for our friends the remarkably decrepit look of the place inside: pipework conspicuously taped up, steam escaping rusted corners in the ductwork, a small oil slick on the floor of the turbine hall.

Beyond the Isle of Grain, with its massive container port and gas storage facility, lies the mouth of the Thames. The Kent landscape of certain Dickens novels gives way here to Joseph Conrad country, an ancient estuarine expanse recalling Roman invasion, medieval industry, prison hulks and malaria — an 'immensity of grey tones', says the author of *The Mirror of the Sea*. The flattened or foreshortened objects before us are getting mixed up with my knowledge of what is out there beyond them, and I turn instead, so far as the distraction of small hands in mine will allow, towards the earthworks, ruins and other artefacts nearby. There is the jetty, almost sunk in the shoreline mud even at low tide, where I suspect (but will need to confirm) that finished shells and bombs and other products of the munitions factories were for many decades loaded onto boats and sent into the Swale for transport to military magazines and thence to war. There are the ditches to our left, with now and then a pathway through them onto the flatness of the marsh and the firmer, higher ground beyond. And for a few minutes there is a distant but thrilling view across one such ditch to some proper ruins: behind a stand of low, wind-hobbled trees a patch of clean concrete, and scattered about it thick lozenges and chunks of cruder concrete, with here and there a squiggled lance of rusted reinforcement tethering it to the base or foundations.

We turn as planned at the jetty. On our way back to Uplees a heron rises clumsily from the ditch and gathers itself on the path ahead of us, astonishingly close. Astonishing for us, that is, and not for the heron, which totters calmly in our direction for a while on its cartoon-bird legs before thinking better of it and labouring up into the air in the opposite direction, till it vanishes among the remains of the old pottery. Not for the first time I wonder at how little of the industrial history of this place remains on the marsh, how much of it has vanished and how swiftly what was left has been engulfed by wildlife. Of course, the land has never within historical memory been left to its own devices, or anything near: it was agricultural first, industrial second, then farmland again with aspirations, realized in the late twentieth century, to an accommodation between nature and culture. It has long, that is, been a reserve of one kind or another, parcelled up and apportioned, charted and chartered.

The writing of the disaster

Our sense of the strangeness of a place may increase rather than diminish with time and intimacy. The way a landscape opens up to myth or invention as well as to historical curiosity, the portals it offers to other stories and other timescales, legendary as well as verifiable, our capacity to get lost in real or fantastical territory: all of this has seemed in the case of

Kent, or at least the eastern, especially coastal, portions of the county that I know best, only to have become more involuted the longer I have lived here.

I have been in Canterbury almost twenty years now, and at first – when I was in my mid twenties – I was almost wholly ignorant of and indifferent to the political, maritime, military and industrial heritage of the place, not to mention its geology, plants and wildlife. At that time I was stuck fast in an unacknowledged, untreated depression that was bound up with the early deaths of my parents and my eager, then laboured, then receding efforts at an academic career. The period is fogged in my memory, but I am pretty sure that I actively despised the sort of attentiveness to my surroundings that might bring with it an appreciation of nature or even the texture, history, day-to-day changes or passing impressions of the world around me. Maybe the names for that are simply immaturity, anxiety, naivety and inexperience, but the tendency seems extreme at this remove and a symptom of my malaise. In one of my lowest periods I had done the worst thing possible: I had left home in Dublin and moved to a small university town – a city, as I thought, and as it calls itself on account of its cathedral – that I had not even mustered the energy or interest to explore before relocating. I felt on arrival in Canterbury, in the autumn of 1995, as though I might as easily have moved to some unexceptional town in Ireland: Drogheda, for example, or Longford. For a few years, with other things on my feebled mind, I was mostly oblivious to the place in which I lived, beyond its potential to fulfil or frustrate my hopes of academic success, friendship, love and, later on, simple survival.

I had been living in Kent for about eight months before I even thought to go for a walk beyond the circuit of campus and

town centre. One Sunday morning early in the summer of
1996 I left my room at the university and set out on foot with
a friend into the countryside, mapless and with no idea where
we were going. We wandered roughly north-west for hours
along footpaths and bridleways, via tracts of managed woodland, through fields of wheat and rape, across bridges and
under flyovers, till we admitted we were totally lost, and had
to be directed towards Whitstable by some teenagers we met
on the path. The coastal town seemed dismal and sleepy to me
then, with its flinty beach and black fishermen's sheds, its
quaint pubs and cafés. (This was a few years before Whitstable's reimagining as middle-class enclave and weekend
destination for certain notable 'creative' and media folk.) I
recall a sign in the window of a twee tea shop informing us that
the horror-movie actor Peter Cushing had visited every day
towards the end of his life.

Whitstable was not quite so grim as Hastings, to the
south-west and just over the county border in Sussex, where
we ended up on another grey Sunday some weeks later. With
time to kill while moving off-campus to a rented house in Canterbury, a few of us drove with our belongings out to the coast
and looked in wonderment at the decayed remains of the famously garish, boisterous English seaside. Here was a dilapidated
seafront on which elderly townsfolk, or maybe day trippers,
were lined up, many in wheelchairs, drinking tea out of poly-
styrene cups and staring at the blank Channel – they were
waiting, I sneered, waiting for death. Posters on the boarded-
up amusement arcades announced that the wrestler Giant
Haystacks, whose television appearances we remembered
from childhood in the 1970s, would soon appear at the local
theatre. None of this endeared me to the idea, fast becoming

a reality as my research and writing faltered and I realized there was little or nothing to go home to in Ireland, that I would have to spend more time, a year at least I thought, in this part of England.

As that year turned into several years, my attitude to my new home did not improve. It was not somewhere I had chosen to make my life but a place, I liked to say when the depression properly took hold, in which I had *ended up*. When my girlfriend, whose outlook was more practical and more optimistic, drove me out to the country in hope of elevating my mood, I reacted with sullen indifference to the pleasures of rural Kent, and loudly announced that there was simply nothing there. We can joke about it now: our first romantic moments by the river Stour, when a rat scrabbled into moonlit view on the opposite bank; an afternoon's escape from the office we shared with others on campus to lie on the stones in the rain at Seasalter, just along the coast from Whitstable. From walks with friends in the country or the woods about Canterbury I seemed always to return muddier than everyone else, drenched and furious, cursing this unplanned life in the sticks. I remember weekend drives to places like Rye, where even Henry James's house did not interest me; I could not connect the great novels with what I thought was the crushing whimsy of the place. I didn't know then that James had written so lucidly about the English landscape, and about the country's already nostalgic or decayed towns, Kent's among them. In the pages of *Lippincott's Magazine* in 1877, he described a visit to Canterbury: 'While I stood there a violent thunderstorm broke over the cathedral; great rumbling gusts and rain-drifts came sweeping through the open sides of the crypt and, mingling with the potent mouldy smell, made me feel as if I had descended into the very bowels of history.'

Something started to change in me around the time, aged thirty, that I finally accommodated myself to the mundane miseries of my past and gave up my academic ambitions, resolving instead on another sort of life. If I was to be a writer of some kind, however small my first progress in that direction, then theoretically I might live anywhere, which suddenly meant to my surprise and relief that I might as well live here, where I already found myself. And with this abstract discovery I began actually to notice where I was, what the landscape looked and felt like, to discover how it had been in the distant and the recent past, what it might be turning into. I do not doubt it is a cliché of the intermittent or former depressive's account of things – the sense that one undergoes on recovery a literal awakening from somnolence, reclusion and detachment as much as a liberation from agony. But I felt and still feel as though for the first time in my life I had become the sort of person who notices the world around him.

It did not matter that what I noticed was as much composed of bland modern infrastructure and retail or leisure precincts as mature countryside and historic settlements. Even the motorways and housing estates began to seem interesting, and also interestingly antique. What I felt most keenly was that I had woken in a field of ruins, brightly lit, and with endlessly surprising associations. At a sanatorium in Ashford – the fact still amazes me – the ascetic French philosopher and political radical Simone Weil died from tuberculosis and malnutrition in 1943. The Grosvenor Sanatorium is long closed, the building turned into a police training facility and later an educational activity centre; but a Simone Weil Avenue was named nearby in 1983, and her hat is on permanent display at the town's civic centre. It was the very dialectic between the run-down and regenerating textures of the region that began to engage me. All of its aspects seemed connected.

Of course, some of what I discovered was part of the official history that the county, and the south-east of England in general, tells and retells itself constantly. In Rochester, on the Medway, which for years had been for me just a glum stop on the train journey into London, huddled around the town's modest castle and cathedral, I found myself one afternoon in the midst of a Dickens Weekend. Half the population, it seemed, had got themselves up as characters from the novels – shoeless orphans, portly beadles, matrons in picturesque hats – and the other half were selling mock-Victorian curios by the side of the street: I recall in particular a display of dried teasels crafted to look like hedgehogs and dressed in tiny Dickensian costumes. At the furthest extreme, or so it seemed, from such eccentricities were the county's monuments to its political and military history: the medieval castles and later manor houses; the Martello towers that punctuate the southern stretch of Channel coast; the vast stone defences at ports such as Dover, with their concrete annexes added during the First and Second World Wars; traces of the Cold War now opened to the public and signposted from motorways – 'This way to the secret nuclear bunker'.

Living for a time in the early 2000s on the outskirts of Herne Bay – another seaside town, this one largely resistant to the gentrification of the coast then under way – I found that any number of twentieth-century ruins were within easy reach, or tantalizingly close even if inaccessible. From the front at Herne Bay one faced a horizon dotted with sea forts from the Second World War, and closer to the shore the skeletal remains of a pavilion that once stood at the end of the town's late-nineteenth-century pier, which at 3,787 feet was for a time the longest in the country after Southend's. The pavilion dated from 1910; when it opened there was music, dancing and skating to divert promenaders, among whom were many language students from across the Channel. As the century went on, Herne Bay, once the most genteel of Kent's resorts, slowly declined along with all the rest. The crumbling pier itself had closed down decades ago and the pavilion finally been orphaned by a storm on the 11th of January 1978.

From a friend – the artist Jeremy Millar, who was making a film on the subject – I learned that the pier had been an unlikely object of attention for Marcel Duchamp, who holidayed at Herne Bay in the summer of 1913. Accompanying his sister, who was studying English at the nearby Lynton College, a few minutes' walk from the front, the artist spent two weeks playing tennis and scribbling notes for his *Large Glass*, the vastly complex composition of mysteriously sexualized motifs, executed on glass, that he would make over the next few years – though in the end it remained 'definitively unfinished'. 'I am not dead; I am in Herne Bay,' Duchamp wrote to the painter Max Bergmann early in August. On the 8th of the month he wrote to a friend, Raymond Dumouchel: 'The traveller is enchanted. Superb weather. As much tennis as possible. A few Frenchmen for me to avoid learning English, a sister who is enjoying herself a lot.' We know the siblings spent four days sightseeing in London, but whether they availed themselves of a road trip from Herne Bay to visit Canterbury Cathedral, or struck out along the shore to see the ruined church and fragments of Roman fort at Reculver, there are no clues. All that remains of Duchamp's time in Kent are the drawings he made for *The Large Glass*, a small photograph

depicting the illuminated pier, which he tore from a local
newspaper, and an enigmatic inscription: 'An electric fête
recalling the decorative lighting of Magic city or Luna Park, or
the Pier Pavilion at Herne Bay.' For his film, Jeremy had
amassed this scant evidence and added a few speculations of his
own. He turned his camera on fragments of the town that
seemed to rhyme with images in Duchamp's work: air vents
above a modern pavilion on the shore; the nested red buckets
of a builder's chute on Downs Park, near the old Lynton College. And he framed the college building itself, now a private
house, and remarked upon its sash windows, an architectural
detail he suspected Duchamp had never seen till he came to
England. The link may be fanciful; but having seen the lights of
Herne Bay and lingered in its decorous streets Duchamp had
written about his unfinished work: 'The picture will be executed on two large sheets of glass about 1m 20 × 1,40 / one
above the other (demountable).'

The idea that this coast, let alone such a tatty place as Herne
Bay, should have had any connection at all with the energy of
modernist art either side of the First World War came as a
shock. (I should have known better, and known it earlier,
because of course there was the example of T. S. Eliot working
on *The Waste Land* in 1921 at Margate – in those early years in
Kent, I taught the poem to undergraduates and never once
thought of the real town close by. It was Jeremy Millar who
later pointed out to me that there is no plaque to Eliot attached
to the seafront shelter where he sat and wrote, only a sign
nearby for some near-anagrammatic toilets.) But it seemed
that the whole territory was opening up in the way that Herne
Bay had done. I had known, as everybody did, about Derek
Jarman's house at Dungeness: a shingled point at the extreme

south-east of the county where, in the decade before his death in 1994, Jarman increasingly retreated and made one of his greatest films, *The Garden*. Around 1996 I had gone there with F, but I now remembered little of the trip apart from the suspicious way locals in the nearest shop had eyed us when we stopped to buy a disposable camera. At that time I was still deep in the phase of my hostility towards Kent, and if I thought at all about Jarman's relationship with the landscape and its inhabitants I most likely imagined his presence and his garden as creative affronts if not to the bleakness of the landscape – the garden was made of detritus from that landscape, after all – then certainly towards what I considered the glum provincial history of the place. In fact, Jarman's house and garden were a homage of sorts to a Romantic ideal of rural and eccentric England with which the artist and film-maker was ambivalently in love.

Jarman's was – and is: his partner still owns it – one of a line of fishermen's cottages that runs along the stones towards a pub, three lighthouses (one working, another decommissioned, a third the stump of the eighteenth-century lighthouse) and in the distance the louring grey hulk of a nuclear power station. I went back to Dungeness ten years ago and found that I tuned in quickly to the obvious and obscure currents of energy traversing the landscape: the maritime history that produced several generations of lookout posts and visible warnings for ships rounding the ness; old railway lines still to be seen among the stones; the location of PLUTO, the pipeline under the ocean that supplied Allied ships on the other side of the Channel in 1944; the panic hiss of power lines overhead and the unthinkable forces at work inside the twin reactors, Dungeness A and B. I seem to have a habit of visiting run-down power stations, because I have been inside this one too. When it closed, the local television news, having got wind a few years ago of my interest in Kent's decaying industrial heritage, invited me to tour the station and be interviewed by their weather presenter. I stood with her in the turbine hall in big white boots and hard hat, declaiming uncertainly about the heyday of British engineering and the decline of British optimism. On a recent visit with students from London we found the turbine hall open on one side, with excised lumps of its rusting machinery lying just inside the fence on the seaward side, like beached cetaceans.

In a county where, wars aside, the most frequently invoked histories were medieval and Victorian, this triangular segment of the Kent coast was a kind of nexus or relay by which the technological ghosts of the past century might become live again, at least in the imagination. When I was there, Dungeness seemed to stand for the way the whole county was haunted by its military past and its wartime ruins. Among these spectres the most thrilling were the sound mirrors at Greatstone, a short walk back up the eastern coast from Dungeness. Here, a few hundred yards inland and surrounded by gravel pits, stand three curious relics of the fretful 1930s. (There are others dotted around the south-east coast, but none so sculptural or massive as these.) Acoustic methods for locating enemy aircraft had been devised during the First World War, and involved soldiers listening from inside deep trenches, where sounds from the surrounding landscape were suppressed. Later, devices were constructed that would do the same job in a more concentrated fashion and were also mobile: bowl-shaped metal noise collectors with simple sound-conducting tubes and ear-pieces attached, like giant stethoscopes. The sound mirrors are versions of these on a vastly expanded scale, executed in re-inforced concrete and facing out to sea. The largest is 200 feet wide, an arcing wall of stained and spalling concrete with the remains of a small hut tucked behind its midpoint. This hut was the listening station inside which a soldier wearing head-phones would sit. It was soon discovered that it was impossible for a technician to concentrate on the task for more than three-quarters of an hour, and so the shifts were shortened. Local legend has it that as single-storey houses and small holiday cha-lets began to appear between the mirrors and the shore, these listeners were ruinously distracted by passing cars, the voices of holidaymakers, even whistling kettles and the clanking of teacups. While such stories may be fanciful, there is no doubt the new buildings, by their simple presence in front of the mirrors, interfered with the job of listening keenly for the approach of German aircraft across the Channel.

Two smaller structures attend the 200-foot mirror still: an upright, flattish concave object like a big Pop sculpture of a plastic spoon, and another that looks like a rendering in crum-bling aggregate of a satellite dish or radar receiver from a later generation of military technology. The whole installation, already doubtful in its wartime application, was made obsolete as soon as the Second World War began and such experiments in acoustic early-warning systems were abandoned in favour of the more precise and practicable machinery of radar. When I looked at these monuments for the first time, they seemed to speak of the whole territory's entrapment in visions of future destruction – also of the visual and aural alertness that the county's vulnerable location had long required. And once I had

seen them I began to spot less dramatic fragments everywhere
I went. Cycling the country roads inland and to the east of
Herne Bay I would stop to admire and explore simple squarish
concrete pillboxes in the summer fields. When we moved to
the outskirts of Canterbury at the end of 2004, I discovered
the flattened points of a concrete tank trap outside a private
school just around the corner. In Blean Woods, across the road
from our house, there was a solitary brick wall that a neighbour said was all that remained of an army firing range from
the Second World War. It is still standing, a few hundred yards
from where I am writing now. A few years ago somebody
knocked a roughly person-shaped hole in the wall, and soon
after the words 'I MISS YOU' appeared in large painted white
letters flanking the gap.

Blast wall

It must have been around the turn of the millennium, when my unexpected interest in the Kent landscape was just beginning, that I first became aware of the archipelago of gunpowder works outside Faversham. We were already in the habit of visiting our friends who lived in Oare village, not yet having moved to Uplees House. An attic bedroom in their house gave a view of the nature reserve, Faversham Creek, the Swale and Sheppey in the distance, and Faversham off to the east. We would always end up standing here at the stroke of New Year, when in the dark the view was illuminated as fireworks went up along the horizon – suddenly you could identify clearly all points as far as Whitstable and Herne Bay in one direction, and Grain in the other. Our walks then would take us along the left bank of the creek, where it always seemed to be low tide, past boats that looked to the inexpert eye as if they were fixed in the mud and would never stir again. There were numerous actual wrecks too: mere sketches of boats, wet black timbers jutting from the slime like animal bones. The arrowhead tracks of waders ran all around the wrecks. Occasionally the birds took to the air en masse as an adventurous dog slithered about on the surface before being called ashore by its worried owner. I always wondered for how long, if at all, the mud might support a human body; I imagined myself trying to run across it, growing comically shorter as I went.

On one such walk, our friends stopped on reaching the creek and urged us in a different direction from usual, inland towards the woods. They had hinted there was something worth seeing there. We descended a short hill to the end of

Church Road, cleared a stile on the right and made for the line of trees at the other end of a partially flooded field. To get into the woods we had to pass by a row of old cottages that looked as though they were sinking into the hillside to escape the inclement weather. At the end of the row was a bigger, darker house at the edge of a large pond or small lake – I thought of Edgar Allan Poe's uncanny House of Usher, with its crumbling facade and attendant mass of dark water interrupting his narrator's approach. A narrow metal bridge extended a little way over the pond, then was lost for a time among the brown, dying reeds that were spreading from the opposite bank. The bridge was gated and locked at our end.

We skirted a cheerless playground that belonged to a small housing estate at the edge of the village, and then found ourselves in the woods, where the wind died, the noise of traffic behind us on the road was quickly muted, and our steps made no sound in the rich black mixture of mud and leaves to which the path had been turned. We followed it for five or ten minutes before there seemed to be a clearing ahead between the trees and we neared a flimsy hurdle fence to investigate. But it was not a clearing, it was a sheer drop of many feet – enough to make us check our footing and clutch the fence – at the bottom of which a sodden concrete floor was scattered with dead leaves. Brick walls enclosed the roughly square area on three sides; to our left on the open side there seemed to be some overgrown structures descending to a cleft or valley at the heart of the woods. The most alarming sight, however, was a massive concrete wall that rose from the floor parallel to, and about six feet away from, the rear revetment. It was clearly meant to defend something or somebody from a force of considerable violence. We drew back from the vertiginous limit, and our friends, amused by our looks of horror, explained that this and a few other ruined structures were all that remained of a gunpowder works that had flourished here until at least the First World War.

I did not visit the ruins in the woods again for several years — during which time the treacherous and impenetrable place had been turned into a heritage attraction. The undergrowth was cleared, fences were replaced alongside sheer drops and around obscure voids, wooden walkways built through the site, and bridges over the network of waterways that meander among the trees. A few of the buildings were fully restored, or near enough; one of these contained a visitor centre full of photographs, models and leaflets; another housed bits of machinery — some original to this place; some merely contemporary with the final phase of the factory — that could be set in motion to demonstrate the process of gunpowder manufacture in the early decades of the twentieth century. (It had not changed much since the eighteenth.) All of this welcoming infrastructure struck me as oddly disengaged from the ruins themselves, and I could easily ignore the colour-coded nature and history trails or even wander off the fenced-in walkways, which for the most part follow the routes of pathways and tramlines that once supplied the plant. You cannot stray too far, however, without reaching one of the canals, or leats, that make up the more ancient transport system. Many have dried up, leaving channels about three feet deep — most likely due to local gravel quarrying, which has reduced the groundwater level in recent decades. Others are shallow bodies of water, still flanked here and there by the horse chestnuts planted in case of a blast. Originally the leats were deep enough to accommodate the narrow flat-bottomed punts; a photograph taken

in 1925 at the nearby Marsh Works shows a worker standing in
the rear of his craft and pushing it with a pole through the
trees. At regular intervals now, signs inform the visitor of the
various creatures that thrive in a tract of woodland bounded
on either side by large ponds and irrigated by canals: the
emperor dragonfly, peacock butterfly, azure damselfly. The
notices announce too the plant life that flourishes here: spear
thistle, wild angelica, the rosebay willowherb that loves disturbed, derelict or ruinous land. Some parts of the wood are
considered ancient (that is, over 400 years old), and these
retain typical species such as bluebell and yellow archangel.
The trees are mostly alder, willow and dogwood: the traditional raw materials of charcoal manufacture.

On returning, I rounded the body of water by the 'House of
Usher' and entered Bysing Wood by a winding path that was
soon blocked with a massive fallen tree. A ragged disc of wet
earth still clung to its upended roots, and the leafless crown
extended almost to the edge of the pond. As I climbed over the
trunk a man approached with his dog and nodded: 'Some mess,
that.' It had been an especially windy start to the year, and all
about me there were other smaller trees that had come to the
same end; some had already had limbs sawn off and carried
away. In their mutilated state the fallen trees matched the
buildings I could see from the near end of the first wooden
walkway. These were the four incorporating mills, where the
ingredients of gunpowder were mixed. All of them had been
ruined: their wooden upper storeys long gone and the lower
brick and concrete partly smashed. In front of each building a
low squat extension in reinforced concrete protruded towards
the footpath; I looked around, saw no sign of the dog owner or
anybody else, then jumped the fence and climbed a pile of

rubble onto the roof of one of these annexes. Walking to the
far side I caught my foot on a big rusted bolt jutting from the
concrete, and for a panicked second flailed at the edge, above
the open interior of the incorporating house, which was
flooded, to what depth I could not tell, with filthy water. Safely
back on the other side of the fence, I paused to let my heart
stop pounding, and to photograph the building. I was hefting
around a Rolleiflex camera from the 1950s – a twin-lens brick
of leather, glass and metal: I had got it in my head to teach
myself photography, the hardest way possible – which now
seized up as I stared down into its gridded viewfinder, so that I

had to make a double exposure to get the mechanism moving again. In the resulting square print, it looked as if the shivering ruin was in the first stages of tearing itself to pieces.

Beyond the incorporating mills, extending south-south-west, roughly along the course of what seemed to be a natural stream, more structures loomed in various stages of desuetude, well spaced, I assumed, so as to minimize the risk of fire or blast spreading from one to others. I knew vaguely that there were several generations of buildings here, and that as late as 1926 much of the complex had been rebuilt, when Nobel Industries Ltd, which had acquired the site six years earlier, was in turn brought under the control of Imperial Chemical Industries. The glazing house – here the powder was made as resistant as possible to moisture: graphite was added and the mixture tumbled for several hours in wooden drums – had been remodelled to form a complex of smaller houses set into a slope, and the surrounding earth revetted in brick. The bricked leats intersecting in front of the glazing house were still intact; ferns sprouted from every damp angle of the canal system, and from a vast circular shaft sunk into the ground nearby: the remains of a water pump from which huge pointed chunks of steel, horribly torn, imitated the surrounding ferns. Other 'danger buildings' – the term for buildings in which explosives are manufactured or stored – had been erased completely, and I had to consult a map produced by the Royal Commission on the Historical Monuments of England to work out their locations.

There was, however, no missing the corning house, where slabs of solidly packed gunpowder were reduced to grains, or 'corns'. This was the dizzying void on the edge of which I had stood that first time in the woods. I approached it now along a sturdy wooden bridge that crossed the bright green algae of a leat-end; on either side of the entrance, a thick wall of earth, with superficies of brick, enclosed the shadowy, claustral pit, full of leaves, filth and an inch or two of water. There was a strong smell of fox mixed in with the rot. At the centre, I stared up at the summit of the concrete blast wall, which was pitted with square holes where beams were once attached, then stepped carefully through the slime to get to the rear, where a control room had once been enclosed and protected. Here the leaves at my feet were dry and even the sound of the wind in the trees above me had ceased.

I have been back many times to the Oare works, and usually in summer, when the walkways are dry underfoot and in the visitor centre a running list of birds and other creatures recently spotted is kept on a whiteboard behind the desk, a list that might include, for example, the woodpecker, treecreeper, reed bunting, water rail, reed warbler and bearded tit. I have never to my knowledge seen any of these, but I have leaned on a rail by the pond at the village end of the woods and watched the swans come sailing towards me in pairs and then spin slowly a few inches away as if proudly showing the effect of tree-light on their dappling backs, before drifting back among the reeds on the other side when it becomes obvious I have no food for them. At midsummer the sunlight falls straight through the trees and the ponds and leats are full of life. The pond skater (*Gerris lacustris*) is a thin, brownish-grey insect about half an inch long with a small head, large eyes and a pair of short front legs with which it seizes upon smaller, dead or dying, insects. The remaining four legs are considerably longer, and the middle pair is commonly compared to a set of oars: with these the creature skims itself across the water, while the rear legs perform the office of hinged rudders. All of its legs are equipped with tiny hairs that repel water and allow the pond skater to sense disturbances in the surface tension on which it depends for its characteristically delicate but awkward posture in, or, as it seems, almost suspended above, streams and rivers and ponds. The insect can fly, but it may also employ these unwieldy-looking limbs to jump out of reach of predators. By far its most impressive feat is simply the ability to walk on water, for which reason it is also called the Jesus bug.

From April to September pond skaters may be found teeming on bodies of water calm enough to accommodate them.

There must have been between fifty and a hundred at a time busying themselves on the lazy water of the leats as I walked through the woods at Oare this past summer, straying as usual from the official route as far as my curiosity took me and the undergrowth would allow. I was still on the path when I spotted them – or rather, when I noticed at first a shimmer at the centre of a sunlit portion of a leat, and crouched to examine it. From a distance the very surface had seemed alive, sending large ripples out along four irregular axes of bright water, towards overgrown banks and the low crumbled remains of a brick-and-concrete bridge to my right. On closer inspection I saw them only a little more clearly: these tiny things flitting apparently at random and plucking at the water, but all the while convening slowly in the middle of the leat, which at this time of year was less than a foot deep and perfectly clear to the bottom. The ripples continued to radiate, while here and there at the edges of this insectal cluster a lone pond skater would light on the surface and cause a competing set of concentric circles to abut the larger pattern.

For some minutes they continued to swarm, till at length they seemed becalmed and I was able to examine the insects as they sat upon the water, their legs creating four tiny impressions as if they were trying to pin the fabric of the stream to its leaf-strewn bed. Everything now seemed held in silence and tension, the woods and ruins and walkways falling away as I focused on this act of convergence, and it was with the greatest care, squatting in the crusted ooze of the bank, that I reached into a pocket for my phone, hoping to photograph the suddenly stilled community of insects. I swiped and prodded the screen and watched the camera trying to focus. In the instant of its hesitation I must have shifted my weight or angled the

device and its shadow a little too far across the leat, because
hardly had the pond skaters come into focus than the screen
erupted in a chaos of light, countless scintillations darting
hither and thither as the tiny beings panicked and scattered.
Nor could the naked eye now focus on the glittering surface. It
was a minute or two before things resolved and the violently
coruscating stream produced ripples like the ones I had seen at
first. The pond skaters, only briefly startled, were gathering
again at the centre of the fractured star of shadow-bound light
until at last I could see individual insects bracing themselves
against the surface, once more attaining that condition of delicate and watchful stillness that I had destroyed.

Summa

Eventually I tried to write about the landscape to the west of
Faversham, the remains of its several explosives factories and
the terrible accident that occurred on the marshes near Uplees
in 1916. I had decided that I owed something to this place, that
although I was just an occasional visitor it had gone to work on
me over the years and now embodied something of my attach-
ment to Kent, an element in its essential strangeness, which
had to do with the flatness of the land, the way everything was
visible, or almost visible, on the surface and at the same time
threatened to sink into the earth or disperse into the air. I set
out to try to reconstruct the events of 1916 and to convey, if
not a comprehensive narrative of its history, at least a certain
atmosphere, a mood, the way the marshes held this story in
reserve and would not entirely give it up. Or so it seemed to
me – perhaps I only wanted or needed the story to be vague

and suggestive, to lead me towards other narratives and other places, thence back to myself, here at the edge of England, where I had never imagined myself. Maybe it was this place I was interested in, and this accident, or maybe it was the nature of accidents and especially the accident of place.

I walked the territory all over again, or rather for now its publicly accessible parts, and began to read up on what was referred to as the Great Explosion. A local historian, Arthur Percival, had written about the disaster in the 1980s, and his account was the one I took with me back to the marsh. Here, in a short pamphlet originally published as an article in the journal *Archaeologia Cantiana*, was the story in miniature, drawn from the official reports – not all of which had yet been released to the public when Percival conducted his researches – and from the accounts of witnesses and survivors, some written in the immediate aftermath, others recorded decades later. There were two separate companies operating on the marshes near Uplees on that distant Sunday morning in spring, the 2nd of April 1916, when a fire started out at the north-western end of the factory complex. The Cotton Powder Company, longer established and with a much larger site, was working flat-out to supply mines and torpedoes. Immediately to the west, the Explosives Loading Company was focused entirely on filling shells with high explosive. The war was then in a phase of vastly destructive stasis, notably on the Western Front. In the spring of 1915 the British army had failed to overcome German defences at Neuve Chapelle in the French region of Artois, and the failure had been blamed in part on a shortage of shells. In the autumn, at Loos, they attacked the Germans with gas, mines and a massive artillery bombard-ment, but gained little ground, and again ran short of shells. In

February of 1916 the French and British began to plan a joint offensive on both sides of the river Somme, in Picardy. The attack would take place in high summer.

The fire on the 2nd of April quickly took hold of a building packed with TNT, and though scores of men rushed to the scene, and fire engines were summoned from Faversham and from within the works, it could not be extinguished in time. The building exploded shortly after one in the afternoon. A pall of smoke rose immediately above the scene, and a vast crater was all that remained where the building had been. At the circumference of this crater, and well beyond it, lay many dead or wounded men, sunk in or stranded on a semi-solid and roughly circular wave of mud. At various distances from the blast site lay more bodies and injured workers. Among the surprises attendant on the disaster was the seemingly capricious pattern of destruction and death. While many were killed in the immediate vicinity, others nearby survived with punctured eardrums and their clothes torn off. And at a greater distance from the explosion, where most picked themselves up with minor injuries, some men were mysteriously killed by the force of the blast.

Though it was certainly the most powerful, the explosion of the TNT store was just the first of many that for several hours threatened factory workers and those sent to rescue them, the initial eruption having set fire to surrounding buildings. The noise and smoke told workers' families in the town and outlying villages across that flat landscape that something terrible had occurred on the marshes. Relatives now raced to the factory gates, and were restrained by guards from rushing onwards towards the crater. The removal of most of the injured and the dead took just a few hours; but efforts to put out the many raging fires, and to make safe the buildings closest to the first explosion, carried on into the night. In time, the number of dead was put at 106, later revised to 108; over half were buried in a mass grave in Faversham, and a large monumental cross raised above them. The rest are dispersed in cemeteries around the county and beyond – these include the one recorded suicide that has been linked to the disaster. In the days immediately following, in the absence of comment by the authorities or the press, rumours circulated about spies and sabotage. It was probably for this reason that the government, reticent at first, responded to questions from the newspapers and in the House of Commons; a short account appeared in *The Times*, putting the number of casualties at over a hundred but omitting to say how many of those had been injured and how many killed.

I bore all of this in mind as I walked out to explore the marsh again, from Oare itself this time towards Harty Ferry, the ancient crossing point of the Swale, then north-west along the shore in hope of cutting inland to the place where I supposed the initial explosion had happened. It was a Thursday, and already at nine in the morning the road through the marsh was filling up with parked cars. The midweek birdwatcher was middle-aged and male, and eyed with some disdain the many moorhens and few swans in the nearest stretch of dark water. At the end of the road a noticeboard recorded some recent sightings: wigeon, pintail, long-billed dowitcher, little stint, greenshank, great northern diver, bar-tailed godwit, avocet, merlin and twite. Also: common seals, a weasel and a hare. I supposed I might come across any of these in the hours ahead – the hare seemed the most thrilling prospect – but as I turned left onto the Swale-side path, it was the unnatural history I was attempting to track. To my right, across the choppy grey water, the Isle of Harty and beyond it Sheppey, then the bridge and the view towards the Medway and Grain beyond. The land was so flat that every structure I could see was in perpetual, slowly spinning consort with every other object: nothing dropped out of view as I moved through the scene.

Perhaps this complicated choreography of reference points was the reason I miscalculated from the start my chances of reaching the location of the 1916 explosion. I struck out past the decayed jetties, the ghosts of concrete foundations against which countless generations of rabbits had bumped their noses as they burrowed, past rusted iron rails that ran to the water's edge, all the while imagining that the prospect to my left, the site itself, though bounded by a dyke parallel to the Swale, would somehow make itself accessible beyond the next slight curve of the shore. It never did, and when I finally gave up, an hour and a half later, and looked back towards Oare, and beyond it to Faversham, with the wind speeding long bands of cloud-shadow and sunlight across the land between, I could not quite believe how far I had come, nor how close everything still looked.

Having resolved to turn back, I first left the bank to investigate a short, narrow wooden promontory that jutted out into the dyke below me. As I stood at the far end above a crowd of swaying yellow reeds, and looked back the way I had come, it dawned on me that – judging by the number of jetties I had passed and by the maps in Arthur Percival's little book – I was at the western end of the former factory site, just a few hundred yards from the seat of the disaster. I would never be able to reach it today: the land between was waterlogged and impassable. I began to open the hard brown leather case of my ancient camera. 'Nothing to see there,' said a male voice behind me. A late-middle-aged couple, dressed in sturdy walking gear, had descended the bank and were approaching the odd-looking structure. I had no idea whether the man, his voice almost carried away on the wind, intended a question or an observation, and so I made what I hoped was a noise vague enough to suit either, and closed my camera case again. All morning the horizon had been dotted with walkers, so that each time a fragment of the gunpowder works appeared on the other side of the dyke, or on the fenced-off agricultural land at the far end of the marsh, I had felt uneasily exposed as I stopped to look at it. Quite prepared to trespass should the opportunity arise, I never got the chance: at no point that morning had I gone unwatched, and I had never been quite sure that one of the dots on the horizon was not a landowner or a representative of Swale Borough Council. The result was that I never got close to the tracery of foundations that showed through the grass, the curious field of short pillars that appeared to have supported one of the larger buildings, the several scattered piles of collapsed concrete and twisted reinforcement, or the point, veiled by low trees, where there may or may not have been a gentle declivity of the ground that was once a hideous, smoking hole.

With so many clearly visible points moving about me in the distance, I had imagined I must be veering towards my destination, when in fact I had made only the slightest southerly declension in its direction. I was left stranded still on the other side of the dyke, photographing numerous indistinguishable horizons, with a few low ruins just discernible in the middle distance. And even those I could not get quite right. Each prospect, when I opened the metal hood of my Rolleiflex and looked down on the grid of its focusing screen, seemed jewel-like in its colours, exquisitely sharp in detail, its composition perfectly arranged according to the faint lines that scored the glass. The German engineers had designed the camera so that the distance between its two lenses – one for focusing, the other for taking the picture – was compensated for by a viewfinder that reframed as the camera focused. Thus portrait sitters, for example, no longer risked having the tops of their heads lopped off. But the apparatus could still flummox a clumsy user, and I consistently misjudged how much foreground I was allowing into the frame; the result, a few days later, was a lot of prints of windblown grass and reeds, as if the landscape had made me look away at the last second from its dismal, grey and distant secrets.

Archive fever

At the National Archives in Kew, I have requested half a dozen documents that seem, according to the online catalogue, to be related to the events outside Faversham in April 1916. It is my first effort at research beyond published or local sources, and I have only the dimmest sense of what documentation might be extant. I had half hoped not to come here at all, imagining that nowadays I could simply request the papers I needed on the archive's website and have them delivered electronically or as photocopies. I liked the idea of poring over documents at home and then exploring the territory myself. It was naive of me, I now realize, to imagine that I could thus short-circuit the labour of research.

I have chosen a number of reports from the immediate aftermath of the disaster. But it turns out I have requested not specific artefacts to do with the Great Explosion but substantial tranches of material covering months or years, and there is simply too much of it to order online or expect the archive staff to photocopy. I dislike visiting libraries and archives for the first time, and get nervous and awkward in the face of straightforward registration and induction procedures. Today I've forgotten my ID, of all things, and have to tramp up and down stairs twice, hot and embarrassed, before I acquire a user's card. Then there is the humiliation of having the ordering process explained to me more than once; I always assume I will get some detail wrong at the computer or turn up at the wrong desk at the wrong time, to find my requested item has been spirited back to a basement or off-site storage facility, or was never actually ordered in the first place.

All of this is familiar to me from previous research projects, but today it is a prelude to the larger problem of not knowing, once I have been to the café and waited the requisite hour or so for my requests to show up, how I am meant to comport myself in the reading room when the archival documents are brought to me. Do I have to wear the white cotton gloves that are available on the way in? Or balance my documents on the wedges of grey foam that I can see many of the readers using? As I am about to sit down, a scholarly-looking older man a few desks away is being sharply rebuked by an attendant for not doing precisely that with the fragile papers in front of him. In front of me, collected from one of the large glass-fronted lockers where orders arrive, are two pale cardboard boxes tightly jammed together at their mouths, and it takes me a few minutes, and some clumsy bracing of one of them against the lip of the desk, to prise them apart. Inside is a fat ragged folder of indeterminate colour, bound in a thin canvas or webbing belt that simply will not undo; its fastening involves an immovable buckle of sorts with sharp metal teeth sunk in the fabric. It takes me an age to ease the belt instead over the end of the folder, all the while trying not to tear the yellowed papers it contains, and hoping that the zealous invigilator is not lurking behind me, appalled and ready to pounce.

Inside are what look to be a couple of hundred mostly typed pages, all of them flimsy and some torn, thankfully not by me. I am sure at first that I have got the wrong report: the first hundred pages or so refer to another explosives factory – the Shell Haven Factory, of Messrs Kynoch, at Kynochtown, Corringham, Essex – where it seems there were accidents on the 17th and 20th of August in the same year. As I flip the pages I jot down stray phrases and sentences about this mirror disaster on the other side of the Thames estuary: 'the ease with which anybody wearing khaki uniform can enter through our gate unchallenged by our own men . . . the looseness with respect to soldiers here, there, and everywhere about the Factory in possession of cigarettes and matches'. I have almost lost hope of finding anything to do with the Kent explosion when the Essex report comes to an end and I reach a title page: 'Factory No. 7 Kent. (The Cotton Powder Co. Ltd.) 2nd April 1916'. At the bottom of the pile are a couple of thick envelopes containing maps, and below these, falling out now onto the desk because I have given up all pretence at handling the contents with care, a photograph album.

The album is a leather-bound volume in what we would now call landscape format. Open it from the back and you discover inside a small sticker in the bottom left-hand corner, bearing the legend 'LUXIA ALBUM Kodak Ltd. London'. Below the printed portion, a little off-centre, is a stamped addition in purple ink that was maybe once blue, or black: 'Made in U.S.A.' The cover is dark brown with a slight hint of red, confirmed along the frayed top edge where a dusty pink shows through. I flip the album over again and examine a thin paper label glued to the front cover, on which is typed: 'Accident No. 110. 1916 Explosion of Tri-nitro-toluol and Ammonium Nitrate at Uplees Marshes – Faversham (Factory 7 – Kent) on 2nd April, 1916.' Below this on the left are recorded, one figure above the other, 106 killed and 97 injured. On the right, a number for the document: 'Sp. Report 217'. At three of the corners some effort has been made to peel the label away with a fingernail.

Each page is a thick black silky card on whose recto a caption is neatly written in white; in many instances a ruled pencil line that guided the writer's hand has not quite been erased below the letters. The pages are also numbered, one to twenty-six. I open the book flat on the desk at the first page, where the caption reads 'General view of site of Main explosion'. But there is no photograph. It has been torn out, leaving behind a fragment of the print's backing; the remainder looks like one half of a Rorschach blot, and I am tempted to read into it a warning about the excessively symbolic opacity of the story I have begun to research. Perhaps the photograph simply fell out at some point in the past century? No, the page is torn, I am sure of it.

Almost all of the other photographs are still there. On page four, the 'Remains of building 862'. The structure in question has been reduced to scattered fragments of wood; a few verticals punctuate the grey mass but mostly the picture shows a

senseless aggregate of earth and debris. It is impossible to
work out whether the building itself has exploded or been
blown away by the eruption of a neighbour; there is a suggestion of lateral movement – almost, you might say, of drift – from
right to left, but what then to make of the two great banks of
earth in the middle distance? Does the space between them
denote the point of eruption? Some type of vat or tank sits in
the middle of the image; it looks like an overturned steel bath.
In the background, the photograph is badly overexposed, so
that a white mist seems to smother a pile of wooden pallets
and two neat frames or lattices in which fragile items may be
stacked.

There are few people visible in most of these pictures, just
scene after scene of churned-up earth, wooden huts or sheds
in various states of collapse, brick structures still largely intact
but missing their roofs, metal-framed buildings skeletally outlined against a sky reduced to a dirty white. But occasionally
they are there, the workers posing in lines in front of the
remains of their workplaces, others ignoring the photographer

and getting on with the job of removing debris, or perhaps
miming it for the camera. On page twelve are the remains of
building number 870: no more than a few sheets of rough
clapboard still standing, and a roof half collapsed onto neatly
arrayed shells. To the left, more of these are stacked horizontally, twelve deep. To the right, a great pile of rescued timbers
and a mound of roofing felt. There are wires still attached to a
telegraph pole in the dead centre. I have to look very closely to
spot a man in a cap, just inside the perimeter of the ruined
building, who stands with his hands in his pockets and his back
to the camera, staring off towards the levels of the marsh. On
page nine, the wreckage of 844: a metal armature with what
was once a curved roof. A large cylindrical boiler stands to one
side of the building, and another lies on its side about twenty
feet away. Among the vacant struts and amputated pipework,
eight men are visible. The first holds a sheet of corrugated iron
that he is about to drag onto a small pile he has begun to make.
Inside the ruined superstructure four men stare directly at the
camera; one of them looks better dressed than the others, and

might be wearing a bowler hat. Off to the right are two more, again facing the camera. And in the middle, by the upright boiler, bent over and with his back to the photographer, the last of the eight, who seems not to have noticed what is happening and now cocks his head as if he has just been told to turn before the picture is taken.

It seems the photographs were taken just days after the accident. I imagine the photographer travelling down from London with the party deputed to investigate the explosion, hoisting his large-format camera and wooden tripod onto a train at Victoria, or piling the equipment into a military truck that jounced along the country roads to the outskirts of Faversham before swerving off towards Oare and the marshes beyond. There is no indication in the album, or the report to which it was appended, of who this man might have been. Perhaps he was a local summoned from the town, unused to photographing such scenes – though this seems unlikely, such is the care with which he has framed the remains of buildings and the detritus around them, the way he has ensured in certain cases that there were indeed figures among the ruins or nearby, so as to provide scale. I hope he had an assistant to help carry his equipment through the wreckage and across mud and debris to the seat of the disaster, steadying the tripod legs as they splayed onto hastily dragged boards, so that his view of the aftermath would remain straight and clear.

Ground zero

I turn back the pages; I am getting ahead of myself in terms of reading, maybe over-reading, these images. I have a sketchy sense so far of what happened where, of which buildings (apart, very obviously, from the first of them to explode) suffered the most damage, which points on the maps in front of me describe the centres of the day's destruction. It is too easy to fit these photographs prematurely into a narrative frieze, without truly paying attention to their particularity. I will have to come back to them, I suspect, time and again. For now, I simply need to look more slowly. Consider the second page of the album, captioned 'Crater at building 833'. The sky, as so often in these pictures, is a thin white strip along the top, hardly to be distinguished from the border around the print. The overexposed clouds bleed palely onto the horizon, so that four buildings regularly spaced across the scene appear as if through a fog; the third, closer to us, might actually be two structures, one of which is just a nest of timbers. Between this sparse line of buildings and the crater that occupies most of the image is a scattering of objects that look as though they might be tree stumps. But this is impossible: though it was customary to shield such buildings from potential blasts

with stands of trees, it could not be done on the marshes. They must instead be cylindrical containers of some kind – they are too squat to be shells – that have been dispersed by the explosion.

Over on the right – it takes me a while to spot him – is a darkly dressed man, a speck in terms of the entire scene, who is looking in our direction. I keep discovering these tiny figures, hardly visible. Not far in front of this man, the ground falls away sharply; a thin, vertically ridged strip of earth runs laterally, much more distinct on the right-hand side and almost lost in shadow and debris on the left. Judging by the height of the figure behind it, this sudden drop is not very deep, a few feet only, but it is remarkably clean and abrupt, as though a disc – 135 feet across, I will discover later – has been cut from the marsh and lifted out. In the photograph, there is simply a wide tract of raw earth, strewn here and there with wood and bricks or stones, with a narrow stretch of water at its centre, perhaps twenty feet long and reflecting brightly the featureless sky. It mirrors too the lower half of a man standing at the centre of the crater, at the cone's upended apex. He is wearing heavy boots, or else he has been walking up to his knees in mud, and his sleeves are rolled up. He also looks straight at the camera, and rests his hand on a long-bladed spade. He is like one of those figures one sees in engravings in eighteenth- and nineteenth-century geology books, perched on the lips of volcanoes to provide scale.

But the most striking and unsettling element of this photograph of the place where building number 833 had been is the much paler ridge of earth that occupies the foreground and takes up more than a quarter of the whole picture. At first I thought it was composed of bricks or shattered masonry, but it seems instead that this dense and twisted mass, made of distinct gobbets of wet earth, has been extruded from a deeper stratum than the dark and more friable soil that flanks it. It is possible I have mistaken something quite ordinary for a vision of hell: these sods may well have been piled up in the days since the explosion, in an effort to clear the area. But I cannot shake the impression that they have been ripped like this from the earth in the instant of detonation, writhing and fleshy and obscene.

In fact, they appear more than once among the documents I have discovered at the National Archives. Jutting out of the package that makes up the official report is a fragment of dark blue paper, stuck to the end of one of the typed sheets and folded over. It is a small blueprint, roughly edged and with a triangular rip at one end, but with the image intact as well as its caption: 'Section of main crater. Not to Scale.' A band of deckled earth subtends the crater, forced down into a shallow 'V' shape and with marshy topsoil still intact on the crater floor above it, this denoted by five roughly lateral lines in the drawing. It looks as if the ground has been sucked down into itself rather than blasted or erupted upwards or outwards – at either side is a sort of wound or fracture in the land, in fact a ring or cylinder scored into the earth. And outside this rim, the great circular mound rises, to a height of five feet above the level of the marsh. For the moment I can make only partial sense of the diagram: I see where the sods or turves of earth have gone, but I do not understand the pattern of forces that has deposited them there.

The photographs exist at one end of a narrative line – or do I mean in the middle of another? They were taken at a time, in the days after the accident, when a certain strand of the story had fully played itself out, when the destructive forces first corralled here centuries before had at last, after a few as it were preliminary accidents, turned disastrously on their masters. The accident was a contraction of history; the explosion sucked into itself the history of gunpowder manufacture in the Middle Ages, the industry's development in early-modern England, its migration into Kent, the turn there in the nineteenth century towards new and more efficiently lethal high explosives, and finally the acceleration early in the twentieth century towards a war in which these new weapons would be deployed with such destructive force and frequency. This is not to speak, yet, of the actual lives of individuals – here are some of them, already, in the photographs of 1916 – who worked with this stuff, who risked their lives knowingly (or perhaps not wanting to know) and who were yet to resolve themselves in any great detail before my archival inquiries.

A natural history

Gunpowder is a mixture of charcoal, sulphur and saltpetre (potassium nitrate), the first usually produced from wood and the latter two substances extracted from the earth in their natural state – though saltpetre may also be manufactured or 'grown'. Charcoal and sulphur provide fuel for the powder's rapid burning, saltpetre the necessary oxygen – the result is a rapid production of heat and gas (nitrogen and carbon dioxide), which accounts for the force of the explosion, and the release of solids (potassium sulphate and carbonate), which emerge as whitish smoke. Gunpowder is a low explosive; that is, it deflagrates or burns rather than detonating like a high explosive, which produces a shock wave whose force is greater than the speed of sound. In practice, the distinction may vanish when gunpowder is exploded in enclosed or pressurized conditions.

'Very few substances have had a greater effect on civilization than gunpowder. Its employment altered the whole art of war, and its influence gradually and indirectly permeated and affected the whole fabric of society.' So begins the entry on gunpowder in the 1911 edition of the *Encyclopaedia Britannica*. It is a notorious edition of that work, celebrated for the erudition and renown of many of its writers – including Edmund Gosse, Algernon Charles Swinburne, Ernest Rutherford and Bertrand Russell – but notable too for the stuffily late-Victorian and frankly imperial orientation of many of its entries. The encyclopaedia, in spite of its faults, which are in part the faults of its age, represents the ideal form of such a work. In its entries on gunpowder, on explosives, and more generally on the methods and machinery of war, one glimpses a culture at an extreme of confidence regarding its place in the world and the innovations that have put it there – a civilization describing to itself the means by which it is about to destroy itself, or all but. It is hard to read these essays, with their exact and elegant accounts of the physics and chemistry by which modern varieties of death and destruction may be wrought, without contemplating the shells and bombs and torpedoes that did not yet exist except as raw chemicals and materials, as plans on paper or as pure theory.

It is frequently asserted that the Chinese had gunpowder before Europeans, and this seems to be the case, though the earliest application of some such substance, in the fourth century, was more likely to have been for the production of toxic fumes than for propellant or explosive purposes. It is probable that knowledge of gunpowder travelled to Europe first via Arab traders and then by direct contact between China and Europe. The first rockets, which are sometimes cited as early instances of Chinese use of gunpowder, were not deployed for military ends until the twelfth century.

The earliest European source referred to in the *Britannica* is by Roger Bacon, the thirteenth-century English Franciscan and author of treatises on grammar, logic, physics, mathematics and philosophy. (He is also said to have invented spectacles and proposed, but did not see built, an early telescope.) The later Middle Ages regarded Bacon as a necromancer, because of his interests in alchemy and chemistry. Among his writings on the latter subject is a treatise, *De mirabili potestate artis et naturae*, completed in 1242, in which he describes an explosive mixture employed for diversion or entertainment, 'producing a noise like thunder and flashes like lightning'. In a passage of this treatise Bacon speaks of saltpetre as itself an explosive substance, but the *Britannica* assures us that 'there is no doubt he knew it was not a self-explosive substance'. The more mysterious aspect of Bacon's interest in and knowledge of gunpowder is his apparent effort to keep the secret of its manufacture from the casual or merely curious reader. In a text entitled *De secretis operibus artis et naturae*, attributed to Bacon, we read: 'From saltpetre and other ingredients we are able to make a fire that shall burn at any distance we please.' In the ninth, tenth and eleventh chapters he turns to practical matters and discloses the recipe for gunpowder; or, rather, Bacon hides it in plain sight by rendering his instructions in the form of anagrams. The ruse is quite transparent, and one must conclude that the philosophical Franciscan did not really believe it would deter any would-be adept of the art who had a less than purely scientific interest. Whatever his intentions, here is the passage in question: 'Item ponderis totum 30 sed tamen salis petrae *luru vopo vir can utri* et sulphuris; et sic facies tonitruum et coruscationem, si scias artificium. Videas tamen utrum loquar aenigmate aut secundum veritatem.' The *Britannica* writer glosses the anagrammatic section thus: ' "salis petrae r(ecipe) vii part(es), v nov(ellae) corul(i), v et sulphuris" (take seven parts of saltpetre, five of young hazel-wood, and five of sulphur).'

Bacon makes no mention, so the *Britannica* tells us, of guns or the use of explosive powder to propel a projectile. It is said that the Moors or Saracens employed machines 'that cast globes of fire' during the siege of Boza in 1325. A document from 1326 refers to the appointment, by the council of twelve in Florence, of persons to oversee the manufacture of iron balls and brass cannon, for the defence of the republic. In 1375 John Barbour, archdeacon of Aberdeen, wrote that cannon had been employed during Edward III's invasion of Scotland in 1327. Two documents from 1338 seem to refer to cannon in England and France, and in London there are 'trustworthy accounts' from 1345 of the purchase of ingredients for making powder and the shipment of cannon to France. And further:

In 1346 Edward III appears to have ordered all available saltpetre and sulphur to be bought up for him. In the first year of Richard II (1377) Thomas Norbury was ordered to buy, amongst other munitions, sulphur, saltpetre and charcoal, to be sent to the castle of

Brest. In 1414 Henry V ordered that no gunpowder should be taken out of the kingdom without special licence, and in the same year ordered twenty pipes of willow charcoal and other articles for the use of the guns.

The early history of explosives in Britain is in part a history of struggle over who precisely ought to be licensed to produce such a valuably lethal commodity. Knowledge of the process of manufacture lay first of all with artillerists themselves, who knew how to make or collect saltpetre, refine sulphur and produce charcoal. In the fifteenth century a German manual, the *Firework Book*, depicts a gunner carrying out by hand all the stages of powder production. In England, the King's or Queen's gunners made and stored gunpowder at royal castles and other notable centres of military power. As early as 1346, powder was being produced at the Tower of London, which remained a site for storage until the seventeenth century. The centre of London was a perilous location for a magazine, though not unusual – in 1548 an explosion in the stores wrecked one of the towers.

To Renaissance writers, says Wayne Cocroft in his thorough history of the explosives industry in Britain, gunpowder was one of a triad of inventions – alongside the compass and the printing press – that marked modern Europe's departure from the medieval; if the technology was to spread, it would require a transfer of expertise and authority from gunners under direct control of the Crown to private entrepreneurs. This is essentially what occurred from the middle of the sixteenth century onwards, with predictable consequences in terms of the state's efforts to control manufacture and dispersal of the material. In 1554 Henry Reve established a gunpowder mill at

Rotherhithe, on the south bank of the Thames. In 1561 Brian Hogge, Robert Thomas and Francis Lee declared that they had erected five new mills, though the precise location of these is uncertain – Lee seems later to have taken over Reve's works at Rotherhithe. Mills sprang up in Surrey, to the south and south-west of the city, towards the end of the century, several under the control of the Evelyn family, which would come to dominate production in the south of England via lucrative contracts to supply the Crown. In 1580 Dublin Corporation paid Robert Poynter, a master gunner, to dig saltpetre and make gunpowder. By the early seventeenth century there were powder works in Devon, Somerset, Dorset, Sussex, and close to the cities of Bristol and Chester. Exactly how many of these were established illegally is unclear. But there are documented cases of remarkable speculative daring, indeed of pure recklessness: 'In 1639 Robert Davies of Thames Street in London was reported for storing all the ingredients necessary to make powder in his house. Perhaps the information was supplied to the Office of Ordnance by his fearful neighbours, as his previous house in Whitechapel had blown up by accident,' writes Cocroft.

A decade later in Tower Street, a ship chandler and provisions dealer named Robert Porter was storing twenty-seven barrels of gunpowder in his house, to be loaded onto a ship in the morning. Nearby, at the Rose Tavern, a parish feast was in progress and many gentlemen, merchants and traders had gathered there when Porter's stock of powder erupted, destroying the pub and many surrounding houses; sixty-seven people were killed. It was said that the blast delivered a baby girl, still in her crib, to the very top of the church tower, where she was found alive and well the next day.

The spirit of the earth

Of the three ingredients for gunpowder, saltpetre was the most troublesome to obtain, and so has left the most detailed historical trail regarding its extraction, manufacture and delivery. By the 1600s the substance was a source of considerable scientific attention and controversy, as well as some fraught politicking.

In September 1662, the polymath Thomas Henshaw, one of the first fellows of the Royal Society, delivered his most celebrated paper. 'The History of the Making of Salt-Peter' begins, as was still common in the middle of the seventeenth century, with reference to classical sources; it is unclear, Henshaw writes, whether the 'Salt-Peter' known today, and used as a preservative for meat as well as an ingredient in gunpowder, is 'the same species' as the 'Nitre' mentioned by the ancients. The question is 'variously disputed by very learned Authors amongst the modern Physitians'. The Germans, he writes, ascribe the first account of saltpetre to one Constantine Autlitzer, or to the 'monk of Friburgh' Berthold Schwartz, who was said to have taught the Venetians to use guns at the Battle of Genoa in 1380. Saltpetre was mentioned by a Moorish alchemist in Spain called Geber, but his dates are unknown, says Henshaw. (In fact there were two Gebers: the first a Muslim polymath of the eighth century, the second a pseudo-Geber writing on alchemy and metallurgy in the thirteenth century; many generations of European scholars confused the two.) Raimond Lully referred to saltpetre in 1333, and it is 'no ill conjecture' that he may have 'had a design to draw a higher Spirit from Peter than the common *Aqua fortis*, and that he might better open the body of *Peter*, he ground it with *Sulphur* and charcoal, by which Composure he soon became the Inventour of Gun-powder'.

Henshaw is more certain of the geography of the substance than its history. He has been told by a refiner of saltpetre 'that near Sophia, *Santa-Cruz*, and several other places in *Barbary*, he hath seen *Salt-Peter* shoot out of the ground (as thick and white as a hoar frost) on many barren and desert lands'. In such places, following the rains in August and September, 'little Chrystals' of saltpetre may be picked off the ground and sold to merchants. And in the floodplain of the river Nile, 'once in a year, it sweeps with an impetuous overflow the burnt and barren Desarts of *Africa*, under the *Torrid Zone*; where, by the relations of Travellers, those lands are visibly full of Nitre, and those Springs and Wells that are to be found there, are by that reason so bitter, that the *Moores* and their Camels are forced to make a hard shift with them in their long journey.'

Closer to home, saltpetre is ubiquitous but hard to extract. 'The Air is everywhere full of a volatile kind of Nitre', discovered as a fine salt, like flour, on plastered walls or between bricks. In wet weather it is washed into the earth: 'I have more than once extracted *Salt-Peter* out of Rain and Dew, but from the latter more plentifully, and yet even there, is Salt-Peter accompanied with a greasy purple Oyl, in great plenty.' In northern countries such as England, he writes, saltpetre is most commonly found in stables, pigeon houses or dovecotes, cellars, barns and warehouses: places, that is, protected from rain, which would dissolve it, and from the sun, 'which doth rarefie it, and cause it to be exhaled into the Air'. He has also been told by an experienced workman that no place yields so much of the stuff as the earth in churches, which might be thoroughly mined for saltpetre were it not for the impiety of disturbing in their 'sacred Depository' the remains of the dead. (As we shall see, some of Henshaw's contemporaries suffered no such scruples.) In a good spot, the nitre may extend six or eight feet into the earth, less frequently to ten. Once mined, and assuming that the site stays dry, saltpetre will return in around twelve to fourteen years. 'And if they mingle with the dried earth store of Pigeons-dung, and mellow Horse-dung, and then temper it with Urine (as was usual before we were supplied with Peter from India) it will be fit to dig again in five or six years.'

Chemical or alchemical descriptions of saltpetre in this period tend towards ambiguity; the substance seems at once base and ethereal, metaphysical and all too corrupt, almost bodily. According to Francis Bacon, saltpetre was the 'spirit of the earth', while the physician Henry Stubbe, a notable polemicist against Bacon and the Royal Society, called it 'one of the most odd concretes in the world'. Robert Boyle wrote of a 'seminal principle' latent in the earth, a self-regenerating principle at that; it ought to be possible, Boyle says, to discover a perpetual mine of saltpetre, ever renewing and ever profitable. Alongside this chthonic and productive quality – remember Henshaw's image of saltpetre shooting, white, out of the ground – the sublime and abstract nature of the substance is insisted upon by the virtuosi of the seventeenth century. The physician William Clarke called it 'ubiquitarian', 'obscure' and 'hermaphroditical'; by the last term he referred to the ambiguity of the material, its propensity to mimic attributes of other natural substances.

By the late sixteenth century, most of the powder used in

English cannon combined one part each of sulphur and charcoal with six parts of saltpetre, and it was becoming harder to feed the state-controlled gunpowder industry's appetite for the latter. During the war with Spain, Queen Elizabeth's army and navy consumed almost 100 tons of gunpowder each. By the 1630s – this in peacetime – the annual amount had increased to 250 tons; by the period of the Seven Years War in the middle of the eighteenth century, it was 647 tons; and in 1828 it was estimated that a major new war would use up 9,000 tons per year. By that time, the problem of saltpetre supply had largely been solved by exploitation of resources and labour in India; this had begun of course, as Henshaw's reference to India attests, much earlier. In Henshaw's century, however, there was a protracted struggle in England regarding the right of the state – that is, the Crown – to trample figuratively and actually on the property rights of private individuals in the search for saltpetre. There was the matter too of the sheer unpleasantness of its extraction and refinement, and the attendant boorishness and brutality of the men employed at those tasks. Saltpetre, in short, was a contentious as well as protean substance.

Digging for saltpetre in the barns, dovecotes, stables and even churchyards of England had been the prerogative of the Crown for about a century by the time Henshaw was writing. In 1531 Henry VIII had instructed one Thomas Lee, the King's gunner, to go in search of saltpetre at home and abroad. An industry, and a set of notoriously corrupt practices, had grown up around the location, extraction and refinement of saltpetre in the intervening decades. Many landowners refused to have their estates and farm buildings disturbed, but their appeals were regularly overturned by judges – though the saltpetre-men were famously open to bribery, so might be paid to move on. In theory they were required to leave the land they dug in the condition in which they found it, and were barred from setting their spades to the floors of private residences. Neither were stores of corn and hay to be touched. In practice the regulations were frequently ignored, and there were many complaints. In the 1630s, saltpetre-men were reported to have torn up the floors of churches, excavated graveyards and invaded the bedchambers of pregnant women, the sick and even the dying. At Norwich assizes in 1607, Lord Coke was said to have delivered – the authenticity of the speech was later disputed by his son – an address on the 'abuses and corruptions' of certain officers in the Crown's employ:

There is also a Salt-peter-man, whose commission is not to break up any man's house, but such as is unused for any necessarie imployment by the owner. And not to digge in any place without leaving it smooth and levell: in such case as he found it. This Salt-peter-man under shew of his authority, though being no more than is specified, will make plaine and simple people beleeve, that hee will without their leave breake up the floore of their dwelling house, unlesse they will compound with him to the contrary. Any such fellow, if you can meete with all, let his misdemenor be presented, that he may be taught better to understand his office: For by their abuse the country is oftentimes troubled.

Such was the opposition to the way these men went about their task that in 1625 Charles I issued a proclamation, 'For the Maintaining and Increasing of the Salt-petre Mines of England, for the Necessary and Important Manufacture of Gunpowder', designed to protect the Crown's interest and those charged with its exploitation. The proclamation states:

. . . for the future, no dovehouse shall be paved with stones, bricks, nor boards, lime, sand, nor gravel, nor any other thing whereby the growth and increase of the mine and saltpetre may be hindered or impaired; but the proprietors shall suffer the ground floors thereof, as also all stables where horses stand, to lie open with good and mellow earth, apt to breed increase of the said mine. And that none deny or hinder any saltpetre-man, lawfully deputed thereto, from digging, taking, or working any ground which by commission may be taken and wrought for saltpetre.

But it seems the populace sometimes interposed itself between the saltpetre-man and his raw material. In Kent, in December 1639, certain 'malignants' with cudgels beat up a gang of salt-petre workers and locked them in the stocks, declaring that 'the king employed more rogues in his works than any man'. Saltpetre-men were commonly despised, called 'undermining two-legged moles' and condemned for their drunkenness and 'saucy unbecoming language'. There were plans and practical efforts to centralize and industrialize production, but as these usually involved the installation of specially prepared nitre beds on the outskirts of villages, towns and cities, they proved no more popular than the habitual exploits of the roving and speculative bands of saltpetre miners.

In 1626 Sir John Brooke and Thomas Russell proposed to Charles I that production be centralized in London. Beggars would be employed to collect the city's urine, which would then be spread on the nitre beds. These would yield, Russell wrote in his broadsheet on the subject, up to 500 tons of saltpetre per year; he asked for £20,000 to set up the scheme. Despite the scale of urine-collecting required, and the necessity for vast and stinking nitre beds in the city's suburbs, the plan was approved by the King. As a result, his landowning subjects felt even more justified in refusing the regular itinerant saltpetre-men access to their land, and within months a proclamation had to be issued to safeguard normal supply. Russell responded with a second plan: every household and every village in England should start its own small-scale saltpetre manufactory, diligently soaking with urine the earth in their stables, barns and hovels. It was an implausible project, and Russell's grand schemes were anyway soon made obsolete: already in the 1620s the East India Company had begun shipments of saltpetre that had been extracted and processed by a lowly caste of workers. This source came to dominate among the Crown-controlled gunpowder works in England, so that when Henshaw speaks, in the title of his Royal Society address, of the 'history' of saltpetre manufacture, he is already describing skills and practices that are starting to vanish.

Under the heading 'The Manner of Making Saltpetre', Henshaw writes:

In the first place you must be provided of eight or ten tubs, so large, that they may be able to contain about ten Barrows full of Earth, each of them. These tubs must all be open at the top; but in the bottom of every one of them, you must make a hole to that side you intend to place outermost, which hole you must fit very well with a tap and spigot on the outside downward.

The tubs in turn should be placed on stands, leaving enough space for workers to move between them, and filled with

'Peter-Earth' and cold water to a hand's breadth from the top. After eight or ten hours the spigots should be loosened; the liquor should run the colour of urine, and if it does not it is to be poured on the earth again. 'When this is done, turn out the useless insipid earth out of the Tubs, which you must fill with new Earth, and continue this Operation, till you have in the same manner lixivated all the Earth.' The liquid is then to be boiled in a copper until it 'hang like Oyl on the sides of the Brazen-scummer when 'tis dipped into it'. From the cauldron the mother liquor is decanted into another tub and left to settle, all its earthy impurities declining to the bottom of the vessel. Finally it is poured into long wooden containers where the saltpetre crystallizes, and any remaining liquid is recycled by pouring onto fresh earth. The vessels or 'separating baskets' may be seen in a series of engravings produced for Lazarus Ercker, the official assayer in Dresden in the late sixteenth century, and published in 1580 in his *Description of the Principle Ores and Methods of Mining*. Here we see a saltpetre worker dipping his brass scummer into the boiling cauldron to measure the progress of refinement. Ercker's work was translated in 1683 by John Pettus as *The Laws of Art and Nature, in Refining and Inlarging Bodies of Confin'd Metals*. The 'sculptures', as Pettus calls his illustrations, depict first the boiling stage: 'By the following Sculpture you are taught how the Tubs are to be set, and the Lees made and boyld from it.' And subsequently: 'The long narrow Tubs wherein to cool the Lees. The Oven wherein the Kettle is placed. The Master that makes and takes out the Petre, puts it into separating Baskets.' In all cases, the job looks remarkably hygienic and orderly, though the boiling and refining house, and the nitre beds tended outside in the sunshine, must have stunk of urine and dung.

Sent up, in silence

Where the refinement of saltpetre was complex, laborious, disgusting and fraught with resentment or even violence, the production of charcoal for gunpowder manufacture was so straightforward by comparison, and so little dependent on special locations or circumstances, that it has left hardly any trace in the historical record. The main users of charcoal in the medieval and early-modern periods were involved in metal-working and not powder manufacture, but its production was carried out in the same woods and forests. Certain areas were notable suppliers to the gunpowder factories: in London, for example, the industry drew on the major charcoal-burning districts of Surrey, Sussex and Essex. As Wayne Cocroft points out, it is possible here and there to discern a history of charcoal-burning from local place names and surnames. In some of these localities, earthworks are still visible in wood-land, or soilmarks to be seen from the air in fields that were formerly forested: the remains of the 'stances', or circular platforms on which charcoal burning was carried out, in some cases for centuries.

The techniques for making charcoal did not change much, if at all, in that time. A series of plates in the *Encyclopédie* of Diderot and d'Alembert shows a process that was generally used, with minor adjustments, throughout Europe and later North America. A circle of ground was cleared, and a vertical wooden pole raised at its centre; in the *Encyclopédie* illustra-tions, two tiny figures rake the ground about this shored-up central spike. Shorter poles were stacked around it, vertically and horizontally at the core, then diagonally in the manner of a wigwam; when these had formed a sufficiently dense cone, the timbers were covered over with earth to form a 'clamp', and the wood was ignited, usually from the top, and allowed to burn for between three and ten days, depending on the size of the clamp and the type of timber. In the *Encyclopédie*, there is a worker perched atop a ladder at the very point of the cone, either firing the clamp or altering the rate of burning. The speed and degree could be controlled by digging holes in the earth to increase the flow of air, or plugging such holes as appeared when the wood inside burst into flame instead of smouldering quietly. After the requisite time had elapsed, the earthy portion of the clamp was dismantled and the charcoal raked out. If the burn had gone as planned the finished product fell to the ground with a characteristic ringing sound.

Faversham and environs

The market town of Faversham, where the gunpowder industry of north Kent originated, lies about nine miles west of Canterbury and two miles south of the Swale, to which it is linked by a meandering tidal creek. London is forty-seven miles away to the north-west. The centre of the town sits on elevated chalk-land which declines northwards into gravel and alluvial clay. There are flooded gravel pits to the west of Faversham, near Oare village, to which a shorter creek snakes south-west from the mouth of the main waterway. For centuries the larger creek – the relic of a shallow river valley that became tidal only a thousand years ago – made this a viable and indeed thriving port; among the products exported via Faversham were wool, hops, beer and oysters. Shipyards were established early, and are still active, though they declined with the arrival of the railway, and faster still in the past half-century.

There seems to have been a settlement at Faversham before the Roman invasion of AD 43; soon after, it became an important staging post for travellers to and from the ports further east in Kent: from Faversham one travelled swiftly to London along Watling Street. Later the town became a summer capital for the county's Saxon kings. By the eleventh century Faversham was well established as a port, controlled directly by the monarch; in 1080 the Domesday Book recorded: 'In the lathe of Wiwarlet in Favreshant Hundred, King William holds Favreshant. It was taxed at 7 solins. The arable land is 17 carucates' – that is, about a hundred acres. Sixty years later, King Stephen granted Faversham to William de Ipres, the newly created Earl of Kent. In 1147 Stephen and his queen, Matilda, repossessed Faversham and environs, and founded an abbey to the north of the town. (All that survives of the abbey is a pair of medieval barns at Abbey Farm.)

Apart from its commercial success and royal ownership – the town was the only one in England permitted to use the royal coat of arms, with its three lions and Old French motto '*Honi soit qui mal y pense*' – early-modern Faversham is probably best known for an event that occurred much later, in 1551. Thomas Arden was a trader living in a former guest house of the abbey; he had served as mayor of Faversham and been appointed the King's controller of imports and exports – he had made his fortune in part from selling off the former property of the monasteries Henry VIII had abolished. On the 14th of February, Arden was murdered in his home by two ex-soldiers from Calais who had apparently been hired by his wife, Alice, and her lover, Mosby. The killers left Arden's body out in a snowstorm, hoping their tracks would be covered, but the snow stopped and they were discovered. Mosby was hanged and Alice burned at the stake. Forty-one years later, an anonymous play was published, based on the events in Faversham. As is the way with anonymous works of that period, certain playwrights have been canvassed as possible authors of *Arden of Faversham*: Christopher Marlowe, Thomas Kyd and, of course, William Shakespeare, whose company, the Chamberlain's Men, is thought to have performed the play.

Arden's house is still there, halfway up Abbey Street as you walk north from the town centre with its remarkable number of well-preserved timbered houses from the period of the unfortunate mayor and merchant's end. Naturally, many of these have been renovated, or rebuilt after one of the town's several historic fires; on Abbey Street itself brick facades have covered the timbers, adding a layer of Georgian rectitude to the rambling mansions behind. Faversham is a necessary counter to the fame of Canterbury: both more rugged and more genteel, it feels like a working town and also deeply attuned to its storied and royal-sponsored past. The town's history of gunpowder manufacture is one of the most frequently evoked elements in that past; at the Fleur de Lis Heritage Centre on Preston Street, you can read about the factories and the disaster of 1916, and examine artefacts from the plants that were dotted around the town.

The area was well suited to the gunpowder industry: it was close to the arsenals in London, the naval ports of the south coast were within easy reach, the land was ideal for growing willow and alder for charcoal manufacture, and the creek afforded ready access for importing sulphur and dispatching the finished product. The earliest powder mills, the Home Works at the head of the creek, were likely set up in the sixteenth century and by the eighteenth they had spread south towards the village of Ospringe. In 1760 the state took control of the Home Works, which became the first royal gunpowder works; in 1786, following an explosion, much of the more dangerous work was relocated to the Marsh Works to the west of Faversham and adjacent to Oare Creek. The Home Works was in state hands until after the Napoleonic Wars; the Marsh Works was bought from the government by a private firm in 1854. And finally, just south of Oare in Bysing Wood, the Oare Works was established in the early years of the eighteenth century. By the nineteenth, Faversham was thus fringed to its south and west by these factories, which expanded during the Napoleonic Wars and again with the outbreak of the Crimean War.

What does such a palimpsestic industrial history do to a town, or to the land around it, the fields and woodlands and the constantly altering shoreline? Of course in one sense all of this is simply what has been: the material remains point to technological, economic and human narratives, a history for the expert enthusiasts at the museum and heritage centre, treading the landscape and trawling the archives. But it is surely also a mythic and metaphoric history, marked by stories told about endeavour and disaster, and by the very materials themselves – the stuff out of which the powder was made. Raw materials have their own stories to tell, their own actual and symbolic progress down the centuries, almost their own ambitions. And Kent is a place impregnated with powder and its near-alchemical origins. I am not the first to have noticed this.

That clevverness what made us crookit

Russell Hoban's *Riddley Walker*, a novel published in 1980 and chiefly known for its invention of an opaque if demotic post-apocalyptic dialect, is also a richly researched envisioning of one possible future for the landscape of Kent. The book is set a couple of thousand years into the future, at a time when England, renamed Inland, is still suffering the consequences of a nuclear catastrophe that occurred towards the end of the twentieth century. Civilization has regressed to something approximating the Iron Age, with ghosts of the country's past – and perhaps the world's: the extent of the disaster is unclear – hovering constantly around language, ritual, technology, landscape and the struggles for power enacted in the resurgent forests and encroaching marshlands of Kent. *Riddley Walker* is in some ways a remarkably self-enclosed novel, as much in the atmosphere of cultural stasis it evokes as at the level of its hectic linguistic texture; but it is also based on Hoban's visionary research into the place he has set it, and so it connects in startling ways with the religious, political, military and industrial history of the county. It describes a version of Kent marked as now by its deep as well as its recent past, but more alert to the persistence and movement of forces or energies in the landscape than to particular events, which have been elided, buried or badly confused.

I first tried to read the book nearly thirty years ago – I had heard it compared, not very accurately, to the novels of William Burroughs – with no idea that I might one day be so familiar with its locations, which are barely disguised by the comic and usually obscene names Hoban gives them. Faversham, at the north-western extreme of the territory the novel describes, has become Fathers Ham; Ashford, directly south of it via Moal Arse (the present-day Molash), is now Bernt Arse. Dotted around the eastern and south-eastern coast are Sams Itch, Do it Over and Fork Stoan: Sandwich, Dover and Folkestone. Canterbury is modified to Cambry; to the north of the city on the coast are Widders Bel (Whitstable) and Horny Boy (Herne Bay). And at the north-eastern corner of the county – all of this is laid out in a map at the start of the novel – is the Ram, formerly the Isle of Thanet, which is once more an island: the Wantsum Channel, narrowed and unnavigable since the Middle Ages, has opened up again and become Ram Gut. The Ram itself is now 'the head of Inland'; it is here that a feared but vulnerable leader or chief, the 'prime mincer', has his base and plots to reinvent or rediscover the technology that has brought the country to this primitive state in the first place.

Riddley Walker's eponymous young narrator loses his father early in the novel; he is crushed to death in a mining accident. Two thousand years from today, the inhabitants of Kent (still a mining county when Hoban wrote the book) dig not for coal but for the rusted hulks of long-dead machines, which they melt down for tools and weapons. This new Iron Age can only find its way into the future through an archaeology of Inland's rotting past. When the orphaned twelve-year-old sets out into the countryside – it is filled with packs of wild dogs, but Riddley is 'dog frenly' and immune from attack – he discovers a landscape everywhere haunted by the myths and rituals according to which his culture tries to make sense of what has happened to it, the catastrophe from which it seems it cannot recover.

Chief among these is the legend of St Eustace, or 'Eusa' in

the novel's parlance, which Hoban derived from a fifteenth-century wall painting in the north choir aisle of Canterbury Cathedral. This depicts, in a narrative that runs from bottom to top, the various trials and violent end of Eustace. The saint and his family present themselves to the Bishop of Rome and renounce their earthly possessions. His wife is captured by pirates. Eustace and his sons must cross a swollen river; when he tries to take them over one by one they are stolen by a wolf and a lion while Eustace is still in the middle of the river. Fifteen years later Eustace is a general in the army of Hadrian, and has recovered his family; but when they refuse to make a sacrifice in honour of the Emperor all four are roasted to death in a brazen bull. The motif of this gruesome end will return towards the end of the novel, but the aspect of the Eustace story that is most present in the book is the first scene, at the foot of the painting. Here the saint comes across a stag, between whose antlers appears the crucified Christ on a cross made of light. In its retelling, which has become a central ritual of the future belief system of Inland, the encounter is understood as a story about knowledge. Eusa pulls the 'littl shyning man' apart in an allegory of both the splitting of the atom and the act of Creation; in the portmanteau style of Hoban's Joycean argot the mysterious figure is referred to as 'the Addom'. The legend – that is, the renewed legend 2,000 years into the future – has it that the disembodied head of the Addom is a repository of knowledge, a kind of oracle which is ritually represented in the theatrical 'Eusa shows' that traverse the country.

Among the dead towns of Kent in Hoban's novel, 'Cambry' occupies a particularly resonant place in the lore of the county and its potential future as a site of technological renovation,

thus also of repeated ruin. It seems that on the outskirts of the
city (Hoban may be thinking of the curve of the half-ruined
city walls, or even of Canterbury's 1970s ring road) there was
once a nuclear facility of some kind, or a particle accelerator:
it appears this was where the disaster took place. The landscape, says Riddley Walker, still throbs or reverberates from
the former presence of this 'Power Ring'. He feels its energy,
'the goast of it' at any rate, as he nears the city. As with other
dead towns, the centre of Cambry has been flattened, but this
city was at the centre of the destruction – it was 'Zero Groun
it ben where the wite shadderd stood up over every thing'.
And at the centre of the ruins, at the heart of the heart of
things, is the former crypt of Canterbury Cathedral, now a
hole in the ground into which Riddley crawls and discovers
pillars and arches still extant, 'stoan trees growing under the
groun'. For the first time he is struck by all that has been lost:
the wealth of knowledge that made the architects of the cathedral, and later the builders of the Power Ring, so much
'bettern us'. Here in this grey-lit 'woom', with the 'girt big
music pipes' of the wrecked cathedral organ tangled and bent
above him, he senses the creative potency that must have been
required to mediate between wood and stone, to make the one
take the form of the other: 'I put my han on a stoan tree trunk.
There wernt no grean rot on it the stoan felt clean and dry. In
the ½ lite in the grey lite it lookit like it wer stanning in its oan
time not the same time I wer in.'

It is here among the ruins of Canterbury that character
and reader alike realize that Riddley's tale, the narrative of
Inland and its decline, is also a story about potential, physical
and spiritual. The stones themselves, Riddley tells us, 'want to
be lissent to. Them big brown stoans in the formers feal they

want to stan up and talk like men. Some times youwl see them
lying on the groun with their humps and hollers theywl say to
you, Sit a wyl and res easy why dont you.' But more than this:
there is an energy in all things – they want to be themselves, to
fulfil to the fullest and perhaps most destructive degree all the
potential they contain. In the language of Inland there is a pun-
ning intimacy between 'wood' and 'would': 'the hart of the
wud' means the force of inanimate will that waits in the landscape. And at the centre of this allegorical world-view is the
perilous search, among the primitive power brokers of east
Kent, for the secret to the '1 Big 1': that is, the explosive technology that obliterated Cambry and environs. 'How cud any
1 not want to get that shyning Power back from time back way
back? How cud any 1 not want to be like them what had boats
in the air and picters on the wind? How cud any 1 not want to
see them shyning weals terning?' But the inhabitants of
post-apocalyptic Inland are very far from such expertise; in
their reading of the landscape and fragments of writing left
from before the disaster, they have mistaken evidence of gunpowder manufacture for the vastly more destructive power of
the atom. Towards the end of the novel the various obscure
elements of this knowledge converge in a lethal experiment.

The ghosts – or 'goasts' – of the gunpowder industry are
still at work in the savage hinterland between the dead towns,
though their products are not only lethal. Dyers – 'them bloaks
what boyl up the pig shit' – produce 'Saul & Peter', or 'the
seed of the red'. Blue smoke rises from the woods where charcoal manufacturers are burning alder for use in melting down
metal from the great machines. In the world of *Riddley Walker*,
as in reality, the most precious and rare of the three ingredients is sulphur, 'the salt 4', or 'the yellerboy stoan' – '1 ce

youve got that salt youre on your way to the woal chemistery and fizzics of it'. Late in the book Riddley comes across the corpse of a man in whose pocket he finds a bag of sulphur. The stuff seems alive with explosive energy: 'Hol it in your hans and you can feal it in them stoans and scrabbling to get out you can hear it hispering to its self and clacking like a skelter of crabs . . . I know theres Power in it.' This power is released at the end of the novel in a potent coming together of all the knowledge and symbolism by which the inhabitants of Kent make sense of their blasted territory. The rulers of Inland – if that is what the primitive warlords of the Ram, such as one Abel Goodparley, really are – have finally acquired, in part thanks to Riddley, the secret of forcing certain substances to fulfil their potential: 'Them wite Kirstels and that black chard coal and that yeller boy theyre coming to gether to show you the Power in the changingness of things.'

Riddley watches the charcoal burner Granser as he goes to work on the ingredients:

He wer pounding that yellerboy stoan to a fine powder. Then he done the same with some chard coal. Done it with a boal and pow-der. He had the Saul & Peter all ready that wer kirstels like salt. He took littl measures and measuring out yellerboy and chard coal and Saul & Peter. Mixing them all to gether then and me watching. It wer like the 1st time I seen a woman open for me I wer thinking: This is what its all about then.

The experiment is meant to condense all the governing myths of Inland, and the half-buried knowledge by which its inhabit-ants struggle towards the future, into a single moment of transformation – it is also, of course, a power grab by the rulers of the Ram. The test succeeds, too well.

I jus begun to roal up a smoak when WHAP! there come like a thunner clap it wer like when litening strikes right close it eckowit up and down the rivver. There come up a cloud of smoak from the fents it wernt the regler blue smoak it wer 1 big puff of grey smoak and things wer peltering down out of the trees like when you shake down nuts. The dogs begun to howl.

The black hut where Granser sat pounding the ingredients has been blown to pieces: 'jus only sticks and sods scattert wide'. Granser's body lies nearby, emptied out like a puppet, and his head is stuck on the pointed pole of a gate. Looking about, Riddley finds Goodparley sitting where he last saw him, outside another black hut – sitting quite still, that is, because the stone pounder with which Granser worked the mixture has been driven into his skull. The dogs carry on howling, 'lorn and oansome', and Riddley slips away.

Blown to atoms

In the early years of the nineteenth century, the search for a safe and smokeless alternative to gunpowder led to a number of discoveries and not a few disasters. The explosive potential of various celluloses had been known for some time: hence various experiments with sawdust, paper and starches. Research in this direction seems to have begun as early as 1813, when a French chemist, Henri Braconnot, investigated

the action of nitric acid on linen, starch and sawdust. A couple
of decades later, again in France, Théophile-Jules Pelouze conducted experiments using the same acid operating on paper,
with explosive results. The greatest success was attributed to
one Christian Friedrich Schönbein, a professor at Basel University, who published details of his discovery in 1846.
Schönbein's method employed cotton waste that had been
cleaned and dried, then immersed in nitric acid. In August of
the same year Schönbein travelled to Woolwich to demonstrate 'guncotton' to the British military and to prospective
manufacturers. (His demonstrations were so successful that he
was invited to perform his experiments again before Queen
Victoria and Prince Albert, and the first pair of partridges shot
using guncotton was sent to the Prince Consort.)

The moments of greatest danger in the process of making
guncotton occurred during the drying and shaping of the
explosive compound. When dry it was easily detonated by a
sudden blow, the more so if it was warm. Moisture made guncotton safer and easier to shape or work into slabs for blasting
purposes or into the forms required of a propellant in military
use. The *Encylopaedia Britannica* notes that a compound containing 2 per cent of moisture might still be detonated on an
anvil; at 15 per cent of water, guncotton would no longer burn
and could be compressed or otherwise worked without danger. It might still be detonated, however, using a smaller dry
charge of guncotton; in fact, the wet and compressed material
was more explosive in such circumstances than the dry, and
could even be used under water. As regards heat and its attendant dangers, carefully prepared guncotton would not 'inflame'
until heated to about 180 or 185 degrees Celsius. When he
arrived at Woolwich in 1846, Schönbein was proposing that

his propellant be used as a compact alternative to gunpowder. But the results were unpredictable. The first practical trial of the new explosive was carried out later in 1846 in a granite quarry in Cornwall. It is said the local miners were not impressed as they watched a hole in the rock being charged with guncotton, and one of them joked that he would happily sit on the hole in return for a pint of beer; he then watched as the granite was shattered into a thousand quite unusable fragments, Schönbein and his associates having badly under-estimated the power of the charge.

I first happened on evidence of the outcome of Schönbein's experiments while I was peering at the photocopies of mid-nineteenth-century newspapers and magazines displayed at the visitor centre of the Oare Works – though the story does not relate directly to that site. Schönbein, having hit upon the innov-ation of guncotton in 1846, pursued British manufacturers, and the following year production began at the Marsh Works, Faver-sham, under the supervision (closely informed by the Professor) of one William Hall. By the summer of 1847, things had begun to go badly wrong. On the 24th of July the *Illustrated London News* ran a short account of what had transpired on the marsh ten days before, accompanied by an engraving 'from a sketch by an artist we dispatched to Faversham'.

At the left, a leafless broken tree frames the scene. On the far side of a leat that crosses the foreground lie three large metal cylinders resembling vats, one of them cracked open vertically. All around is mud and fragments of wooden build-ings, with here and there an upright timber or the remains of a brick chimney. Small groups of men busy themselves in this ruinous landscape: digging with pickaxes, hefting something into a barrow, setting off with a pallet raised on their shoulders. Two large mounds of earth dominate the picture, but they seem to shrink from the vacancy at its centre. In the bottom left corner lies what might be the skeleton of another tree; its roots have more than a hint of human limbs about them. Above the whole, the sky has been rendered in thin meandering lines, less like a cloudscape than a miasma drifting across the desolate prospect. A small lock has been built across the canal, and a lone figure stands inside it, thrusting a pole at the water.

Ten days before this image was published, at around eleven o'clock in the morning, two buildings at the Marsh Works – they were formerly 'stoves' where gunpowder had been dried, now adapted for the manufacture of guncotton – had exploded without warning. The *Illustrated London News* reported that twenty people had died and another fourteen been injured, noting too that the toll would surely have been greater had not many persons employed by Hall been making hay in the surrounding fields – though one such worker, as we shall see, had also died, and in 'very peculiar circumstances'.

The *Illustrated London News* devoted just five short paragraphs to the disaster, but *The Times* offered a fuller version, including a detailed account of the coroner's inquest, which had failed to settle the precise cause of the explosion. The buildings involved, so the newspaper reported, were numbered 3 and 4; when the latter went up, its neighbour followed almost immediately, this despite the pyramidal mound that separated them. According to *The Times*, the two buildings were 'blown into the air, leaving literally not one stone upon another. The immense bars of iron forming the machinery were rent asunder and broken as if they had been mere twigs, and the massive beams of timber were rent asunder and lay scattered about in small pieces in every direction. Indeed language is incapable of depicting the scene of desolation.' The writer resorts to this last cliché again just a few lines later: 'The scene now was scarcely to be depicted' as hundreds hurried to the spot and then as rapidly retreated, fearing that buildings nearby might explode at any moment.

Fire engines were called from the town and adjacent factories, and once the remaining buildings had been made safe 'all hands were directed . . . to the rescue of the sufferers beneath the ruins, whose cries for help were heart rending in the extreme'. The living and the dead were pulled from the earth, among the latter a boy of about sixteen, 'too much disfigured to be recognized'. Searches began of the marshes and fields adjoining, where mutilated remains were discovered 'many yards' from the seat of the explosion. We may imagine that the figure in the foreground of the *Illustrated London News* engraving, who is about to breach the surface of the canal with his pole, has made one such discovery. In the hours and days that followed, many smaller body parts were collected in baskets from the site itself and the surrounding fields.

At the inquest, William Hall was 'much affected' as he gave his evidence. He had been at the factory, he said, between six and eight o'clock; during this time, concerned that the younger members of his staff were not as careful as might be in their filling of tubes with guncotton, he took pains to instruct them in the safest method. At eleven o'clock (having gone home for breakfast) he returned, and was half a minute's walk from stove number 4 when it exploded. 'I saw the materials of the building ascend into the air and fall in all directions. I paced to and fro for a minute or a minute and a half, until I thought it safe to venture. I then went up to the buildings, and heard cries under both of them.' Hall called for others to help, and 'several hundred persons soon came to assist. We used our utmost endeavours until the fire drove us away.' Stove number 3 was now in flames; Hall sent for the fire engines. As soon as it was safe he supervised again the efforts at rescue and recovery: 'We got out fourteen persons alive from the ruins and several dead.' Hall seems genuinely shocked that the explosion could have happened at all; the temperature inside the buildings was monitored constantly, and was at the time about a hundred degrees below the limit set by Schönbein. Hall ends his testimony with an anxious statement of his own bona fides and those of the new explosive itself: 'The gun-cotton is manufactured by the French government and also by merchants in America. I have had three applications from the English government for gun-cotton, and have executed several hundred orders in all parts of the kingdom.'

Several other staff members gave evidence to the coroner, among them Robert Cheeseman, who had lost his wife and himself 'suffered most severely'. He told the inquest: 'I was in No. 3 stove when the accident occurred. I heard no explosion. It was momentary, and I cannot tell how it took place . . . I was buried in the ruins of the weighing room of No. 3, about four or five feet from where I had just previously been standing. I was greatly injured, and removed to my home.' Cheeseman confirmed that the temperature in the two buildings had been kept within safe limits; his wife, he said, had made no complaint of the heat during the morning. Finishing his testimony, the widower declared, 'I cannot attach any blame to any person in connexion with the accident.'

Of the stories told to the coroner and jury, the fate of one George Ransom was the most detailed and the most mysterious. Like many of the factory workers on a fine July day, he had been given leave to work in the hayfields not far from the works. Labouring beside him was John Batt, who recalled:

We both fell down with the concussion. On recovering, I went towards the stove on the south side, and told Ransom to follow me. He, however, went on the other side of the mound (the north-west side), the mound being between us and the explosion. The wind was then blowing in the direction towards where Ransom was, and I lost sight of him, in consequence of the smoke. I never saw him after this.

Ransom had, though, been seen by Frederick Francis Giraud, a doctor from Faversham who swiftly attended the scene with a fellow surgeon, Snape. While Giraud was tending the wounded, Ransom had come up to him 'and said he felt great inconvenience from the acid he had inhaled and asked if I could do anything for him'. Giraud advised getting as much fresh air as possible. It seems Ransom followed this advice for some hours before returning home and (not without reason) taking some strong drink. Giraud heard nothing of the man that evening, but at four o'clock in the morning he was sent for by Ransom's wife: the man had hardly slept, and had begun coughing and vomiting. Giraud treated him as best he could – he does not say how – and returned at seven o'clock, but found his patient no better. 'Mr Snape and I used all the means in our power for his recovery, but without success, and he expired about 12 o'clock.' A post-mortem examination had shown that Ransom's lungs were badly irritated and 'filled with an exudation resulting from that irritation, and thereby causing suffocation, which was the immediate cause of death'. Giraud concluded that Ransom must have inhaled a 'mephitic' (that is, noxious or poisonous) gas formed in the reaction of sulphuric acid with straw packed around the bottles in which it was stored. The effect, he said – the works' chemist, Alfred White, agreed – would have been worsened 'by the subsequent taking of stimulating drink'. This latter opinion did not appear in the final verdict of the jury, which found 'that the deceased died from suffocation produced by the inhalation of the fumes of mephitic gas'.

The funerals of most of the deceased – there were in the end twenty-one of them – took place nearby at Birchington on the Saturday following the explosion. *The Times* reported:

The melancholy scene was attended by many hundred persons from the town and neighbourhood of Faversham. The remains of those deceased had been coffined on the previous day, by Messrs Hall's direction; and this morning, at 10 o'clock, a numerous caval-cade of sorrowing mourners assembled at the works to pay the last tribute of respect and affection to their unfortunate relatives.

The procession left the works at a few minutes after ten, the coffins being borne by fellow labourers and followed by their managers, including Hall himself, whose kindness towards the bereaved is noted by the *Times* correspondent. 'The procession was met at the entrance of the churchyard by the officiating minister, who read the solemn service for the dead in a very impressive manner, tears being drawn from nearly every one present.'

The inquest reconvened on the 9th of August, having been adjourned in the hope that some of the injured might suffi-ciently recover as to give evidence; it was to this second meeting, and the jury already impanelled on the 16th, that the widowed and wounded Cheeseman gave his account of the day's events. The jury, like Cheeseman, attributed no blame to William Hall, nor to any other person; nor could they say why the explosion had occurred. *The Times* concludes its account of proceedings with a gruesome vignette from the aftermath:

The total number of deaths resulting from the accident has been 21. Only 11 bodies have been discovered, the remaining 10 having been blown to atoms. Portions of the human frame are still found in the corn fields at an enormous distance from the scene of the catastrophe; and it is a disgraceful fact that some inhuman wretches, since the accident, have actually possessed themselves of mutilated fragments for the purpose of exhibition. At Sittingbourne and Whitstable, portions of limbs were exhibited for some days to a depraved crowd at so much per head. The disgusting affair was, however, promptly put a stop to by the local magistrates.

A second disaster occurred at the Marsh Works just weeks later. Robert Cheeseman was again badly injured; he had been removing a small portion of explosive, a remnant from the first accident, when it ignited. According to *The Times*, he would now likely lose his sight. The accidents spelled the end, for now, of guncotton manufacture at Faversham and beyond. The new explosive had proved catastrophically unstable, and the Kent disasters were quickly followed by two more in France, at Vincennes and Le Bouchet. Commercial interest declined, but research continued under the direction of the Austrian government. Baron von Lenk, an artillery officer who had been experimenting with guncotton since 1853, had some success in using it as a propellant, and in 1862 the

Austrians approached the British government with a proposal to put into manufacturing practice the methods he had devised. The War Department dispatched a chemist, Frederick Abel, to inspect von Lenk's plant at Hirtenberg, near Vienna. The following year, manufacture began again, this time at Waltham Abbey and under Abel's supervision. As Wayne Cocroft tells us, Abel's crucial innovation was to pulp the guncotton before nitration, allowing it to be thoroughly washed to remove the nitrating acids, residues of which seem to have caused the fatal instability; machinery from the paper industry was adapted for the purpose. These new processes had economic as well as military advantages: they allowed manufacturers to use cotton waste as the raw material instead of the expensive cotton skeins used previously; and the pulped product could now be moulded to fit into shells, mines and torpedoes.

But guncotton was still a volatile substance. A decade after the state-run Waltham Abbey factory opened, the properties of the explosive remained imperfectly understood. A private enterprise, the Patent Safety Gun-Cotton Company, had begun production according to von Lenk's system at Stowmarket, Suffolk, in the early 1860s. On the 11th of August 1871 there was an explosion in one of the site's three magazines: twenty-four people were killed and fifty injured; the small wooden buildings, erected just fourteen feet apart, were blown to pieces, and considerable destruction caused in the nearby town. The works, however, were soon rebuilt, and the factory became a leading supplier to the army, the navy and the mining industry. Guncotton manufacture resumed on the marshes outside Faversham in 1873, when the newly established Cotton Powder Company built its low clusters of fragile timber buildings on the shores of the Swale, far enough from the town and from the gunpowder factories to the east. Supplies of acid, cotton and other raw materials were easily transported in the Swale, and the finished product carried back along the coast and into the Thames estuary. The obvious disadvantage of the site, and of the marshes in general, was that it was impossible to plant trees between the danger buildings – the traditional method of shielding buildings and bodies from any future blast.

And there an end of all

In 1852 Richard H. Home, a regular contributor to Dickens's magazine *Household Words*, spent some hours at a powder works at Hounslow, Middlesex, on the outskirts of London. The complex, owned by the firm of Curtis and Harvey, was situated on the river Crane, and its mills were powered by water and steam; by mid century, Hounslow was among the most important privately owned gunpowder factories in the country. In the article Home wrote for *Household Words* – soon reprinted for American readers in *Harper's* magazine – he is not much interested in the technology, infrastructure or economics of gunpowder manufacture. 'How Gunpowder is Made' is purposely, sometimes luridly, impressionistic; the journalistic model is Dickens's own brand of reportage, as practised in his early court reporting and perfected in *Sketches by Boz*. In his sketch of the Hounslow factory and its workers, Home borrows from his editor's repertoire of near-Gothic imagery; the banks of the Crane might be the setting for a 'sensation novel' or a story by Poe. Which is not to say that Home has merely exaggerated the atmosphere he found in the woods in Middlesex; his article is as much a portrait of his readers' fears and fantasies regarding such places as it is an attempt vividly to describe the works and their setting.

Accordingly, 'How Gunpowder is Made' is a lavishly figurative piece of writing; everything Home sees reminds him of something or somewhere else, as if the strangeness of the place, and all that it suggests of destruction visited here among the trees and leats or at the furthest reaches of empire, could be expressed only in terms of inflated simile. This is, in a sense, appropriate: sites such as the Hounslow works were both extraordinarily dangerous and necessarily obscure and secretive – they were in their way among the wildest places in Britain. And it is with this impression that Home begins: 'We never met a single man in all our rambles through the plantations, nor heard the sound of a human voice. It is like a strange new settlement, where there is ample space, plenty of wood and water, but with scarcely any colonists, and only here and there a log-hut or a dark shed among the trees.' The 150-acre site looks, says Home, 'like the strange and squalid plantation of some necromancer in Spenser's "Fairy Queen"'.

As he sets out across this enchanted land, Home spies some way off among the winding paths and clusters of osier willows a stand of black and shattered trees, distorted, writhing, partially stripped of their bark. Amid the confusion of these bizarre but apparently natural features, he spots a 'great, black, slanting' thing that he is told is a blast wall – there will be more of these. In the distance he observes an enormous mill wheel, 'the queen of all the rest', silhouetted black against the grey sky like an 'antediluvian skeleton'. Beneath its lower spokes, 'as if disgorged before its death', bursts forth a torrent of water. Flanking this monster are lower structures, also black, and at some distance a chimney or tower. 'Over all this there float clouds of black smoke, derived from charred wood, if we may judge of the effect upon our noses and eyes.' Altogether, Home writes, there are ninety-seven buildings, spaced between 30 and 150 yards apart so as to minimize loss of life and materials should one of them erupt. Many of these buildings are sturdily constructed but have flimsy upper storeys and light roofs, so that the force of an explosion will be directed upwards. Others have concrete roofs, or shallow water tanks above them to quench a fire as soon as it takes hold.

The scene is a Gothic one for sure. It is also at first entirely silent. Not only are the wooded precincts between the danger buildings unpopulated, but the whole complex, interior and exterior, presents an unsettling hush. 'Here no shadow of a practical joke, or caper of animal spirits, ever transpires; no witticisms, no oaths, no chaffing, or slang. A laugh is never heard, a smile seldom seen. Even the work is carried on by the men with as few words as possible, and these uttered in a low tone.' There are no instructing voices raised inside the buildings, no calls or shouts directed across the intervening woodland or along the leats from one powder punt to another, because when a man shouts it is understood by all his colleagues to mean just one thing: imminent and likely mortal danger. Inside, Home finds the powder workers 'creeping about' without a sound, whispering orders or questions to each other, and communicating in a language of 'mute gesticulation' like actors in a well-drilled mime troupe.

Home passes rather cursorily over the manufacture and preparation of raw materials for gunpowder: 'After visiting successively the mills where the charcoal, saltpetre, and brimstone, are separately prepared, we plash our way over the wet path to the "incorporation mill" — a sufficiently dangerous place.' Here two great millstones turn on iron beds, with three inches of powder packed at all times between the stone and metal. Otherwise, sparks would be inevitable, 'and there an end of all'. The time required for incorporation is precisely known, so there are no workers needed in this room to over-see the process. All reasonable precautions are taken. And yet, says Home's guide Mr Ashbee, 'five of them – just such mills as these — went off at Faversham the other day, one after the other. Nobody knew how.' Home responds with a bit of Dick-ensian sarcasm: 'This seasonable piece of information naturally increases the peculiar interest we feel in the objects we are now examining, as they proceed with their work.' Though in the Faversham case the cause was obscure, Home tell us, the circumstances of such accidents are routinely communicated to the proprietors of other gunpowder mills; those involved in the industry 'all display the same consideration for each other'.

His guide now leads him towards the buildings reserved for corning and graining – the latter 'a very nice, and, it would appear, a sufficiently alarming operation'. The two men ascend a pathway and pass over a mound planted with firs, then descend to the riverside and arrive at a black timber blast wall, twenty-five feet high and 'set up in the shape of an acute angle'. There is a similar structure on the other side of the river. Home turns towards the corning house: low-roofed and black, like so many of the buildings here. In front of this dismal edifice, he has the impression it might be a place of torture, 'devoted to the service of the darkest pagan superstitions'. Inside, a black framework hangs from the ceiling; it would be 'just the thing to hang the dead bodies of torture victims in'. Just as Home is giving himself up to these grisly fantasies, a shout goes up from Ashbee: 'Put *on* the house!' The whole building starts to vibrate, filled with the noise of machinery shuddering into life. Home, startled out of his reverie, just about holds himself together: 'Nothing but shame – nothing but shame and an anguish of self-command, prevents our instantly darting out of the house – across the platform – and headlong into the river.'

He escapes instead to the glazing house, where the powder revolves in barrels and is coated with a thin layer of graphite. A curious-looking company of men presents itself: 'The faces of the men here, being all black from the powder, and shining with the addition of the black lead, have the appearance of grim masks of demons in a pantomime, or rather the real demons in a mine. Their eyes look out upon us with a strange intelligence. They know the figure they present. So do we.' Home is suggesting, of course, that the workers look like natives, or imported slaves, in the colonies he invoked at the start of his article. He moves on to the charge house, where the barrels of finished powder are stored: 'We enter the house alone; the others waiting outside. All silent and dusky as an Egyptian tomb. The tubs of powder, dimly seen in the uncertain light, are ranged along the walls, like mummies – all giving the impression of a secret life within.'

All of this mock horror is in fact a prelude, designed to heighten his readers' worst fears and expectations of the place, to Home's account of a genuine and recent catastrophe. Passing through the fir groves on his way out of the factory, he notes again the strange appearance of many of the trees, which have been twisted or had their crowns cut off. In places 'there are large and upright gaps in a plantation'. The previous year, the separating house had blown up, then the granulating house a hundred yards away. How the fire was carried between the buildings, and thence to another four of the danger houses, Ashbee cannot imagine, 'except by a general combustion of the air'. Within forty seconds – it is not clear how Ashbee can be so precise about this interval – the press house, mixing house, glazing house and another granulating house had all erupted. An iron waterwheel, thirty feet in circumference, was blown through the air to a distance of fifty yards, cutting the tops off all the trees in its way, finally coming to rest between the upper boughs of a large tree where, Ashbee recalled, 'it stuck fast, like a boy's kite'. He now dropped his voice, says Home, and spoke in a whisper, 'in short detached fragments', about the men who died that day. They were horribly mutilated – 'more than mutilated, some of them' – and their limbs and other parts distributed 'hither and thither', so that they could not be identified with any certainty. One man escaped from a building mere seconds before it exploded, and ran forty yards before he suddenly dropped dead, killed by the invisible blast wave. Some of those missing were never found – 'blown all to nothing'.

Home now turns his gaze on the huge gaps among the firs, where trees have been reduced to half their height:

Some trees, near at hand, we observe to have been flayed of their bark all down one side. Others have strips of bark hanging dry and black. Several trees are strangely distorted, and the entire trunk of one large fir has been twisted like a corkscrew, from top to bottom, requiring an amount of force scarcely to be estimated by any known means of mechanical power. Amid all this quietness, how dreadful a visitation! It is visible on all sides, and fills the scene with a solemn, melancholy weight.

In case we have not already grasped the significance of the ruined trees that Home observed on his way into the works, it is now made stark and clear: the trees not only record the force and pattern of the explosion, but their naked, burned and twisted limbs are meant to stand for human bodies maimed or killed.

Throughout his essay Home has insisted on the silence, or near silence, here among the firs and waterwheels and low black buildings. 'How Gunpowder is Made' – he has in fact told us very little about how it is made – concludes with a last invocation of that silence, which we must now imagine interrupted by the first hideous report:

The dead leaves lie thick beneath, in various sombre colours of decay, and through the thin bare woods we see the grey light fading into the advancing evening. Here, where the voice of man is never heard, we pause, to listen to the sound of rustling boughs, and the sullen rush and murmur of water-wheels and mill-streams; and over all, the song of a thrush, even while uttering blithe notes, gives a touching sadness to this isolated scene of human labours – labours, the end of which, is a destruction of numbers of our species, which may, or may not, be necessary to the progress of civilization, and the liberty of mankind.

An explosive archipelago

By the end of the nineteenth century the Cotton Powder Company factory at Uplees was one of the largest munitions works in Britain, with about 150 buildings dotted across the marsh, producing thirty-five types of explosive. The factory, as Cocroft describes in his account of the industry, was equipped with a Swale-side acid plant, a gasworks for heat and light, three sets of hydraulic accumulators, air compressors, and a high-pressure water system to serve a network of fire hydrants in case of emergency. (As we shall discover, the location of these hydrants would be crucial on the 2nd of April 1916.) The buildings themselves were linked by a tramway with a gauge of three feet and three inches. The whole complex, in other words, had been the object of considerable investment, in common with many of the older powder works, and the newer guncotton factories, around the country. By the late nineteenth century the explosives industry had changed radically, with new chemistry, new machines and vastly expanded commercial applications. Although the United Kingdom fought no major foreign wars between the Crimean War in the mid 1850s and the Boer War commencing at the end of the century, fear of conflict with European powers meant it was easy to justify politically a vast expenditure on defence and the continued stockpiling of weapons and explosives.

Production of guncotton and its successors was best suited to sites like the one at Uplees: sufficiently distant from the town, but with ready access to transport by water and rail. The new ingredients – including glycerine and the basic raw material of cotton waste or wood pulp – required not just new technologies but a degree of expenditure that could not be borne by the old family firms that had dominated the gunpowder industry. The chemical-explosives producers tended to be limited companies, and in many cases they acquired factories from family firms. It was these companies, Nobel chief among them, that devised or perfected the best-known, and the most notorious, explosive compounds of the period. Nitroglycerine had been invented in Turin in 1847 by Professor Ascanio Sobrero, but it was so volatile that no practical use could at first be found. In 1864 Alfred Nobel came up with a mercury fulminate detonator for nitroglycerine, and then a means of stabilizing it by adding a siliceous sediment known as *Kieselguhr*; the result was dynamite, which Nobel patented in 1867.

Nobel's new high explosives were too sensitive and too violent for use as propellants. Late-Victorian manufacturers, and the military forces they supplied, dreamed of a smokeless propellant that would neither give away a gunner's position nor obscure his vision. In the late 1880s, while living and working to the north of Paris at Sevran-Livy, Nobel produced 'ballistite': a blend of nitrocellulose, nitroglycerine and camphor. The following year in England, a committee of the War Office drew in part on this research of Nobel's to come up with cordite, an explosive made of nitroglycerine and guncotton, stabilized with mineral jelly. Nobel Explosives took legal action against the British government for infringement of patent, but lost the case because of a single difference in the type of nitrocellulose employed.

The British army and navy soon adopted cordite as their principal propellant. Production began at Waltham Abbey, but was slowed by an accident in May 1894. Curtis and Harvey converted their powder works at Tonbridge in Kent for the manufacture of cordite, and opened an extensive plant at Cliffe (also the site of a small powder factory), out on the marshes by the Thames estuary. The Cliffe complex had a river frontage almost a mile long, and was furnished with two jetties and a loading bay. A remarkable amount of this complex still survives on the bleak and almost treeless marsh: huge circular earth traverses, ponds formed in the borrow pits from which this earth was dug; and the remnants of danger buildings built in brick that were once roofed with corrugated iron, lined with zinc and floored with lead. The complex hovers in my imagination thanks to aerial photographs in Cocroft's book and a vertiginous zoom via Google Earth from the mass of Kent and its estuaries to an amazingly legible grid of buildings, earthworks and the ghosts of tramlines.

Already, by the early years of the twentieth century, the new chemical-explosives industry had replaced or cannibalized much of the infrastructure and land devoted to traditional powder production. The works at Uplees formed part of a widely dispersed archipelago of factories built – if that is the word for these buildings practically floated atop saturated countryside – on marshland at the edges or in the interstices of the kingdom.

This special form of warfare

Some more detailed sense of what was afoot on the marshes at Uplees in the early years of the twentieth century may be gleaned from a fat volume published in 1909 by the International Congress of Applied Chemistry. According to *The Rise and Progress of the British Explosives Industry*, the Cotton Powder Company, registered in 1872, was originally involved in the manufacture of Punshon's Patent Controllable Guncotton, which it seems was not so controllable as its inventors had hoped: 'Owing . . . to the extremely hygroscopic nature of the finished product, this explosive proved a complete failure and had to be abandoned.' But the company carried on, and began manufacture of nitroglycerine at Uplees in 1892, and cordite four years later. There was a second, smaller, works at Melling in Lancashire. In 1909, between the two establishments the company employed 10 chemists, 3 scientific engineers, 25 commercial and administrative staff, 352 workmen (including foremen) and 75 women workers. At Uplees, it produced 850 tons of guncotton each year, 800 tons of cordite, 500 of nitroglycerine, 350 of tonite, 3 million detonators, 40,000 distress signals and a million 'sound signals of all descriptions'. Most of this output was sold within the United Kingdom for military and industrial use, but the Cotton Powder Company also traded with the governments of New Zealand, Australia, Canada, Chile, Peru, Argentina, India and Japan. Almost a decade into the century – and five years from the outbreak of the Great War – the factory comprised over 200 buildings, and occupied 400 acres along the Swale.

In 1912 the Cotton Powder Company was joined at its western end by the Explosives Loading Company, which had been formed expressly for the purpose of filling shells with TNT. Until the outbreak of the war it was the only plant to specialize in that task, and so in August 1914 was able to supply the government with 100,000 pounds of TNT from its stock. The company's head office was in Parliament Street, in the heart of Westminster, and among the founders was one Captain T. G. Tulloch – known as 'Tri-nitro Tom' – who had been chief experimental officer at the Royal Arsenal at Woolwich, and then served on the board of the Chilworth Gunpowder Company near Guildford. In the years before the war, Tulloch visited Germany many times and saw at first hand the army's turn there towards TNT as its main shell propellant; he passed on everything he knew to the British military authorities, but could not yet convince them to adopt fully the new explosive.

Tulloch seems to have had an eye for the future of technological warfare – during the coming war he would be involved, in his post at the Ministry of Munitions, in the development of tanks – and the plant at Uplees was thus among the most innovative in the country. As at the neighbouring factory, the Explosives Loading Company's buildings were low and spread generously across the marsh, most of them lightly constructed in wood on concrete bases. Among these were more substantial brick-built magazines and offices, steel-framed boiler and power houses and the shell-filling buildings themselves, which were of thick reinforced concrete and surrounded by earth traverses, nine feet high and six feet thick at the bottom.

On the 8th of August 1914, just four days after the declaration of war, the first Defence of the Realm Act secured state authority to acquire land and resources for munitions manufacture. Within the space of four years, the country would be covered by a network of 200 state-controlled factories on which the government had spent £60 million. Some of these were privately owned establishments that had been taken over and converted under powers outlined in the Act, their staff numbers, scale and capacity increased, and overtime and night working introduced. At Woolwich, Stowmarket and Cliffe new structures appeared, and on the marshes at Uplees, where the factories remained in the hands of private companies, concrete slabs were laid to support the new danger buildings. Most of the factories were newly built and resembled towns, with residential streets and barrack houses as well as industrial plant and storage. High-explosives factories were set up late in 1914, followed early the next year by the National Shell Factories, devoted to ammunition for the lighter types of field gun, and National Projectile Factories for the heavier artillery.

On Friday the 14th of May 1915, *The Times* published an article by its military correspondent Colonel Charles Repington
that would lead to the collapse of Herbert Asquith's Liberal
government, a distinct shift in the balance of power between
Britain's principal military commanders, and a reorganization
of munitions manufacture and supply across the country and
the empire. The 'shell crisis' or 'shell scandal' is well known,
but it is worth briefly describing its causes and effects. Though
Repington did not mention the fact in his article of mid May,
he had been told by the Commander-in-Chief, Sir John French,
that the recent Allied offence at Neuve Chapelle had been
ruinously compromised by a shortage of munitions. (This despite the fact that more shells were fired in the initial
bombardment, lasting little more than half an hour, than had
been discharged in the whole of the Boer War.) The *Times* correspondent cast the matter in terms of immediate, present
danger: 'It is important, for an understanding of the British
share in operations of this week, to realize that we are suffering from certain disadvantages which make striking successes
difficult to achieve.' At present, he wrote, the Germans occupied mostly the higher ground along an undulating front, 'and
are provided with every scientific and clever device for arrest-
ing an attack'. The German defences had formed a 'hard crust'
that would only be broken if the British forces were sent more
men, more large guns and more high explosive: 'This special
form of warfare has no precedent in history.'

The *Times* article seems to have been the result of both private grief and political manoeuvring. The paper's proprietor,
Lord Northcliffe, privately blamed Lord Kitchener, then Secretary of State for War and still venerated as the hero of
Khartoum, for the recent death of his nephew at the front.

And Northcliffe was sympathetic to the view of David Lloyd George, the Chancellor of the Exchequer, that munitions policy was being mismanaged. The *Daily Mail*, Northcliffe's other paper, was more explicit than *The Times* in its levelling of blame: the headline of the 21st of May read, 'The Shells Scandal: Lord Kitchener's Tragic Blunder'. One effect of such reports was to turn some readers against Northcliffe and his newspapers, and circulation declined for a time. But the more dramatic consequence was the swift collapse of the government and its replacement by a coalition – though Asquith remained as Prime Minister. Kitchener retained his post as Secretary of State for War but was now sidelined, and ceded control of munitions production to Lloyd George, newly appointed Minister for Munitions. (Before the year was out, Sir John French was removed from his role as Commander-in-Chief and replaced by Sir Douglas Haig.) There now began the wholesale reorganization of munitions manufacture – including the production of high explosives – that was necessary for the fullest prosecution of the war, and which would transform industry, infrastructure and landscape, not to speak of the lives of all who worked in the factories. Just a month after Repington's article appeared in *The Times*, a cartoonist for *Punch* depicted Lloyd George as a pharaonic slave driver, brandishing a whip over his factories and their harried (but contemptuous-looking) workers.

At the outset of the war, the main high explosive used in British shells was picric acid, known as Lyddite because it had first been tested at a firing range in Lydd, Kent. (The range is still there; you have to drive, or in my case cycle, inland of it for a few miles to make your way south along the coast to Dungeness.) In the nineteenth century, the substance had been used as a yellow dye for clothing, but a series of factory explosions put an end to this, and it was soon taken up by the military. During the early years of the war, picric acid was superseded by TNT, though it continued to be used in naval shells and as a powerful detonator in other contexts. TNT, which had been used by the Germans since 1902, was considered a relatively safe explosive in manufacture: it seemed that it could not be detonated by violent percussion or merely by being set alight. As Cocroft recounts, there were ten TNT plants in operation at the start of 1915, and sixteen by the summer in the wake of the shell crisis; by June, production had already quadrupled. But TNT was expensive to manufacture, and as the shell crisis was addressed and production stepped up considerably, the explosive began to be mixed with ammonium nitrate to make amatol for use in shells, mines and aerial bombs. Thus was introduced a powerful, economical and apparently safe high explosive that would come to dominate on the battlefield and so also affect work and life in the factories on the home front.

The success of TNT as a replacement for the earlier high explosives, especially in its modified form as amatol, meant that it was also involved in some of the worst accidents of the war. By Cocroft's calculation, 600 people died in accidents at explosives and ammunitions factories; about one-sixth of those were women, and the same fraction were civilians not actually working at the plants in question. At Ardeer, in 1915, an explosion on the railway that ran to and from the factory stopped the production of TNT for the duration of the war. An explosion in 1917 at the complex in Silvertown, in the east end of London, killed sixty-nine people, of whom fifty-three were local residents. Twenty-four workers and nineteen locals died later the same year at a TNT plant in Ashton-under-Lyne. And at the National Filling Factory at Chilwell in Nottinghamshire, 134 workers died in an explosion on the 1st of July 1918. The new explosive was not only lethal in the case of such accidents; TNT could also induce severe jaundice in those who handled it: 106 'canary girls', and maybe more, died in this way during the war. It was said that some of the canary girls who made it through the war subsequently reverted to their yellowed aspect whenever they fell ill, sometimes decades later.

The plant at Uplees was directly affected by all of these circumstances: the accelerated demand for high explosives after the shell scandal in 1915; the state regulation of privately owned factories; and the switch to TNT and later to amatol, with their attendant dangers. The Explosives Loading Company plant grew, new buildings appearing within its pre-war limits, the whole expanding to the west along the Swale – but the buildings were low and lightly put together, still modest compared to the larger structures of the cordite and guncotton works of the Cotton Powder Company. Infrastructure was extended and ramified too: the tramlines, paths and roads that traversed the site; the texture of telephone and telegraph wires that delivered instructions from outside and within the complex.

The devil's porridge

Of the explosives factories built across Britain in response to the shell crisis, the largest was the cordite plant near Gretna, spanning the border between Scotland and England. The completed site stretched for twelve miles and included two townships where many of its workers – most of them women – lived in newly built barrack houses. At the height of its production the Gretna plant was turning out 800 tons of cordite per week. Towards the end of 1916 the Ministry of Munitions allowed Arthur Conan Doyle to visit the factory and write about it for a local newspaper, the *Annandale Observer*. Doyle's article pits the workers at Gretna against the enemy's Chief of General Staff and the might of German industry:

We can never defeat Hindenburg until we have beaten Krupp, and that is what these khaki-clad girls of Moorside and elsewhere are going to do. Hats off to the women of Britain. Even all the exertions of the militants shall not in future prevent me from being an advocate for their vote, for those who have helped to save the State should be allowed to guide it.

Doyle had been shown the new townships built for the workers, and watched the women mixing the noxious ingredients:

The nitroglycerine on one side and the gun-cotton on the other are kneaded into a sort of devil's porridge which is the next stage of manufacture. Those smiling khaki-clad girls who are swirling the stuff round in their hands would be blown to atoms in an instant if certain very small changes occurred. The changes will not occur and the girls will still smile and stir their devil's porridge, but it is a narrow margin between life and death.

A month earlier, on the 6th of November 1916, the *Daily Chronicle*, then by some distance the best-selling newspaper in

Britain, had published a short article by Rebecca West entitled 'The Cordite Makers'. West does not name the place, though it is clearly also Gretna. She begins thus:

The world was polished to a brightness by an east wind when I visited the cordite factory, and shone with hard colours like a German toy-landscape. The marshes were very green and the scattered waters very blue, and little white clouds roamed one by one across the sky like grazing sheep on a meadow. On the hills around stood elms, and grey churches and red farms and yellow ricks, painted bright by the sharp sunshine. And very distinct on the marshes there lay the village which is always full of people and yet is the home of nothing except death.

With this last statement, West practically begins where Home concluded: with a reminder of the ultimate destination and purpose of the factory's products. But she is also keen at the outset to capture the near-poetic unreality of the place: 'In the glare it showed that like so many institutions of the war it has the disordered and fantastic quality of a dream.'

How does she interpret that dream? As if all its elements are examples of symbolic or metaphoric displacement – nothing quite what it seems. Like Home in 1852 turning the danger buildings into a colonial settlement, West immediately wants to compare the low huts now looming into view with other sorts of building: they are like, she says, the barrack huts that house Irish labourers, or like the well-spaced chalet-type structures of a modern, airy sanatorium. 'They are connected by raised wooden gangways and interspersed with green mounds and rush ponds' – the ponds presumably excavated to form the mounds. Barbed wire surrounds the huts and mounds, and guards patrol the perimeter. Surveying the complex as a whole, West writes: 'Its products must have sent tens of thousands of our enemies to their deaths. And it is inhabited chiefly by pretty young girls clad in a Red-Riding-Hood fancy dress of khaki and scarlet.' They start work at six in the morning and finish twelve hours later: a working day the girls vastly prefer to the prospect of a normal eight-hour shift, mainly because they earn more money this way, though the work is physically and mentally a deal more taxing than even the exhausting domestic service in which many of them would otherwise be engaged. There is also a degree of pride, and of competition between the huts; in the final few hours of a shift, spies are dispatched between huts to report on the day's production, and if need be their colleagues quicken their rate accordingly.

From a distance, as West records, the work itself looks oddly domestic. In tidy rooms, dressed in their bright uniforms, working with powders and pastes, the women might be labouring away in a huge bakery. 'The brown cordite paste itself looks as if it might turn into very pleasant honey-cakes, an inviting appearance that has brought gastritis to more than one unwise worker.' Can this be true? Perhaps boredom or the austerity of a wartime diet, maybe just curiosity or bravado, led the odd girl to pinch off a morsel of explosive dough and cram it into her mouth. Or maybe this is just an authorial indulgence in the dreamlike unreality to which West has already alerted us. The factory, she now writes, 'must be the place where war and grace are closest linked'. Improbable gardens have been created around the danger buildings, containing neatly trimmed shrubs and a sundial, while 'within there is a group of girls that composes into so beautiful a

picture that one remembers that the most glorious painting
in the world, Velazquez's *The Weavers*, shows women working
just like this'. The scene inside a cordite shed resolves itself,
before the intensity of West's gaze, into an arrangement of
lines and forms and coloured planes: the women 'laying out
the golden cords in graduated sizes from the thickness of rope
to the thinness of macaroni'. The wet floor of the hut reflects
the girls' dresses in patches of scarlet and khaki. The dresses
make them look like diligent children. They are fireproof,
or meant to be: 'There had been one of those incalculable
happenings of which high explosives are so liable, an inflam-
matory mixture of air with acetone, and the cordite was
ignited. Two huts were instantly gutted, and the girls had to
walk out through the flame. In spite of the uniform one girl
lost a hand.'

'The Cordite Makers' is a curious piece of reportage, punctuated by moments of painterly or photographic stasis and
some stark reminders of the destruction caused, deliberately
or accidentally, by the 'devil's porridge'. But the article is also
a polemic on behalf of the women themselves, whom West
considers to have sacrificed 'almost as much' as enlisted men.
If they are not in as much danger as soldiers at the front, their
situation is certainly as perilous as that of any man engaged in
home defence. Finally, West has a message for the Prime Minister in the wake of the 'shell crisis' of the previous year: 'It
was all very well for the Army to demand high explosives, and
for Mr Lloyd George to transmit the demand to industry; in
the last resort the matter lay in the hands of the girls in the
khaki and scarlet hoods, and the State owes them a very great
debt for the way they have handled it.'

A congested state

It rained hard and long on the marshes of east Kent in March 1916. I have walked the land in mist, drizzle, steady downpours and gales full of sea spray, and felt as if the inundation might never end, such is the sense on this spongy expanse that water, ground and air are simply returning to some natural unity. After weeks of rain the landscape looks strewn with fragments of mirror. You can feel here as though you are picking across an oddly delicate and airy lattice of land; that is, until you sink ankle-deep in the soaked and sucking earth beneath you. On such days it seems hardly credible that anybody built anything out here, let alone structures belonging to an industry that depended on keeping its product dry.

Towards the end of March the rain stopped, and on the 29th a snowstorm covered much of the country and badly affected telegraph and telephone communications. By Friday the 31st the land south of the Swale was comprehensively sodden. That morning, Major Aston Cooper-Key, His Majesty's Inspector of Explosives, travelled to Kent to make an unannounced inspection of the Explosives Loading Company's factory. We may imagine the melting snow still dropping from the rooftops of Chatham and Gillingham as the Major's train passed through the Medway towns, and the naval base and its industrial hinterland giving way to the drowned, half-frozen fields as he neared Faversham. A car or army truck must have taken him out to the Uplees marshes, where he surprised the soldiers and civilian workers when he presented himself at the gate.

The factory, Cooper-Key would later write, was in 'a very

congested state', the Ministry of Munitions having sent supplies 'much in excess of the requirements of the works'; though the managers had objected and tried to slow the influx, there remained scarcely any storage space, indoors or out, that was not completely filled with explosives, shell casings, primers or empty packing materials. About fifty tons of TNT had lately been received for which no magazine or other accommodation could be found, and so it had been left in the open, protected as far as could be with waterproof fabric. In fact, sixty tons of TNT and forty of ammonium nitrate passed into the factory each week; the nitrate barrels were frequently found to be damaged and could not be returned, so accumulated at the site. The empty TNT barrels were mostly intact, but the irregularity of the railways meant that these too piled up in the spaces between offices, danger buildings and boiler houses. The complex, Cooper-Key estimated as he made his rounds, was extended to about four times its operational capacity: 'Very great pressure was being exercised to secure the greatest possible output, and, in consequence, the limitations and precautions observed under normal circumstances were not possible.' Cooper-Key noted the relevant quantities of materials and their locations, including 150 tons of TNT stored inside building 833, and 50 tons stacked high in wooden cases outside the same building. Inside the cases, the TNT was packed in linen bags, and to the north of building 833, directly against the wall, was a pile of these bags about six feet long, three deep and two-and-a-half feet high. It was covered:

. . . by a green rotproof canvas sheet which covered the top but not the side of the heap. The TNT is packed in these bags before being put into cases. A little TNT dust always adheres to these bags and the heap was stained brown and the ground around it. There had been a large accumulation of these bags in this position for some months. It was there when Mr [George] Evetts, the present manager, took over charge of the factory in October 1915. The pile was being reduced as the empty cases were returned and was about one fourth of the size it had been.

Notwithstanding his concerns about the storage of TNT, Cooper-Key declared himself satisfied with the general condition of the Explosives Loading Company factory as he found them on 31 March 1916. After all, such ramping up of production was exactly what had been called for by the Ministry, and the consequent dereliction of certain standards, rules and habits was entirely to be expected. Mindful of the delays in the setting up of government-run factories, the Major would have boarded his train at Faversham station secure at least in the knowledge that the Explosives Loading Company and its workers were not shirking out there on the marshes.

If you don't look out

The sun shone on the morning of Sunday the 2nd of April, two days after the visit of His Majesty's Inspector of Explosives, and a fresh breeze slanted in along the coast from Whitstable, Herne Bay and Margate. Sunday was a full working day, though with certain variations from the midweek schedule and work practices. There were 150 men at the Explosives Loading Company that day, although during the rest of the week there would normally have been 270 workers: Sunday was a day off for the canary girls. At 7 a.m. the men teemed onto the site.

Many detrained from the Davington Light Railway, which terminated at the edge of the Cotton Powder Company plant, just east of the main gate. From here they spread out among the buildings to the west, reporting for duty, taking up their stations, addressing themselves wearily to familiar machines as they thrummed into motion, shell cases to be filled, crates and bags to be moved, trucks and trams to be driven about the complex. On a Sunday morning in the middle of the war, the men at the Explosives Loading Company could look forward to working until noon, pausing for dinner and then embarking, as they did every Sunday, on a general clean-up of the overworked and overstocked factory.

For the workers already present at seven o'clock, the night had not gone by without incident. The factories were patrolled regularly and would not have fallen into complete darkness. Lamps burned here and there, and an orange glow was visible from each of the boiler houses, where sparks escaped the flues and were intercepted by the plates of specially installed spark arresters. At some point during the night two patrolmen happened upon, and quickly put out, a small fire between a boiler house and a TNT store. It had clearly been caused, not for the first time, by sparks that the boiler-house arresters had failed to catch. The guards reported the incident at the start of the working day, but it was not thought so alarming as to require any rearrangement, in the course of the morning, of the explosives or packing materials stored in the open around the factory.

The manager at the Explosives Loading Company, George Evetts, started home for dinner at noon, deputing Rickman Palowkar to look after the factory while he was gone. Evetts intended to come back in the afternoon and oversee the weekly tidying of the factory. Before he left he spent three-quarters of an hour in a general inspection, and stopped in again briefly at his office, in building 826, before striking out towards the main gate and his home at Uplees Lodge.

Evetts walked along the tramline that ran to the gate at Uplees, passing close to building 833, where he saw nothing out of the ordinary. When he had got about a hundred yards east of a boundary dyke, he met a man called Underwood, foreman from a firm of pile drivers then at work on extending a jetty. Evetts carried on and arrived at Uplees Lodge at a quarter past twelve. Underwood was walking in the direction of building 833, and must have reached it, says the report, at about seven minutes past twelve. As he passed he noticed that the edge of the pile of bags stacked against 833 was burning. The bags were crackling, he said later, and flames were advancing towards the building. He does not seem to have left the tramline, or tried to put out the fire, which, Cooper-Key asserts in his report on the disaster, must only just have taken hold. Underwood now walked to the Explosives Loading Company office and, finding no one there, to the staff mess room. He put his head in at the door and remarked, 'You are sitting here enjoying yourselves, but if you don't look out you will have one of your buildings alight.' The manager's deputy, Palowkar, was in the mess room, and on hearing this news made his way at once to the larger canteen used by manual workers, sent a gang to fetch a manual fire engine, and ran towards building 833.

According to Cooper-Key's report, Palowkar 'called up' Evetts at twenty past twelve. (This seems to mean that he telephoned him, though in 1916 the phrase also meant to fetch or rouse directly.) The manager had by this time reached Uplees

Lodge and was sitting down to dinner. He started back at once towards the factory, and at the gate requested that the Cotton Powder Company's fire brigade be sent out. He saw nobody as he rushed back among the Explosives Loading Company buildings to the north-west; men not already alerted to the emergency and at work fighting the fire were either still at their midday meal or had gone back to work. As Evetts recalled, he had reached building 223 when he saw the fire about 250 yards away; it appeared to be burning strongly. Palowkar was at that point in charge of between thirty and forty men with buckets, chemical fire extinguishers and a manual fire engine. Their efforts were having little or no effect; the bags 'were still burning, and appeared to burn readily in spite of the exposure to the weather'. At half past twelve, the Cotton Powder Company fire brigade arrived, but the nearest hydrant was 700 yards away and they had to send for an additional hose. In the meantime, more buckets arrived by truck from the Cordite Department.

'It was then about 12.35,' Evetts recalled, 'and at this time there was a temporary slackening of the fire, probably due to the fact that the end of the building had burned out, and the Nitrate of Ammonium barrels had not yet fully caught fire.' He saw clearly that the building could not be saved, and so employed his men instead in removing the explosives stored inside 833 and nearby on three sides of the building. Goldfinch and Pover worked on the eastern side with the men of the fire brigade; Palowkar and his party to the north; and Evetts took charge of the remainder, to the west. For about fifteen minutes the men went back and forth, removing the crates. Evetts again: 'I was last there myself at about 12.45. Jarvis was looking after the men in the building. There did not appear to be any more fumes inside, but the smoke was very thick. It got too thick for the men, and I told them to come out.' To the east, the Cotton Powder Company brigade broke down a door and tried to reach the explosives inside, but the heat was too great and they were forced to retreat; the best they could do was to move the TNT stored outside.

By this time, so Evetts recounted to Cooper-Key, the whole of building 833 was burning fiercely, 'and the bulk of the Nitrate of Ammonia was alight. The heat was intense, with great masses of flame. I do not remember much smoke. This would be some time after one o'clock.' Forty yards away, trucks were reported to have caught fire as the wind blew sparks to the west. Evetts, afraid now that surrounding buildings were also in danger, ordered his men to shield them with what they could find of corrugated iron and flat sheets of aluminium. 'I was fully occupied protecting the buildings to leeward of 833, and did not know what was going on just then to the east and north of the building.' His attention was focused on building 868, onto which sparks had begun to rain. Evetts ordered a Private Wiltshire onto the roof to extinguish the debris, then called to him to lie down and face away from the heat, smoke and sparks of 833. Evetts continued:

Palowkar came to me at this time for instructions. I said to him – 'we have done all we can for the building; there is nothing more to be done now.' The building was then almost completely burnt out. The upper tiers of barrels and boxes had disappeared. It was possible to see right through the building. The fire had considerably decreased and appeared to be dying down. I said to Palowkar 'I am going to clear my men out – you had better do the same.' He left me and went to his gang at the north end of the building, and I did not see him again. I told my men to go, and saw them on their way from the building. I turned back to have a look at the east side of building 868 to see if it was still safe. Wiltshire was still lying on top. I walked round to the north of the building and some little distance towards building 833. When I was about 40 yards from it the explosion occurred.

F. B.

Steve Epps of Faversham had married in the new year; his job as a charge-hand at the Cotton Powder Company factory, where he had begun work towards the end of 1914, paid a good deal better than his previous job driving a horse-drawn dray for one of the local breweries. Among his duties at the factory was a role in the part-time fire brigade; like his fellow charge-hands, Epps wore a badge – 'F. B.' – so that he could be identified in an emergency. On the 2nd of April, he was summoned from his dinner by a hooter sounded in response to Evetts's request for help as he dashed back into the complex. Half a century later, Epps told the story to a researcher from the Faversham Society. By the time he arrived at 833, he said, 'the stuff inside the shed was already alight'. Again at Evetts's command, Epps joined the effort to remove as much TNT as possible from the immediate vicinity. 'We was chucking it to one side, handing it down – it kept falling all round about you. They were slamming it around, and one old chap – he could see I was a bit nervy – he said: "That won't go off unless it's detonated, old chap." I said: "Right, I feel safe enough."'

Another local, Syd Twist, was seventeen in the spring of 1916; his father, who had been working at the Cotton Powder

Company works for thirty-five years, was foreman of the Blasting Powder Department. Young Syd had joined the Maintenance Department as an apprentice fitter and turner in 1914. In 1977 the Faversham Society published his recollections of the town where he grew up. At six decades' remove, Twist's memory of some details is considerably awry; he recalls being told there was a fire at the Explosives Loading Company as early as nine o'clock, and going upstairs at the fitting shop to see smoke rising to the west. But he offers another intimate perspective on the decisive moment: 'I had managed to get off at twelve o'clock and as I was walking towards the gate, which meant passing the cordite ranges, I saw the firemen laying the hose from the hydrant nearest the ELC – a distance of 400 to 500 yards. They collected the hoses from all over the factory and by about 12.15 to 12.20 had laid enough for one nozzle. I had got home by cycle and was just washing, about 12.30, when we heard and felt the explosion.'

An immense volume of flame

'We'd just got the water on it – and up she went.' This was how Steve Epps recalled the moment of the first explosion. His is one of several accounts of the disaster that encompass the instant of detonation. In some of these narratives, the explosion itself is a sort of lacuna: one moment the workers were engaged on averting disaster, the next they found themselves already in the aftermath. George Goldfinch had been running alongside a dyke with a colleague; decades later his niece Betty Bax told Arthur Percival: 'The next thing he remembered was finding himself on the other side of the water and seeing the other man quite near him with all his clothes blown off him, and just his shoes and socks, and his collar at a strange angle round his neck.' Goldfinch's own clothes were in tatters, and he had a broken arm; he remained partially deaf for the rest of his life.

According to Cooper-Key's report, there appeared to have been 'some change in the nature and appearance of the fire immediately before the explosion'. A number of workers who had been watching from a distance recalled that an immense volume of flame suddenly shot up from the building, sending out fiery streamers that rose to a great height and then broke off; the resulting detached and glowing masses remained visible in the air above 833 'for an appreciable time', perhaps a minute and a half.

At the moment of the explosion, Evetts was about forty yards from the building:

I was on the point of turning away to go back, but just saw a puff of dense black smoke which immediately preceded the explosion. This was about 1.15. I did not hear the explosion at all. I was struck by the flying debris and knocked down. I do not remember falling till the debris struck me. My coat was entirely blown to pieces, my waistcoat torn in halves, and part of my trousers were torn to rags, and I was covered with falling mud blown from the crater. I was not unconscious and got up at once.

Building 833 had vanished. The surrounding buildings – stores, mess rooms, offices and power house – were not alight, and looked as though they had not suffered serious structural damage, though all of the windows had been blown out.

No use at all

Evetts picked himself up to the west of building 833. To the north, Palowkar and the survivors among his party came to their senses and assessed the scene before them. Among their number was one Robert Allen, a cordite hand and member of the A Section of the Cotton Powder Company fire brigade. In the pages of Cooper-Key's report that are devoted to eyewitness statements by factory managers, staff and firemen who attended from the town, Allen provides a short but clear account of events as he experienced them. Like many of the others, Allen's statement is more detailed regarding what happened immediately before the first explosion than it is about the aftermath: the explosions that followed, or the dead and injured that he saw. Of course, the report was meant to gather evidence of how the disaster had come about and whether it might have been averted, and only secondarily – beyond an account of lives lost and materials and buildings destroyed – to describe its physical effects upon the men or the land on which they had lately stood. Still, it is not hard to imagine that the comparative reticence of survivors on the subject of the dead and injured must arise in some part from the unspeakable nature of what they had witnessed. We shall have to return to this subject later, and try to picture just what a man like Allen had seen that he does not tell us. For now, let us trudge back in time with him an hour or so. It is a fine spring morning and there is work to be done at the Cotton Powder Company.

Allen first knew that something was wrong when from inside the mess room he heard a hooter blast, as he recalled, at about twenty past twelve. He went outside immediately, and started off with a hose truck along the tramline to the main buildings of the factory, where he supposed the fire must have broken out. But on the way he met a colleague, Seabury, who gestured to the west, in the direction of the Explosives Loading Company buildings. The two men now transferred the truck to another line and started over. When they arrived at building 833, Allen remembered, it was obvious that the bags to the south of the building were at the seat of the fire: 'The end and about 2 ft of the inside of the building were well alight.' Great volumes of flame, as Allen put it, roared from the interior; such was the heat and the density of the smoke that it was hard even to approach the building. But approach it they were forced to do, because, as Allen said later, 'our appliances were of no use at all as we could not get a connection from the pumps so we started in with buckets and with the chemical extinguishers belonging to the Explosives Loading Company, which were of no use'. Having given up for the moment, Allen enquired of Palowkar whether the building, which he now knew to be packed with TNT and nitrate, was in danger of exploding. Palowkar replied, 'No, it will only burn.'

Whether Allen and the firemen of A Section were guided by this specific assurance, or whether they persisted out of a feeling that the fire simply had to be put out, remains unclear. We can say for certain that Allen and his colleagues now went to fetch hoses in hope of connecting to a hydrant belonging to the Cotton Powder Company, close to building 421. Others ran towards Uplees Lodge, where they knew more hoses were stored. In total they were now furnished with over 2,000 feet of hose. This was enough to reach the hydrant; the question was whether or not the men charged with directing the hose

could get close enough in the great heat to take aim. The heat
was now so intense, Allen reported, that a fire truck thirty
yards from 833 burst suddenly into flames, apparently
untouched by sparks or airborne debris. By this time, said
Allen:

. . . the building had nearly burnt out and a small piece only of
the roof remained – I could see right through the building.
There appeared to be none of the upper tiers of barrels or cases
remaining – boxes and cases 30 yards away were also burning but
no other buildings were alight. I returned along the line of the hose
to make good any defective lengths.

When the explosion occurred, Allen was with Palowkar;
both men were thrown to the ground. Allen recalled hearing a
series of small explosions followed straight away by the main
catastrophic one. The air was filled with flying debris, and so
Allen and Palowkar leaped into the covered hose truck for
shelter. 'Palowkar laid down at the side of it – when I got out
he seemed stunned. I shook him up and we commenced to
clear out but we saw the injured crawling about the marsh and
turned back to help.' The men they encountered, said Allen,
had all been knocked out, including Goldfinch, whom they
took to the Cordite Office and then to the main gate. Allen
helped dispatch the wounded to Mount Hospital, others to the
Salvation Army barracks. In his statement, in common with
some of the other survivors and perhaps in response both to
rumours and to explicit questioning or instructions from the
Inspector of Explosives, Allen was careful to append a final
assertion: 'I did not at any time see anyone who was looking
on – everyone there was doing something.'

The limits of total destruction

George Bethell, General Works Manager at the Cotton Powder Company factory, begins his statement by noting that on
the day in question he worked from 7 to 9 a.m., as usual, and
then went home, 'intending to return at 2 in the afternoon'.
Before Bethell left, the company's Night Superintendent, Cremer, had passed on to him a complaint from a patrol at the
western limit of the complex, where it abutted the Explosives
Loading Company site. Sparks from a chimney had set fire to
waste material outside the boiler house, and the man in charge,
said Cremer, claimed he 'couldn't help it and that it might
occur again – he can't stop it'. There had been similar reports
before, but the events, as Bethell put it, 'not being on our
premises had not previously been reported to our Night
Superintendent'. Bethell reports that his counterpart, Evetts,
was aware that such incidents had taken place – though it is not
obvious how Evetts knew, or how Bethell knew that he knew.

At about twenty past one, Bethell was at White Hill to the
south-west of Faversham, cycling towards the town, when he
heard a single loud report. When he turned to look, 'There
was a dense volume of black smoke followed by a mushroom
shaped cloud of grey smoke similar to that seen when the
"Princess Irene" blew up and which remained visible for a long
time.' (We shall return to the *Princess Irene*.)

The road towards the spot where a grey mushroom cloud
now rose took Bethell through the centre of Faversham. He
reached the main gate at 1.40 p.m. and telephoned the Admiralty at Sheerness; the consequence of this call was that 120 men
were sent at once by car. No doctors or ambulances were yet at

the scene. While Bethell was still in the gatehouse, the second explosion occurred. He set out now towards the Explosives Loading Company's building 833 and soon came upon injured men who were making their way towards the gate, some lame or weak enough to need support, all of them cut and shaken and with clothes torn or missing. He saw the first stretcher cases as he neared building 205, the nitroglycerine plant. Soldiers and Cotton Powder Company staff, he recalled, were by then arriving on trucks, carrying more stretchers.

Bethell could see at least three buildings alight nearby, and to the west a lot of burning debris. 'Quantities of explosives

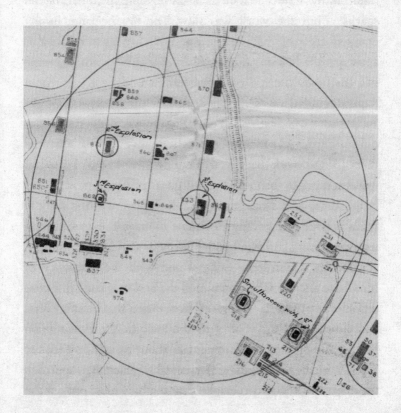

were lying about in the burning area and heavy minor explosions were continually occurring.' Bethell was joined by Evetts, and together the two managers hurried to the power house: 'While there the third explosion occurred, scattering primer tubes in all directions from some of which we had a narrow escape.' The offices, power station and stores in building 830 were all alight, and in the open air there were numerous charges from submarine mines, all burning fiercely and then expiring, as Bethell put it, 'with a kind of squib explosion'. The most pressing danger now was to magazines filled with TNT, which soldiers were doing their best to remove and dump in the empty marsh, as far as possible from flames and sparks – but the work was slow. The fire brigade, having dragged their engines over adjacent fields, now refused to approach the burning buildings, from which explosions were still frequent. There is no suggestion in Cooper-Key's report that this refusal was unjustified. Bethell simply notes, 'Of the 11 Brigades which attended only 2 got to work, the remainder did very little. As a matter of fact there were too many people there for the work that was to be done.'

Bethell is less than exact about what happened next: 'I find it difficult to give a clear or consecutive account of the work in the afternoon.' Regarding the danger to magazines in the vicinity, which were still filled with high explosives, he says simply, 'Evetts and I got some buckets and with the assistance of Mr Chant and Mr Clarkson placed the first magazine in a condition of safety.' Bethell neglects to mention that he and Evetts had noticed that the roof of the building in question was on fire, a building they knew to contain about twenty-five tons of TNT. With the fire brigade understandably reluctant to approach the magazine, the two managers realized they must put out the fire themselves, and that in the absence of hoses the only way to do it was to climb onto the flaming roof itself. In one of the most astonishing episodes in the drama of the 2nd of April, Evetts and Bethell hauled themselves onto the roof and enlisted Chant and Clarkson to hand them the buckets. In addition to having caught fire, the roof was still being rained on by burning debris from which the men no longer had any shelter. Cooper-Key notes with absurdly inadequate sobriety that 'Their gallantry is much to be commended.'

Given Evetts's and Bethell's laconism on the subject, we must imagine what it was like to stand, if briefly, on top of a building that had become a smoking and crackling bomb. It is said that time slows down at such moments, and most of us have likely experienced something of that sort at the moment of an accident, of actual or narrowly averted violence, at the moment we're told of a loved one's death or other intimate catastrophe. So we may justifiably wonder if there was time for Bethell and Evetts – both, let us recall, badly shaken, and Evetts deafened and half naked – to pause even for an elongated second, at their elevated and extremely tenuous vantage, and survey the devastation that surrounded them.

What might they have seen? The magazine on which they stood, building 875, was about 250 yards west-south-west of the locus of the original explosion at 833. It was the first, that is easternmost, of seven such magazines that ran in a straight line to the west, just south of a drainage ditch. A tramline ran along the other side, and seven small bridges linked the two banks of the ditch. The point where the two men stood overlooked a stretch of buildings between twenty-five and seventy yards away – offices, stores, mess room and power house – that were all now burning and would be soon consumed. On

Cooper-Key's map they are a little way inside a blue circle that denotes the 'limits of total destruction'. Smoke and flames may thus have obscured the view of the main explosion site; the sparks and debris were blowing in the direction of the magazine, which was why the two men were perched atop it with buckets in the first place.

Assuming, however, that there were at least intermittent views of the landscape to the north and east, a glance in the direction of building 833 must have disclosed an appalling scene. The intermediate ground was dotted with small fires and fragments of smoking debris. Had Bethell and Evetts been able to focus on this first of several concentric rings of destruction, they would have seen too that the earth was scattered with clothing. Beyond this circle the ground darkened where it had been torn up and strewn in clods. Not much more than fifty feet inside this area, in turn, was a wave of soft clay in which many of the dead were still embedded. At least one man was found alive in this zone, and as the two managers flung bucketfuls of water on the burning roof of 875, in the distance workers and soldiers were advancing into this morass, sunk to their knees in mud and who knows what gore, or struggling to bridge the mire with planks and fragments of wood from the buildings blown apart further out. Beyond this sucking rampart of mud, like the final defence of some half-finished prehistoric fort or burial site, the two men saw nothing, because there was nothing to see even from their raised position. Here was the crater itself: 135 feet across at its widest – it forms a rough circle on the map, somewhat flattened on its south-east quadrant – and 13.5 feet deep at the centre, which we may guess was already filling with water.

II

To the Heart of Things

On contingency

When reading narrative accounts of disasters, I often have the absurd sense that catastrophe may yet be averted. A hungover soldier or civilian guard will think twice before flicking his unspent fag away; a trail of smoke will lead an alert young officer to the seat of a small fire that has not yet reached the fatal magazine; an inspector sent from the Ministry of Munitions, days or even weeks earlier, will have ordered chemical tests on explosives that some obscure hunch, born of years in the job, tells him may be lethally corrupted.

Why this counterfactual urge when faced with the actuality of violent, especially accidental, destruction? It is perhaps more than a simple fantasy or desire that things were not thus. It has something to do, I think, with a fundamental if nonsensical refusal to accept that things have to be this way: events being events, chemistry and physics emphatically themselves, cause and effect lining up as usual, the past after all being past, irrevocable, unchanging and unchangeable. It is as if there are cracks in the narrative that allow through some light and hope. In fact, without this perverse feeling that things might still somehow transpire otherwise, whole genres of literature and film, for example, whether fictional or documentary, would simply cease to have a narrative hold on the imagination. The attraction of a story such as that of the *Titanic*, for example, consists partly in our feeling that the ship might not, this time at least, strike the iceberg, or that even after the collision events might take a different turn: distress flares might not be mistaken for fireworks, rescue vessels will speed to the scene hours in advance of the historical record. And the feature of such narratives that gives us this odd hope is precisely the level of detail they possess; it is in the smallest pivots of history that we glimpse a world in which all might have been well.

Time passes

It is said that time slows in the moment before disaster strikes. This is to assume, of course, that we see the precipice yawning at our feet, the axe raised above our heads, or the engine speeding towards us on fate's clean and level rails. Which in a sense, in retrospect, we (the survivors) will always have done, no matter the circumstance: that's to say, narrative demands suspense, even when its editor is the Home Office and its author His Majesty's Inspector of Explosives. The story slows as it picks up details, digresses towards fresh evidence; perspectives multiply as the dread moment nears, as if one of them might divert the course of events at the last instant. One might say that writers have always known this – philosophers too, as for example Zeno's paradoxes regarding the flight of an arrow or the race between Achilles and the tortoise – but it seems the nineteenth century grew increasingly preoccupied with the timescale of split-second catastrophe, and with the nature of the instant in general, until the new century turned up to provide unprecedentedly violent examples, and some answers. In this sense there is a curious continuum between literature, scientific research, photography, sound recording

or measuring and vast innovations in the field of explosives and
their military deployment.

Here is one telling prose example, from the middle of the
century. In 1849 the essayist and autobiographer Thomas De
Quincey published the three articles that make up *The English
Mail-Coach*. In the first, 'The Glory of Motion', he surveyed
the history and present importance of the mail-coach: until
the advent of the railway, the principal means by which news
was carried around the country. In the second essay, 'The
Vision of Sudden Death', De Quincey turns to an incident that
he insists really occurred, 'in the second or third summer after
Waterloo'. The author was travelling, he tells us, as a passenger on the box of the Manchester and Glasgow mail. Halted
for several hours at Manchester, De Quincey loses his way in
the dark and almost misses the coach. Once he is seated on the
box, he takes (as is his habit) a small quantity of laudanum, and
observes his neighbour: a one-eyed coachman whom De
Quincey in his tired and now drugged state likens to the
Cyclops, or a figure out of *The Arabian Nights*. The coach sets
off, the moon begins to rise, and the traveller drowsily settles
himself for the hours ahead: 'On this occasion, the usual silence
and solitude prevailed along the road. Not a hoof nor a wheel
was to be heard. And to strengthen this false luxurious confidence in the noiseless roads, it happened also that the night
was one of peculiar solemnity and peace.'

When De Quincey wakes, it is to 'a sullen sound, as of some
motion on the distant road'. He listens keenly for a moment,
and the noise dies away. But he is now unsettled, and makes an
observation that is curiously precise: the coach is travelling
at thirteen miles an hour. More startling: it is advancing at
this perilous speed on the wrong side of the road, and the

coachman is asleep. De Quincey is not, he pauses now to tell us, a man of action. He lacks the presence of mind, and is too addicted to doubt and given to distraction, to be able to react swiftly when events so demand. But what he does possess and deploy is a synthesizing, instantaneous mode of thought: he sees the course of events whole before others have begun to grasp what is about to unfold. 'The sounds ahead strengthened, and were now too clearly the sounds of wheels. Who and what could it be? Was it industry in a taxed cart? Was it youthful gaiety in a gig? Was it sorrow that loitered, or joy that raced?' The seconds are hardly to be discerned in which these questions occur to De Quincey; it all rushes on him at once, while the coachman slumbers beside him, oblivious.

Certain physical details now intervene in De Quincey's story, the tale expanding in the telling at exactly the moment it has seemingly contracted towards the point of catastrophe. Should he not wake the coachman, or seize the reins from his grip? There is no time left to rouse and warn him, no hope of pulling the reins out of his hand, which is 'viced between his upper and lower thigh'. The coach has at this point reached a straight avenue lined with trees, like a Gothic aisle. And framed by its cathedral arches is 'a frail reedy gig', in which are seated a young man and woman. 'The little carriage is creeping on at one mile an hour; and the parties within it being thus tenderly engaged, are naturally bending down their heads.' De Quincey calculates that there is a minute and a half left before the vehicles collide. He begins to shout. At his second warning, the young man in the gig lifts his head: 'He saw, he heard, he comprehended, the ruin that was coming down: already its gloomy shadow darkened above him; and already he was measuring his strength to deal with it.' He stares, De Quincey estimates, for seven seconds, then falls into a kind of reverie for another five, 'like one that mused on some great purpose'. Still another five: his eyes fly up to heaven, looking for guidance. At last he acts: stands up, pulls hard on the reins and slews horse and gig around at right angles to the onrushing mail-coach. But a second action is required – the horse's hooves are still in the air, and by the time they have crashed to earth it seems the young man knows his fate is sealed; at the last second he slumps in resignation. The mail-coach strikes the rear of the gig. Both horse and driver remain curiously still, but the little carriage shivers and trembles as though it might fly apart. And in the moment that his coach speeds past the quaking vehicle in its path, De Quincey sees for the first time the terrified face of the woman 'as she rose and sank upon her seat, sank and rose, threw up her arms wildly to heaven, clutched at some vision-ary object in the air, fainting, praying, raving, despairing'. The prospect of violent death had leaped suddenly upon her out of the quiet night and the sweet moonlight; she had seen nothing until the very last second, while for the man of action beside her, and the doubtful, ruminative De Quincey, everything had unfolded with amazing slowness, the disaster or near-disaster appearing to dilate in time so that it could fill the twenty or so printed pages of its subsequent retelling. This single isolated moment had expanded as if filmed in slow motion, half a cen-tury before the birth of cinema.

A couple of decades after De Quincey wrote 'The Glory of Motion' and 'The Vision of Sudden Death', the American pho-tographer Eadweard Muybridge began his experiments to freeze on photographic plates the movements of humans and animals. Following initial attempts in 1852, Muybridge started in 1878,

using rows of twelve to twenty-four cameras, to capture movements too fast for the eye to see. He famously proved that the
hooves of a galloping horse all leave the ground at once, though
not in the splayed fashion that painters had traditionally depicted.
The results of Muybridge's experiments – including photographic series showing men and women walking, running,
wrestling and carrying out actions such as pouring water from
a pitcher – were published in 1887 in his book *Animal Locomo-
tion*. In Paris, meanwhile, Étienne-Jules Marey had similarly
begun to analyse the movements of certain animals – birds,
insects, expressive aquatic creatures such as octopuses and
rays – using a single camera instead of Muybridge's multiple
devices. Marey's 'chronophotographs' showed many instances
of the same object on a single plate; the action was at once
slowed or separated into its constituent phases (like De Quincey's
startled young man, whose moonlit face records the stages of
his fear and resolve) and captured in one image, all its fleeting
poses seen together.

Around the same time, several scientists and photographers
sought to reduce the duration captured by a single photographic image as far as it would go, using electrical sparks to
arrest the object in motion. In 1891 Lord Rayleigh succeeded
in photographing a soap bubble at the moment of bursting. A
year later Charles Vernon Boys of the Royal College of Science
in London photographed the moment a bullet, travelling at
around 1,800 miles an hour, pierced a sheet of plate glass. It is
possible to look at such images today and see them as punctu-
ating moments in the history of photography; but we only have
to reflect for a moment on the wider effort to immobilize the
moment in nineteenth-century art, and literature, to realize
they are part of a much larger pattern.

Shadows pointed

Of course explosions, whether on the battlefield, in the factory or on the street, do not typically announce themselves in advance; it is in their nature, mostly, to take us by surprise. Even when, as on the marshes at Uplees in 1916, the explosion is feared or expected, the exact moment of detonation still cannot be computed; one does not see it coming like a small frail carriage along a country road at night. Things remain uncertain till the very last. How to write about these intervals of time, the period of waiting and the moment of arrival? Is it even possible to describe the latter, to say what has gone on in that tiny span? Could we look sideways inside the explosion, like De Quincey turning to stare into the face of a terrified young woman, and say what we have seen? Will such a small morsel of time expand in the telling, as if it has been photographed by Muybridge or Marey? Will it stay sufficiently still before the writer's gaze to pose for the prose or poetic equivalent of a high-speed photograph?

Here is how Tolstoy, in *War and Peace*, presents one such moment: the ultimately fatal wounding, at the Battle of Borodino, of Prince Andrei Bolkonsky. Actually, it is the second such moment for the Prince, and the reader. At the close of Book One, Andrei is badly injured at the Battle of Austerlitz. He feels a blow to his head, and falls flat on his back. There ensues a strangely peaceful interlude in which the Prince stares up at the slowly drifting clouds and thinks, 'How quiet, solemn, and serene . . . How is it I did not see this sky before? How happy I am to have discovered it at last! Yes! All is vanity, all is delusion, except those infinite heavens. There is nothing but that. And even that does not exist; there is nothing but still-ness, peace.' Andrei is famously discovered after the battle by Napoleon himself, who summons doctors to save him. Seven years later, at Borodino, a shell lands smoking at his feet, and he waits aghast for it to explode. (Though he does not die till much later, at home.) This time the Prince is frozen in apprehension of the worst, after an adjutant warns him to lie down. 'Prince Andrei hesitated. The smoking shell spun like a top between him and the prostrate adjutant, near a wormwood plant between the field and the meadow.' The wormwood is more than a nice example of realist precision; it is the distracting invita-tion, while the shell fizzes before him, to a reverie not unlike the one he fell into at Austerlitz: '"Can this be death?" thought Prince Andrei, looking with a quite new, envious glance at the grass, the wormwood, and the streamlet of smoke that curled up from the rotating black ball. "I cannot, I do not wish to die. I love life – I love this grass, this earth, this air . . ."' As these thoughts form, the Prince recalls that he is not alone: '"It's shameful, sir!" he said to the adjutant. "What . . ."' At which point the shell explodes, an event that is instantaneous but at the same time composed of discrete, separable incidents:

He did not finish speaking. At one and the same moment came the sound of an explosion, a whistle of splinters as seen from a breaking window frame, a suffocating smell of powder, and Prince Andrei started to one side, raising his arm, and fell on his chest. Several officers ran up to him. From the right side of his abdomen, blood was welling out making a large stain on the grass.

Prince Andrei's wounding is the classic novelistic example of what happens when a writer tries to describe an explosion:

everything slows and fragments as we approach the decisive moment, details multiply and distractions intervene, the principal actors cease to act and start instead to think, and not only or necessarily about whether they can still escape the spinning and smoking thing that has suddenly entered their lives. When the explosion itself arrives, it is hardly there at all: a sound – but what does it *sound like*? – and a whiff or more of powder, a shower of fragments and we are already in the aftermath, surveying the damage to human bodies, what is left of them. But how could it be otherwise? How could you concentrate hard enough on the moment of detonation that it would open up in front of you and linger like this sufficiently to allow you, the writer, to describe it? Isn't the preliminary stage, before the explosion, meant to imply all the horror that is to come? And afterwards, there is enough evidence, enough wreckage and scattered body parts, to imply all that occurred in the moment. The disaster itself is really nothing compared to the course of events before and after. These are the only timescales that matter: approaching the moment, and emerging on the other side among its consequences. The event casts a shadow, but in opposite directions at once. Between the two: very little, almost nothing.

In the early twentieth century, the classic literary example of this phenomenon is Joseph Conrad's 1907 novel *The Secret Agent*, with its pivotal attack, recounted in flashback, on the Royal Observatory at Greenwich. Conrad's tale was based (more exactly than he later allowed) on a real event in 1894, when a French anarchist, Martial Bourdin, was discovered gravely injured near the observatory. His anarchist comrades seemed as surprised by the incident as the authorities. He may only have intended to test the explosives in the park, and not to attack the symbolic edifice of the observatory, with its relationship to time and to empire. Even more confoundingly, the whole affair may have been engineered by some foreign power – Russia, for example – in order to encourage the British government to expel anarchists who had sought asylum in London. It is this tortuous conjecture that provides the motive in *The Secret Agent*. The spy Verloc, agent of an unnamed European state, dispatches his wife's brother Stevie – a childlike 'idiot' in the parlance of the time – with a bomb to Greenwich, hoping to discredit his anarchist brethren.

The explosives are supplied by the Professor, a member of Verloc's anarchist group who travels always with a bomb inside his coat, which he can detonate at will by pressing a button inside his pocket – like a photographer using a cable release. (The bomb, were he ever to use it, would go off twenty seconds after he pressed the button; the reader is left to wonder what the Professor would do or say in that interval: gloat, pray, beg or cower?) Stevie has no such control over his device, and though it seems to have gone off by accident, only Verloc can be blamed. When his wife discovers what he has done with Stevie, she stabs him to death and later drowns herself. The hapless unknowing bomber is blown to pieces, which must be shovelled up by a police constable – the park-keeper who hands him the spade retires to vomit against a tree – and partially reassembled on the mortuary table: 'Another waterproof sheet was spread over that table in the manner of a table-cloth, with the corners turned up over a sort of mound – a heap of rags, scorched and bloodstained, half concealing what might have been an accumulation of raw material for a cannibal feast.' Once again, however, as in life, the moment of the explosion

itself, this violent event that was meant to interrupt meta-
phorically the flow of time itself, remains necessarily absent
from the tale.

A View of Delft

At the National Gallery in London I have frequently stood
before a painting that offers dismal proof of the depredations
wrought by the explosion of gunpowder stores in peacetime,
and points, nearly two and a half centuries in advance, to the
scale of destruction that would one day be visited deliberately
upon the densely peopled cities of Europe. The picture in
question is modestly sized – roughly thirty-six by fifty
centimetres – but depicts a vacant immensity. It is mostly

made up of grey sky: a pallid stretch of cloud at whose centre a darker pall seems to rise, becoming almost black at the top of the canvas. Beneath this sinister mass nine glyphic birds are flying towards us, two or three at a time. Little more than a quarter of the painting is taken up by the cityscape — or what was once a cityscape — from which the birds have taken flight. On the horizon is a line of tiny roofs that seem to be intact, though it is hard to tell because they are silhouetted against the brightest portion of the sky. From this semi-obscured stratum there rise four spired buildings: three on the left, one considerably smaller than the others, and one on the right with its summit pinned to the clouds like a carpet tack. Some way forward — or some way further down, according to my slow scanning of the image in the gallery — is a pale grey square of a building with large windows (they seem undamaged, but this cannot be true) which has had its roof reduced to four A-frames and a few lateral beams. A radically curtailed chimney probes the skeletal remains but fails to reach the roofline.

The foreground is a mess. To the left a small humpbacked bridge abuts on its far side the blank walls of two houses; behind these in receding parallel more walls are all that remain of a street whose rafters and other timbers are piled chaotically on the thoroughfare. From the right-hand row of these dwellings or shops a moraine of rubble and wood extends across the canvas, along the bank of the waterway spanned by the bridge. On the near side: more timbers, fragments that might be clothing, a single boot. But the eye is drawn most readily to the flat expanse on the right, where some way back from the bank a vast crater filled already with water reflects the clouds, and at least a dozen white trees, quite bare, stretch their brittle limbs to the sky. To their left is a dense mound of beams and rubble and above it a whitish patch that might be plaster or masonry still intact or just as plausibly a small cloud of smoke or dust. Beyond that once more, a thick black shadow out of which smashed timbers bristle: a void that cuts its way, V-shaped, into the streets behind.

Large and small groups of stunned citizens are scattered about the scene. The waterlogged hole that we may assume marks the precise locus of the disaster separates two such gatherings; we can just make out their hats and tiny blank faces as they stare into the depths of the crater. On the other side two men, close together, look down at the raw earth, and one of them appears to prod at something with his stick. Further left – that is, south, as we shall see – a line of perhaps twenty people is straggled out in front of another bridge: I cannot be sure, but they may well be standing back while city officials, or militiamen, investigate the crater itself. But it is the figures in the foreground that properly tell us what has happened and that, allowing for the masterful composition of the austere and terrible whole, keep me coming back to this painting. On the left, coming over the bridge, two exhausted men, one dressed in red and the other in blue, are hefting between them a large basket of stones. Behind them a figure runs with outstretched arms towards another, who, if one squints very closely, is smiling or laughing in greeting. A little to the right on the near bank a man and woman clasp hands while a smaller person – more dwarfish than childlike – looks on. Two men converse nearby. A shape that might be a bloodied individual seems to be coming out of the water. There are two men trying to help to her feet a woman who has collapsed. On the opposite side of the picture: a man being comforted by his wife (his hat has fallen on the ground behind him) while their child, definitely a child this time, hunches or maybe sobs. A well-dressed man in cape and rakishly brimmed headgear stands with his back to us, regarding the crater and the trees and the destruction in the distance. Immediately to his right a small figure runs or staggers towards the edge of the painting, head in hands.

Has the world come to an end?

On the morning of the 12th of October 1654, Cornelius Soetens, a clerk employed by the city of Delft, approached the buildings of the former Clarissen Convent – now converted to an arsenal belonging to the States General, or national assembly – on Doelenstraat in the north-east of the city, not far from the headquarters of the city militia and just a block from the protective curve of the Schie River. Less than half a mile to the south-east – across three canals and through a mixed commercial and residential district that included the houses and studios of some of Delft's most notable painters – lay the main marketplace, bordered by the town hall, the Nieuwe Kerk and St Luke's Guild Hall: the premises of an association that regulated among other professions the city's painters, bookbinders and glassmakers. To the north-west of this administrative, religious and mercantile hub the spire of the Oude Kerk leaned (as it still does) a little way from the vertical, though not enough to worry the citizens who passed it by that morning. They may well have included one Simon Decker, lately retired as the church's verger, who by mid morning had made his way to Doelenstraat to sit for his portrait by the painter Carel Fabritius.

A little before half past ten, the clerk Soetens reached a

tower in the convent garden, known as the Secret of Holland. The tower contained 90,000 pounds of gunpowder, much or perhaps most of it in underground stores beneath the building proper. On this autumn morning Soetens and a companion from The Hague were charged with the task of extracting a two-pound sample in order to test its quality. Before they went down the stairs a lamp was lit for them, and the gentleman from The Hague handed his expensive red cloak to a servant for safekeeping. Then he and Soetens advanced into the dark.

What happened inside the powder store remains a mystery. Soetens may have dropped his lamp, or one of the men struck a spark – from a lock, from the stonework at the entrance or the brick walls inside. In an instant the clerk and his visitor, the tower and convent, the surrounding streets and their inhabitants were no more. The earth shook and the masonry, bricks, timbers and tiles that had been Doelenstraat and its surrounding district became airborne, taking with them the contents of houses and shops, bodies and body parts, as well as a considerable quantity of water from the nearby canals and river. A wave of flame and dust and steam sped through the streets. Above ground, the blast wave crossed the meadows, roads and waterways of the flat countryside beyond the city – it was said later that doors had slammed in Delfshaven, ten miles to the south, and even in Haarlem, thirty miles to the north. Windows shattered in The Hague and rattled in Gouda. In Delft itself, the shock passed beneath the streets and caused all the houses inside a radius of a few hundred yards to collapse; beyond that, buildings and trees caught fire, roof tiles and timbers rained down, and windows were smashed in the two main churches and the civic buildings of the market square. Black water filled the crater where the Secret of Holland had stood.

Citizens from outlying, less damaged, districts now rushed to the scene and despite the real danger of further explosions began to dig in the rubble, from which rose the screams and sobs of those trapped and wounded. Many of the dead and injured had worked in the textile and clothing trades; in one house, a manufacturer of serge was discovered with his wife and children and their servant, all dead. Nearby, a seamstress and four of her apprentices had been killed, another three surviving, one having crawled under a loom. At the local girls' school twenty-eight children had died. And in the Doelenstraat Simon Decker the verger, sitting for his portrait at the time of the explosion, was found dead along with Carel Fabritius's mother-in-law, Judith van Pruijsen, and his assistant Mathias Spoors. The painter himself had survived, but was badly injured; he was taken away to the hospital near the Koornmarkt, in the south-west of the city. He died less than an hour later.

As the day turned to evening, and heavy rain and wind extinguished the torches of those still searching in the wreckage or assisting the physicians who had arrived from neighbouring towns, there were instances of near-miraculous survival. In a ruined house twin babies were discovered unharmed in their cradles, not far from the corpse of their mother. A 75-year-old man had survived in his bed, where he still lay when rescued, though his house had collapsed around him. And a girl just over a year old was dug out sitting in her high chair, with hardly a scratch on her. She may be seen in a pen-and-ink drawing by the artist Gerbrand van den Eeckhout, probably completed later in 1654, which shows piles of rubble, orphaned gables, vacant arches, buckled trees, a whiskered old man being pulled from the earth, and a mother racing into the foreground with her arms raised, because in the bottom right-hand corner is the high chair — like a decorated wooden bucket or a crude miniature pulpit — in which her daughter sits, clutching an apple in her left hand and paying no attention to the man who leans over her, but appearing instead to gaze at the chunks of broken masonry at the bottom of the picture. It was said that when she was pulled out of the rubble she was laughing. The last person to emerge alive from the wreckage was an old woman discovered four days later, who on being found looked up at her rescuers and asked, 'Has the world come to an end?'

It is not known how many people were killed by the Delft Thunderclap, as it became known. One report stated that only fifty-four bodies had been identified; thirteen years later the city historian Dirck van Bleyswijck claimed that between 500 and 1,000 had died. Many had simply been vaporized by the explosion itself. Others had been burned or mutilated beyond recognition, dismembered or decapitated, so that a final tally was impossible. Among those who survived was a neighbour of Fabritius's on Doelenstraat: the painter Egbert van der Poel, who was born in the city in 1621 and whose *View of Delft after the Explosion of 1654* is the one in the National Gallery described above. Here, too, Fabritius and van der Poel are neighbours; Fabritius's own *View of Delft*, with its strangely skewed perspective of the Nieuwe Kerk and the stall of a musical-instrument seller, is at present exhibited next to van der Poel's. (This room at the gallery also contains a curious and intimate glimpse into the interiors, or the sorts of interiors, in which so many citizens of Delft were blown to pieces. Samuel van Hoogstraten's peepshow or perspective box, one of only six surviving from a veritable artistic craze in the middle of the seventeenth century, is a five-sided model of a domestic interior. The sixth side is open, but would originally have been covered with paper through which the interior was lit. When visiting the gallery, I cannot now hunker down and squint into the little viewing holes in the short sides of the rectangular box without picturing the force and flame of an explosion ripping the house apart.)

Van der Poel painted or drew at least twenty pictures that refer to the Delft Thunderclap, including one that shows the same view as the National Gallery painting, but this time at the moment of detonation. Or rather, it shows the explosion – a burst of pale fire, a roiling black cloud, a wide funnel of flying debris – and at the same time its aftermath: there are the same piles of timbers, the same rubble and comparable if not identical townspeople in attitudes of shock and disarray. One or two of the prone figures might be corpses, but none is so much as charred or bloodied, let alone mutilated. We might conjecture that despite his obsessive return to the subject van der Poel, whose daughter had been killed by the explosion, baulked at painting its effects upon the human body. His several renderings of the disaster and its consequences are all like this: views of small figures strewn or busying themselves about the central catastrophe. If you visit Delft today you will find at the Prinsenhof Museum that van der Poel was not alone in painting his city in peril or in ruins: a century earlier, following a lightning strike on the wooden spire of the Nieuwe Kerk, fire had ravaged the city and destroyed well over 2,000 wooden houses. (The fire is one reason there is so much rubble as well as timber in the later paintings of the explosion: much of the wooden city was rebuilt in stone.) In fact, depictions of fire and firefighting practically constituted a distinct genre in the Netherlands in this period, with numerous paintings showing civic fire brigades at work to save churches, guildhalls and private residences.

There exists still a further perspective on the same event, drawn by the Dutch artist Jan Luyken, which seems to broach, maybe crudely, the problems that attend any effort to depict an explosion. Here, the eruption is a white flash surrounded by smoke, toppling masonry and bystanders hurled to the ground by the blast. The most striking feature of Luyken's version, however, is just how much of the city is actually airborne, including large portions of the military magazine itself and several persons, physically intact at the centre of the explosion, but surely already dead. Luyken's drawing is a modest example of one possible means of representing an explosion: as an agglomeration of articles suspended in space.

There are instructive precursors to Luyken's drawing among paintings of battle scenes, where the problem of the vanishing moment has been dramatized to spectacular, and sometimes absurd, effect. Consider Cornelis Claesz van Wieringen's painting *The Explosion of the Spanish Flagship during the Battle of Gibraltar, 25 April 1607*. On that date, thirty Dutch ships took the Spanish fleet by surprise in the Bay of Gibraltar, destroying all twenty-one of the Spanish ships and killing (in many cases while they swam for their lives) or capturing 4,000 Spanish sailors. The Spanish and Dutch admirals were also killed in the battle. Van Wieringen's painting shows the moment – a rather elongated moment – when the Spanish flagship, its powder magazine having been struck by Dutch cannon, exploded. In the painting a Dutch ship strikes the Spaniard from the port side and sends it listing, so that the tattered angel on the flag at its stern is clearly visible. Flames burst from the flagship's deck and are reflected in the roiling

sea below, making it seem as though it has been turned to blood. The waves are full of floating bodies and flailing limbs. A Spanish monk falls into the sea with his buttocks bared.

All of this detail is rendered with partisan glee on the painter's part. But the most curious aspect of van Wieringen's composition is to be found in the painting's upper portion, where a collection of debris and human forms is dispersed, aloft. Here are chunks of the ship's mast and decking, powder kegs, and people in a terrifying variety of bodily attitudes, all engaged in their own oddly detached adventure in the air's uncharted ways. Some of the sailors are still clutching weapons, others grasping at the empty air as if to save themselves. At the top of the Dutch mast a tiny figure reaches hopelessly for the rigging as he falls, or perhaps ascends. The whole scattering of objects and frail humanity seems to occupy an entirely different picture plane and compositional universe from the conventional, lurid battle scene below. The explosion itself is no more than a lateral burst of flame and a pall of smoke, van Wieringen in no way attempting the graphic radial representation of a flash or blast that Luyken would deploy in his drawing of the Delft Thunderclap, and which by the nineteenth century would become the standard means by which such disasters as mining accidents, anarchists' bombs and the destruction of naval craft full of gunpowder were to be drawn or painted. Here instead it is as if the blast and its propulsive effects form an alternative story, which takes place at some imaginative as well as physical remove from the firestorm below.

Van Wieringen's figures, briefly and perilously suspended above the Battle of Gibraltar, look as though they might in fact hang there indefinitely, perhaps discussing among themselves the possibility of their survival and the questionable verisimilitude of the composition in which they find themselves. But what would a more realistic depiction involve? Less corporeal integrity, more body parts? What of the explosion itself, its force and flames? The painters of the seventeenth century may have succeeded in rendering the latter, but the energy of the event was figured only by its effects: ships or buildings shattered, bodies dispersed about the scene. For an effort to depict the actual force of an explosion, we have to return to the early twentieth century, and to the Great War. Paintings and illustrations from the nineteenth century already show lines of radiating energy when they portray disasters and exploding shells in battle. Now, under the influence of abstract painting, this desire to paint the violence itself of detonation produced a signature motif: a starburst of radiant energy, superimposed on the chaos of buildings and bodies.

We see it most clearly in the work of the English war artist

Christopher Richard Wynne Nevinson, whose paintings of the Western Front attempted to find some graphic correlative for the violence of high-explosive shells and bombs. His painting *Bursting Shell* of 1918 shows a bare stretch of no-man's-land in the foreground: a brown and grey slope with barbed wire atop it like a thin hurdle fence in winter. Directly above the wire, there is a single point from which the rest of the canvas erupts into a black wedge of earth and energy, flanked by fire and topped by a constellation of fragments: stones, or metal, or worse. And at the outskirts of this eruption is a series of blurred arcs that might correspond to a blast wave, distinct from the cone of fire and earth and other matter at the centre of the painting.

Bursting Shell is a strikingly violent, and apparently unpopulated, image. It is actually, however, a belated and weaker version of a much more extreme painting, similarly void of any living or dead bodies. In 1915 Nevinson had painted another picture with the same title. Here there is no suggestion of battlefield, landscape or other context, apart that is from some glimpses of toppling houses and erupting street: brickwork, roof beams, pavement and cobbled street below. A good part – perhaps a quarter – of the painting is taken up by the abstract black wedges that denote the blast, each of these bordered on one side in orange or red. These five black forms are birthed roughly from the centre of the painting – reverse the visual logic and they seem to gesture towards this centre, their points not quite meeting. From the central area, too, light spits in straight lines: the sort of scintillation you might see pictured around the Sacred Heart, a saintly body or relic. But there is nothing there, or nothing recognizable; instead, a spiralling wave made of pink and blue lines, coiling out of the darkness and dissipating as it meets brick wall and window frames. *Bursting Shell* was exhibited at the Goupil Gallery, London, in November 1915, and reproduced in the *Daily Graphic* newspaper. Towards the end of the month, the *Observer* commented: '"Bursting Shells" [*sic*] is Futurism pure and simple, without a remnant of realistic tendencies. An extraordinary sense of irresistible, destructive force is conveyed by that revolving rainbow-coloured spiral from which radiate black, orange bordered shafts.' Without a remnant of realistic tendencies? The claim seems to be overturned in the very next sentence: it rather depends where you situate your realism, and reality. In his effort to depict the flash, the force and the sound wave in the detonation of the new high explosives, Nevinson seems to have known or intuited something about the multiple energies and timescales involved in such an explosion – factors with which scientists, soldiers and physicians were then contending.

Slow, slow, slow

Prose accounts of high-explosive detonations on the Western Front exhibit all the features we've seen in De Quincey, Tolstoy and Conrad: a certain slowing of narrative time before the lethal event itself, the brief confusion of the explosion, the dazed aftermath giving way swiftly to efforts to save oneself or others, the hideous visual and aural detail of the dead and the dying. In at least one case, the moment of detonation elongates and opens up, taking on a strangely dreamlike, placid aspect at the crucial juncture, and both author and characters are only too well aware of how unreal the moment seems – and also how close it comes to a technologically mediated or even invented occurrence.

Ford Madox Ford's novel *A Man Could Stand Up* was published in 1926, the third volume in a four-part work, *Parade's End*. Towards the end of the novel's second part, Ford's protagonist Christopher Tietjens is serving as a captain on the Western Front. An artillery barrage is in progress, the Germans are rumoured to be testing a big new Austrian gun, and Tietjens in his trench is wondering whether to write to Valentine Wannop, a woman he would like to seduce, and whom perhaps he loves. The sound of gunfire is so loud that it oppresses the mind. 'It was like being a dwarf at a conversation, a conflict – of mastodons. There was so much noise it seemed to grow dark. It was a mental darkness. You could not think. A Dark Age! The earth moved.' Tietjens has just been brought a sandwich and a cup of coffee by a lance corporal, Duckett. He has balanced the cup in the trench and begun talking to a young second-lieutenant, Aranjuez. 'He felt the earth move a little beneath him. The last projectile must have been pretty near. He would not have noticed the sound, it had become such a regular sequence. But he noticed the quiver in the earth . . .' There is no warning, or transition to the next phase; Tietjens now simply seems to be looking at Aranjuez from a considerable height. The boy's face has a rapt expression; he looks, Tietjens thinks, as if he is composing poetry.

Long dollops of liquid mud surrounded them in the air. Like black pancakes being tossed. He thought: 'Thank God I did not write to her. We are being blown up!' The earth turned like a weary hippopotamus. It settled down slowly over the face of Lance-Corporal Duckett who lay on his side, and went on in a slow wave.

It was slow, slow, slow . . . like a slowed down movie. The earth manoeuvred for an infinite time. He remained suspended in space.

Tietjens now recalls a recurring fantasy or reverie that has occupied him in the trench: he has found himself staring time and again at a small irregular splash of whitewash just above the level of his head – it looks, he thinks, like the comb of a healthy rooster – and imagining that if he were suspended above the earth, at the level of this random but enigmatic mark, he would somehow be safe, he would occupy an inviolable sphere cut off from the chaos of the battlefield around him. But he is assuredly earthbound in the aftermath of the shell-burst: 'The earth sucked slowly and composedly at his feet. It assimilated his calves, his thighs. It imprisoned him above the waist. His arms being free, he resembled a man in a life-buoy. The earth moved him slowly. It was solidish.' Aranjuez stares up at him and mouths silently, 'Save me, Captain!' A private soldier pulls Tietjens from the earth, and they start to work on the Second-Lieutenant, who comes out unable to stand, drooping like a flower covered with slime: 'Shell shock, very likely. There was no knowing what shell shock was or what it did to you. Or the mere vapour of the projectile.' The boy will live, though he will probably lose an eye, and is so spooked by the continued sound of shells and bullets around him that as soon as he can stand he runs and hides behind a mound of earth with his hands over his face, screaming like a horse trapped in a burning stable. Tietjens must now set to work to extract Duckett from the mud: only his feet are visible, and he may yet be saved if given artificial respiration. 'This man had been buried probably ten minutes. It seemed longer but it was probably less. He ought to have a chance.' Everything has unfolded with amazing slowness – including, this time, the explosion itself.

III

Blown All to Nothing

Down, and down, and down

In his report, Major Cooper-Key does not linger too long at the edge of the hole where building 833 had been. In describing it, his task is to extract what information the crater yields about the nature and possible causes of the explosion, then to move on to discuss the blast wave itself and its effects. The Inspector of Explosives gives us just a couple of paragraphs on the crater, and of course the accompanying photograph in the Kodak album, to which he does not directly refer. Here are his initial thoughts:

The formation of the crater of the main explosion presents some unusual features, probably due to some extent to the nature of the ground, and the fact that the buildings being unmounded and the site perfectly flat, the explosion was entirely unconfined, but they also suggest that the velocity of detonation was not excessive.

The result was a basin-like depression that did not present the sharply conical profile Cooper-Key asserts is usual in such cases. The building itself was blown into fragments small enough to be held in the hand, and the earth beneath it blasted into clods between a foot and a foot and a half across.

For the most part the surface soil had been forced bodily downwards with a clearly marked line of shearing all round the edge – much the

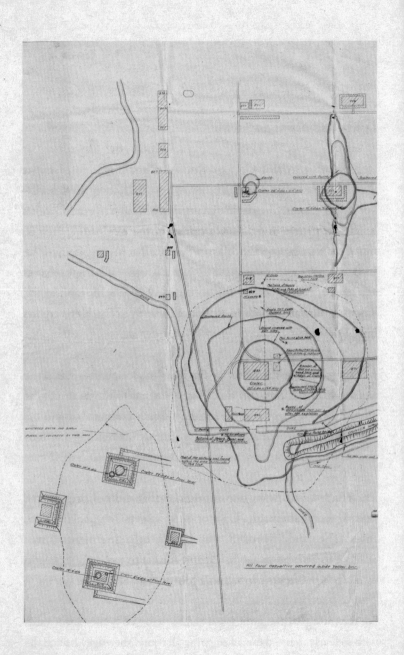

same effect as the detonation of an explosive charge in a lead plate – and the underlying silt was spewed out of the crack in a wave of mud which surrounded the edge of the crater in all directions and buried everything beneath it.

The Inspector estimates that there were 5,000 cubic yards of silt in this wave. We know that it was filled with fragments from building 833, with bodies alive and dead, and we must assume too with body parts, solid or dissolved. And we know that in the minutes and hours that followed, timbers were thrown across this mire in efforts to reach the injured and the dead, some of whom had been completely buried. We cannot say exactly what the wave looked like, however; as noted earlier, the first picture in the report's attendant photo album – the photograph that showed a 'General view of site of Main explosion' – has vanished from the album. So that if we return to the remaining images, we have to peer first just under the horizon behind 833 in the hope of some clue to the scale and horror of the eruption of sodden earth and sand and water. It's impossible: the image lacks the detail in that upper portion; I have the sketchiest impression of rough ground dotted with indeterminate artefacts that might be explosion debris or, just as likely, examples of the munitions scattered everywhere in this part of the factory. But in the foreground is that complex wave of mud of a lighter colour, seeming to writhe towards the camera, and it is this somehow grotesque substance that I assume has covered the ground in the immediate vicinity of the crater.

It is hard to say if the same stuff is what is visible in subsequent photographs: the crumbled agglomerations of earth surrounding the crater at building 861, for example – the photograph of which also shows a huge rend in the earth at the extreme right, like a grike slowly weathered into a natural limestone pavement. Elsewhere one can observe the craters with more customary conical shapes; the crater at building 217 has sharply raked sides covered in lumps of earth that look more like boulders than the smaller clods the Major describes. In each of these photographs a single figure is standing, usually near the bottom of the hole beside the central flooded portion, in order to give us a sense of the scale of the eruption.

What these scenes most resemble, whether pictured in the Kodak album or in the fading typescript of the report, is the familiar landscape of the Western Front. Though of course the mud itself was a localized phenomenon, and much of the worst of the fighting – including the summer horrors of the Somme that in April 1916 were just weeks away – took place on drier and at least initially firmer ground, it seems at a century's remove that the First World War took place in a sea of mud in the same way that it happened in black and white, or sepia: the colour of mud. In ancient footage, it may look like mere background: it stretches in the distance behind figures in the trenches, it fills craters in photographs where the real subject is a corpse or skeleton, it spatters and smirches the uniforms of soldiers who nonetheless keep on marching, through mud and more mud, to rest in muddy trenches or die in muddy holes. Mud looks like the more or less neutral medium in which the war occurred.

In fact, mud was as much a protagonist as the other inhuman elements that contended on the battlefields of the Western Front, chief among them lead, steel, gas and high explosives. In the poetry of the war its main agency or action is that of sucking: Siegfried Sassoon speaks of 'sucking mud', Wilfred Owen of 'sucking clay', Richard Aldington of 'sucking squelch', David Jones of 'aquatic sucking', Herbert Read of 'sucking, clutching death'. Stories proliferated, during and after the war, of men swallowed alive by the mud. In his *Battlefields of the World War*, published in 1921, Douglas Wilson Johnson notes that mud had already presented the advancing German army, in the autumn of 1914, with 'a liquid trap which yawned to engulf them':

Beneath the muddy waters were hidden ditches and canals into which men would suddenly plunge over their heads, and bottomless mud which would hold them fast in the flood . . . Notorious accounts of individuals and animals sinking to their deaths in large mud holes exist, and although few ever strike a note of credibility, some accounts are authentic.

More often, mud simply made things worse: slowing the progress of troops and vehicles, creating real traps that, if they did not suck the victim dramatically into the earth, at least held him long enough to make him vulnerable to enemy fire or attack, mixing with human waste and human remains to form a toxic slurry that even when it did not immediately threaten men with contagion must have been disgusting and horrifying in the extreme, that is until the point when the soldier became used to living with such filth. After seeing for the first time the mud at Passchendaele, Lieutenant-General Sir Launcelot Kiggell, who was Chief of General Staff for the British army and later dismissed for his failure in that campaign, exclaimed, 'My God, did we really send men to fight in that?'

A chain reaction

In his account of the events of the 2nd of April, George Bethell noted that what he had seen of grey smoke rising above the wreckage was 'similar to that seen when the "Princess Irene" blew up'. This is another reminder that the accident at Uplees was not the only extraordinarily destructive explosion that took place in Kent during the war. The wreck of the *Irene*, which we shall come to in a moment, was preceded by the eruption of HMS *Bulwark*, a 15,000-ton battleship launched in 1899 at a cost of £1,000,000. The *Bulwark* was officially based at Portsmouth, but having been refitted at Chatham was considered locally a Kentish vessel. On the 26th of November 1914 she was lying at anchor, with other ships of the Fifth Battle Squadron, just off the coast at Sheerness. The crew had been on leave the night before, and at seven in the morning many of the men had only just re-embarked and were eating breakfast. At 7.35 the *Bulwark* exploded. Later the same day Winston Churchill, then First Lord of the Admiralty, reported the disaster to the House of Commons:

The Vice and Rear Admiral, who were present, have reported their conviction that it was an internal magazine explosion which rent the ship asunder. There was apparently no upheaval in the water, and the ship had entirely disappeared when the smoke had cleared away. An inquiry will be held tomorrow which may possibly throw some light on the occurrence.

The loss of the *Bulwark*, Churchill noted, did not 'sensibly affect' the country's military position, but the loss of life was severe: out of a full crew of around 750 men, only 12 survived. John Budd, a sergeant in the Royal Marines, reported that he had not heard a thing; the deck had opened up beneath him and he found himself in the water. The ship's eleven magazines had exploded in chain reaction. Nobody would ever know why; a shell might have been dropped, a small fire started, or the explosives, as was still too frequently the case, may have become chemically unstable. What was certain, and attested for example by a Lieutenant Benjamin Carroll, an assistant coaling officer at Sheerness, was that the explosion had been an internal one, as Sergeant Budd recalled and Churchill later told the House. As at Uplees, as in all these instances of the unthinkable acceleration of events and energy, it is hard not to imagine that the disaster began slowly, with a sort of mundanity and obviousness, so that things surely could have been set right before that raw void opened at the centre of the ship.

Witnesses to the explosion of HMS *Bulwark* reported a roaring or rumbling sound, and saw a great sheet of flame and debris projected into the sky. The ship, it was said, rose briefly out of the water before it vanished, leaving only thick grey smoke. As the smoke cleared, a small portion of the vessel could be observed protruding about four feet above the water. Sailors on the ships nearby stared hard and long at the waves in search of survivors, but only fourteen were found; two of them later died.

The *Princess Irene* exploded six months later, off Port Victoria Pier on the Isle of Grain. The ship had been a Canadian Pacific liner, lately converted to a mine-layer. Once again there was a vast eruption of flame, a ship lifted out of the water and blown into countless fragments. On land nearby, oil tanks belonging to the Admiralty were damaged by debris, and a hunk of metal weighing ten tons was later discovered. A passing collier was felled by part of the ship's boiler. A labourer on one of Grain's farms was recorded as having died of shock. And little Hilda Johnson, aged nine, was playing in the garden at her home when she was struck and killed by a piece of metal. One eyewitness, a W. G. Moore, reported:

The whole thing was too awe-inspiring for me to appreciate the horror of it immediately. It started with stabs of flame spurting up from her deck from bow to stern, then a colossal roar, and everything was hurled into the air – a column of smoke then went up, up, up, spreading out to a mushroom head at about 1,200 feet.

When Moore, aboard a launch dispatched from the nearby air station, reached the scene, there was next to nothing to be found: 'There might never have been a ship there at all, save for the flotsam and oil. She had just disintegrated and sunk.'

Fragments of the *Irene* were discovered miles from the spot where she had exploded: books, papers, uniforms, furniture and even a case of butter (discovered six miles distant) were strewn across the coastline, the inland towns and countryside. So too with bodies and parts of bodies; human heads were found on the Isle of Grain and the village of Hartlip, about four miles south of the estuary. Parents in the Medway towns kept their children indoors until they were confident no more gruesome discoveries awaited them on the shoreline or in the streets and fields beyond. Meanwhile, explanations were canvassed, the most likely that an improperly fused mine – there were 500 mines aboard – had spontaneously exploded.

An appalling report

Like many of the workers, rescuers and witnesses on the 2nd of April 1916, Charles John Evers was at lunch when events began urgently to unfold. Evers was Medical Officer of Health for Faversham, a post he'd held for nearly a quarter century. A native of Stourbridge in Worcestershire, he had married in 1886 and moved to Faversham; at the town's museum, there is a photograph of the young doctor at the turn of the century in a deerstalker hat and striped blazer, perched on an elaborate adult tricycle. Evers was himself a keen photographer, and recorded many local landscapes and details of life in Faversham – but not, it seems, anything of the events of the 2nd of April.

There was an anti-aircraft battery at Oare, on the alert for bombing raids by airship and aeroplane – in fact, just the previous day the first Zeppelin to be shot down over Britain had been struck above Dartford and crashed into the sea about fifteen miles north-east of Margate. Late on Sunday morning the lookouts at Oare telephoned Evers to warn him of the fire and the fact he might be needed on the marsh. He decided to carry on with his meal because, he later wrote, 'there had been bad explosions on previous occasions and comparatively little damage done to life'. But a few minutes later the sound of the explosion was unmistakable, and the doctor's chauffeur, Amos, did not wait for instructions before rushing to get his car ready. Evers paused only to telephone the town's two hospitals, the Mount and the Cottage Hospital, and alert them that the wounded would soon be with them.

The two men had just passed through Oare, heading for the

main gate at Uplees amid a stream of bicycles bound for the factory, when the second explosion occurred. Evers recalled that neither he nor the driver felt the shock wave, though as Arthur Percival points out in his account of the day, they may have been too preoccupied with what they saw to have registered it – before them, beyond the entrance to the Explosives Loading Company site, 'a tremendous volume' of flame and smoke from the first eruption was already being carried away on a southerly wind. Now, as they drove up to the factory gate, a crowd of workers was moving in their direction, then was suddenly dispersed at the appearance of a 'tremendous burst of flame, followed by, at what seemed ages long, an appalling report'. Here is how Evers describes the scene that greeted him as he rushed to do his duty:

A continuous stream of injured men were dribbling in – pitiable objects. Some had been blown into dykes and were wringing wet and shivering with shock; many were shaking all over. Some were brought on trolleys, some carried, some helped along. One man cheerfully proclaimed that he had a broken leg, which I set Amos on to put up (it was not compound). Others were bleeding and some had half their clothes torn off or burnt off – an awful procession . . . Even then we did not realise the full extent of the disaster, as we had not penetrated to the heart of things and could do no more than attend to those who kept coming up faster than we could deal with them. We had not time to realise that behind that curtain were the worst stricken men, who could only be moved very slowly, and a number that need never be moved at all, for no help could restore them . . . Five of the national reserves who were on guard were killed instantly: of one, nothing but his rifle was ever found . . . The vagaries of the explosion were many: two men side by side – one killed instantly, the other hardly hurt; a number of men between 30 and 40 yards away from the explosion unharmed, while men 100 yards away were blown to pieces . . . men had all their clothes blown off them and were yet unhurt.

The injured were now being ferried to hospitals in the town and various infirmaries beyond – including several men transported by barge to Sheerness on the far side of the Isle of Sheppey – so Evers elected to return to Faversham and begin treating those he could help. Amos was nowhere to be found, so the doctor bundled a wounded man into the back seat of his car, ordered a soldier to sit with him and hold him up – 'otherwise he would have sat down in a heap at the bottom' – and drove himself back into town, where the roads were filled with cars and trucks heading out towards the factory. Evers's wife, Annie, was at work in the Cottage Hospital, and once he had let her know he was safe he made his way to the Mount, where he held another post as medical officer.

The scene there was awful – every bed was full, and still they came. We put down mattresses in the lounge. We had about 20 empty beds and took in 36 . . . Doctors and helpers kept turning up from all directions – Canterbury, Margate, Ramsgate, Maidstone, Ashford, Sittingbourne, Herne Bay, Whitstable – there was work for everyone . . . At last the rush ceased and we began to tackle the poor men in earnest.

The men were dirty, wet, cold and bleeding; some of them groaned, others lay insensible in beds now covered with mud or soaked in marsh water. Their clothes, Evers recalled, had simply been thrown out into the garden: 'those of the 8 men in Ward 2 would not have made one decent suit amongst them'. He began injecting them with morphia and strychnine – the latter was then used in small doses as a stimulant – while nurses of the local Voluntary Aid Detachment went to work with bandages. Melice Telfer, one of their number, later recalled:

One man had been blown through a window, clean through a window, and Mrs Andrews, the [Borough] Surveyor's wife, spent practically the whole afternoon taking small pieces of glass out of his face. [With] others we were told to do just whatever we could. We took our scissors and slit up their clothes to get them out. One man had been thrown straight into water, so you had to get him out of his very wet clothes, in which he was shivering . . . We were given more or less *carte blanche* to do whatever we could for them . . . and we were busy, oh, until quite late at night.

When Evers made his rounds of the Faversham hospitals the next morning, he was told six of the injured had died in the night. At all of these hospitals were relatives who had not yet found their husbands, sons, fathers or brothers:

People going from one hospital to another, tramping about for hours in search of those whom they might never find – and some have not been found at all . . . But as long as there remained one man not named, of course people kept asking to see that man, in case he was the one they were in search of. Now and then someone found what they wanted and departed joyfully if he was not too bad.

All of a quiver

At about one o'clock in the afternoon on the 2nd of April, Stephen Tuck, aged fourteen, was sitting down to lunch with his parents at their house in Trinity Street, Norwich, ninety-three miles from Faversham, when an open sash window began to rattle. Nearby, a locomotive cleaner named William Stowers had slept till noon, having worked the night shift; not long after his mother woke him, he recalled nearly seventy years later, the windows started to shake. Near Great Yarmouth, Dorothy Smith, then a child, was on a family excursion to see her aunt and uncle at St Olave's when a loud bang interrupted the midday meal. In Essex, across the Thames estuary from Kent, the cross was said to have fallen from the altar at St Peter's church, Shoebury.

These accounts, and other reminiscences like them, were sent to Arthur Percival in the summer of 1984, in response to an advertisement he had placed in the *Eastern Daily Press*, soliciting any memories elderly readers might have had of the events of that Sunday sixty-eight years earlier. The fragments compose a belated addendum to a report by Tom Robinson for the Faversham Society, written up in 1963: a Mrs Browning told him she had been dishing up potatoes for her husband, who was home on leave, when suddenly 'you couldn't hold anything – it was all of a quiver. And . . . it was dust – matter of fact, I had to take all my curtains down, they were so dusty.' Melice Telfer remembered that she had been walking up Newton Road, near the centre of town, and was about to go on duty when 'people ran out of their houses wondering what in the world had happened'. On the French coast, if the *Faversham Magazine* of the summer of 1967 is to be believed, a strange sound and sensations were also reported.

I had read all of this in Arthur Percival's account of the disaster, and more besides regarding the way the blast and sound waves had behaved in the seconds after 833 exploded. Across the Thames estuary at Southend-on-Sea, in Essex, two plate-glass windows were smashed, and the event reported on the 7th by the *Southend and Westcliff Graphic*. In the meantime, so I discovered among papers now held at the National Archives, the owner of those shattered windows had written to the Ministry of Munitions; he was among the first owners of damaged property to do so. George Jackaman's shop was located at 16 London Road, Southend; his letterhead announced that the 'complete house furnisher' sold the latest in 'Osram and other electric lights'. Here is the shopkeeper's letter of the 5th:

Dear Sir, on Sunday last April 2nd, two of my shop windows were blown out through the concussion caused by the explosion at Faversham, Kent (this may be verified by the Chief Constable of the Borough) and the damage done is estimated at £40. I am advised that the proper procedure is to apply to you for compensation. If this is so I shall be glad to hear from you at your convenience.

At the Ministry, one Lambert Middleton was tasked with replying on behalf of the Director of Munitions Finance:

Sir, in reply to your letter of the 5th instant regarding to [*sic*] your premises caused by the explosion at Faversham, I am directed to inform you that your claim for damage should be addressed to the firm on whose premises the explosion occurred. The Department can take no responsibility in the matter.

It seems Middleton had drafted his reply for more general use, for alongside the letter to the Southend furnisher is another to a Mrs Swift of 31 Milton Road, Sittingbourne, and here Middleton has corrected himself: 'regarding the damage to your premises'. Mrs Swift had written on the 6th, 'the glass fronts of my shop property ... have suffered rather bad damage' – though she omits to mention what kind of shop she kept.

The letters, as we shall see, establish a pattern at the Ministry, and at the Home Office, of official response to local claims for recompense in the wake of the explosion. But for now it is enough to note the explosion's reach: the blast wave racing inland towards Sittingbourne and Faversham (where there was surprisingly little damage), and the Medway towns to throw open doors at the Chatham dockyards; and in the other direction, out over the Isle of Sheppey, troubling the waters of the Thames estuary and reaching the front at Southend. But is that what had occurred? As Percival tells us, the two nearest seismographs, at Kew and Guildford, registered nothing unusual. It seems that the witnesses further afield had felt a shock wave refracted downwards from the upper atmosphere, or perhaps transmitted through the chalk that underlies both Faversham and Norwich. Melice Telfer and Mrs Robinson, in Kent, had heard the sound first, as it raced across the fields, through the woods and over the creek. But a more oblique effect was responsible for doors and windows rattling and dinner things set quivering many scores of miles away.

The island is full of noises

Queen Victoria died on the 22nd of January 1901, on the Isle of Wight, where, as was her custom after the death of her husband, she had gone for Christmas. En route to its final resting place at Windsor, her body was conveyed to Portsmouth aboard the royal yacht HMS *Alberta*. On the 1st of February, as the vessel and its convoy headed east in the Solent, a line of thirty warships drew up along the coast and began to fire their six-inch guns, at intervals of a minute, by way of salute.

In the days that followed, newspapers in London and around the country received letters reporting a remarkable phenomenon. The firing had been heard well over a hundred miles away: in Cambridge, at St Ives, and near Woodbridge in Suffolk. But on the south coast not a rumble was reported, and many who turned out to hear the cannonade in Winchester, Bournemouth or Chichester had gone home disappointed.

This story quickly entered the annals of acoustical research; in time, however, the original incident was haloed with apocrypha. It became common in popular literature on acoustics to ascribe the strange effect to guns fired in London during Victoria's funeral the following day, or at Windsor where the funeral actually took place, and even to assert that the sound had been heard in Scotland. But the incident had a more profound afterlife during the First World War. The war afforded ample and grisly opportunity to study the behaviour of energy at a distance, and it was frequently found that sound and shock waves behaved capriciously, their force being unpredictable in terms of distance from the seat of an explosion or a fusillade.

The scientific literature of the war is full of instances of explosions heard, and people killed, at quite unexpected distances.

The silence of the Solent guns to listeners along the south coast in February 1901 was the consequence of an 'acoustic shadow', which can usually be traced to one or more of three causes. First, absorption: the sound is muffled for a time by intervening soil or forest or snow, but is heard further away on solid or open ground. Second, wind direction: sounds are more likely to be heard downwind than upwind. Third and most complex is temperature inversion, when the air near the ground becomes cooler than air higher up, causing sound waves to bend back towards the earth. In certain cases alternating rings of audibility and silence will radiate from the source as sound is refracted upwards and then down again.

On future wars

As the nineteenth century neared its end, the improvements, if that is what we must call them, that had been made in methods of propulsion and detonation became the subject of medical interest. In its edition of the 5th of March 1892, the *British Medical Journal* published a set of observations by the retired surgeon-general Sir Thomas Longmore; his remarks, the editors noted, had been written in advance of the International Congress of Red Cross Societies, to be held in Rome the following month. Longmore urged delegates to consider new arrangements regarding volunteer aid on the battlefields of the future, where there would be more casualties, spread over larger areas, and with more complex injuries, than had so far been encountered in any previous theatre of war.

Such is the velocity 'impressed' by the new firearms, writes Sir Thomas, and so great the destructive force of modern bullets, that even the 'fearful wounding' seen two decades earlier in the Franco-Prussian War will be cruelly magnified in future conflicts. The new bullet, he says, is afforded a 'very high velocity, both of translation and rotation'; the speeding and spinning object now travels further, so that from a distance for example of 2,000 yards a good marksman may hit his target at least half the time. And at the sacrifice of precision the effects are still vicious or deadly; Longmore cites the recent case of a labourer, near Aldershot, accidentally struck in the thigh at a distance of 2,500 yards. 'How many wounds may be expected to occur at or near similar distances in war of the future?' There is then the matter of the shape and texture of the projectile: 'In addition to the improved qualities of the new rifle bullets which have already been mentioned, their diminished areal section, together with the hardness and smoothness of their envelopes, have conferred on them a penetrative energy far beyond the penetrative energy possessed by any previous rifle projectiles.' Such narrow bullets can easily pass through several men in succession. Finally, as regards rifle fire, smokeless powders mean the battlefield will present a relatively unclouded environment, further improving the rifleman's chances.

Longmore turns then to the changes lately wrought in larger projectiles. The precise effects of the new chemical explosives, he notes, are not yet very widely known: 'It is generally understood, however, that shells under the action of such explosives will be broken up into a far larger number of fragments, and that the fragments will be propelled with far greater force, than when gunpowder was used as the disruptive agent.' We must imagine, in other words, a field of fire more saturated by deadly particles – and this before Longmore had even considered the effects of the blast wave, which will turn out to have been one of the most potent, and highly unpredictable, effects of the new explosives. The former surgeon-general's first consideration is the treatment of wounds caused by speeding projectiles, and the problem of recovering injured soldiers in the first place. 'Everything thus tends to show that while the number of sufferers urgently requiring help will be vastly increased in future wars, the means of affording them shelter and surgical attention will be pushed back to a greater distance than has ever before been necessary.' Neutral volunteers, Longmore writes, were accepted by both sides in the war of 1870–71; this system, he concludes, ought to be enlarged and more generally applied, 'in case, unhappily, hostilities on a large scale should again arise in Europe'.

There were, meanwhile, more specialized scientific efforts to understand the action of powerful new weapons on the human body. As early as 1848 – in consequence of the revolutionary violence of that year – it was known that improvements in the design of rifles and bullets produced novel and devastating types of injury. In their efforts to understand the nature and scale of destruction inside the body, military doctors began to borrow from the physics and the terminology of hydrodynamics. The French doctor Pierre Charles Huguier hypothesized in 1848 that it was the watery aspect of certain tissues that caused them to expand and rebound in catastrophic fashion when pierced by a bullet.

By the end of the nineteenth century Huguier's theory had led several researchers to try to replicate experimentally the action of a bullet or shell fragment passing through flesh. Many kinds of 'flesh simulant' were tried. The American Charles Woodruff shot at tomato cans and cattle bladders; he was convinced that something like the process of 'cavitation' – the term was used by marine engineers to describe the vacuum produced behind a ship's propeller – occurred inside the volume in question. In 1894 the pioneering British neuroscientist Victor Horsley set out to describe the violent stretching of tissues around the path of a bullet; he chose modelling clay as his medium, and having fired a bullet into it made a cast of the resulting cavity. Also in Britain, Arthur Keith and Hugh Rigby fired bullets into blocks of soap and into specially prepared cadavers. In 1916, the US army doctor Louis B. Wilson began using blocks of gelatin in which he had embedded cotton and silk fibres to imitate the paths of nerves and blood vessels. The softer the organ or tissue under attack, Wilson wrote, 'the further away from the track of the missile will serious secondary results of injuries occur'; the surrounding tissue was 'pulped' and became a nidus for the growth of bacteria carried into the wound by fragments of clothing and dirt. At the same time, pulped muscle and shredded organs – especially soft, glandular organs such as kidney, spleen and liver – gave out toxic products that were likely among the causes of 'so-called secondary traumatic shock'.

Such experiments continued after the war. In the United States, George R. Callender and Ralph W. French, under Wilson's supervision, began shooting at anaesthetized pigs and goats; these were found preferable to cadavers, as the absence of rigor mortis allowed the study of physiological effects. Later Callender and French mounted electrically wired screens in front of and behind their targets, so that they could calculate the velocity of a projectile, and submitted the dead or dying animals to X-ray. Among the pair's discoveries, published in the journal *Military Surgeon* in October 1935, was the gruesome fact that liquid-filled cavities such as the bladder and the rectum suffered particularly terrible injuries, in fact were apt to explode when full, thus confirming the decades-old cavitational hypothesis. In an aside to the description of the main results of their research, Callender and French noted that the nature of wounds altered considerably when the projectile was travelling at over 2,500 feet per second. In the case of high explosives, they wrote, 'Experiments indicate that shell fragments may have velocities well in excess of 3,000 feet per second to which is added this great irregularity of shape.' The era of the modern wound had begun.

A Study of Splashes

On the 22nd of January 1916, a letter appeared in the *British Medical Journal* from one Lionel F. West, concerning 'the divulsive effect of projectiles' – the adjective describes a rending or tearing action. West's letter was a response to a lecture, published by the journal a week earlier, in which Sir Anthony Bowlby had commented on 'the general character of gunshot wounds'. West moved swiftly to the heart of his disagreement with Bowlby, who had asserted: '[I]t has been shown that the injury caused by a bullet is largely due to the wave of compressed air which the bullet drives in front of it, and which expands within the tissues.' Could it really be the case that air is responsible, to use Bowlby's precise but abstracted phrase, for the 'divulsive and expanding nature' of these wounds? West believed he had isolated the real process at work when a metal projectile hit vulnerable flesh at high speed, and he had found it in an unlikely place.

A Study of Splashes is a 130-page volume published in 1908 by A. M. Worthington, then Professor of Physics at the Royal Naval Engineering College, Devonport. Worthington had first bruited his studies of liquid splashes in 1894 with 'The Splash of a Drop', a talk delivered to the Royal Institution and illustrated by drawings and 'shadow photographs' showing the profiles of drops of mercury as they fell directly onto photographic plates. By the time he embarked on the book, he had devised a complex system that used the spark from a Leyden jar as a flash to photograph successive stages in various types of splash: water on water, water on milk, milk on smoked glass. The book is a catalogue of forms produced when the speeding world is arrested for the tiniest of intervals. The shapes are by turn beautiful and grotesque: concentric waves and declivities; columns of liquid topped by little spheres that float free in space in one photograph then cease to exist in the next; spitting, flaring or frilled edges that resemble the coronets of sea anemones; bulbous asymmetrical forms that suggest swollen body parts – and chasms opened fleetingly in the surface of a liquid that look like wounds excavated in flesh.

Worthington's photographs and text are less well known than the images and research produced later, and over many decades, by the American Harold Edgerton, who is generally credited with having invented ultra-high-speed stroboscopic photography. Edgerton's technology, developed in the early 1930s, was certainly faster than Worthington's: he captured events with exposures as short as one hundred-millionth of a second. Among his most famous images are many that repeat Worthington's experiments, freezing in far greater detail the strange domes, minarets and crowns created when a tiny drop of milk or water breaches the meniscus of the same substance. The history of such researches is closely bound to the advancement not only of military photography but of the machinery of war itself: Edgerton worked on stroboscopic aerial photography during the Second World War, and later, with his 'Rapatronic' camera, produced images of atomic weapons tests that are quite unlike the mushroom clouds of popular iconography. In 1953 he photographed a nuclear explosion 0.00001 seconds after the moment of detonation; the bulbous, deformed thing at the centre of the picture looks more like a slowly growing cyst or vengeful tumour.

The history of extremely high-speed photography, in other words, involves unexpected meetings, real or metaphorical, between human bodies, everyday objects and the destructive innovations of military technology. The long hours that Worthington spent training his machinery on drops of milk and mercury were hardly devoted to pure research: *A Study of Splashes* begins with two photographs of the effects of shell impacts on armour plating. In the first image a circular hole has been torn in the metal and its raised circumference perforated with curious regularity; the frilled steel looks like fabric or potter's clay. The second photograph seems to have been substantially retouched, so that it hardly looks like a photograph at all. The hole is cruder this time, the surrounding fringe barely formed, and in the centre, like the pupil and iris of a ruined eye, is the shell or bullet – there is no indication of scale in the picture – still lodged, having failed fully to penetrate the metal. The photographs look less like close-ups of test firings in research conditions than like aerial views of ruined grey landscapes.

Permanent Splashes
left where a Projectile has entered an Armour-plate.

[*See page* 120.

When Lionel West looks at Worthington's photographs in the pages of the *BMJ*, instead of landscape or metal he sees human flesh. He notes the rigour and ambition of the photographer, who has captured every phase of the splash, whether caused by a drop of water falling into water or a modern projectile penetrating armour plate. Somewhere on the continuum between water and steel lies, says West, the human body: 'its several constituent tissues represent subdivisions of the degree'. But how is a wound like a liquid splash? Human tissue, he says has the same tendency to 'bubble', forming briefly a raised and thickened ring around the point of entry. This ring will inevitably break into fragments or drops: thus is explained the 'divulsive effect'. The pattern of such disintegration will be irregular; the object does not enter the body at such a carefully determined angle as it did in Worthington's experiments, and the projectile may be of any size and shape:

. . . it may spin, wobble, or trip over itself at any velocity or angle, but the general phenomena at the moment the wound is made will, considered generally, be the same; any stone thrown into any pond will convince of this – there will be details of 'pattern' at the point of entrance of the stone, but the concentric waves will still travel to the confines of the pond . . . The human body consisting of such different substances as muscle, bone, fat, fascia, nerves, brain, etc., all bound up in a tangled mess, would lead one to expect a very complicated and modified form of splash, just as happens when a stone is thrown into a pond, the surface of which is covered with floating and semi-submerged articles of different size and specific gravity.

What then of Bowlby's theory regarding the ruinous effects of compressed air forced into the body at the nose of a bullet?

West reverts to the example of a stone thrown into a pond; Worthington's photographs show, he says, that air does not precede a projectile but follows it. Here we have to look again at the ragged voids that open in the water behind a 'rough sphere' as it descends, and imagine the same in human skin and its immediate substrata, or even deeper inside muscle and organs and bone. Worthington ended his penultimate chapter by turning at last to the practical results and application of his photographs of water, milk and mercury. Steel, he wrote, will behave in the same fashion; that is, like a liquid. But the obvious analogy did not occur to him as it does to West eight years later; instead Worthington saw only the possibility, which is hardly to be underestimated, for shielding that body in battle: 'what I desire to suggest is, that from a study of the motions set up in a liquid in an analogous case, it may be possible to deduce information about the distribution of internal stress, which may also apply to a solid, and may then lead to improvements in the construction of a plate that is intended to resist penetration'.

The soldier's heart

In February 1915, Charles Myers, founder of the British Psychological Society and then an army doctor with the rank of captain, published an article in the *Lancet* entitled 'A Contribution to the Study of Shell Shock'. Myers's is among the earliest uses of the term in print, and the first in that journal. He describes three patients admitted to a military hospital at Le Touquet. The first had been pinned down by barbed wire while shells burst around him; a shell had caused the trench in which the second man was standing to collapse; the third was blown off a heap of bricks fifteen feet high, and flung into a pool of water. Their symptoms were almost identical. All three suffered a diminution of the visual field, which Myers represents in circular diagrams that resemble nothing so much as maps of blast sites: a series of rings and spokes with irregular shapes denoting the extent of each patient's vision. The three men also presented with their senses of taste and smell diminished or entirely gone. Memory was affected in the three cases, and they all complained of constipation and insomnia. They were by turns excitable and morose; one of them had been declared 'off his head' by comrades in the trenches. Comment on these cases, Myers writes, 'seems superfluous':

They appear to constitute a definite class among others arising from the effects of shell-shock. The shells in question appear to have burst with considerable noise, scattering much dust, but this was not attended by the production of odour. It is therefore difficult to understand why hearing should be (practically) unaffected, and the dissociated 'complex' be confined to the senses of sight, smell and taste (and to memory). The close relation of these cases to those of 'hysteria' appears fairly certain.

'Shell shock' is of course one of the phrases and phenomena that comes most readily to mind when we think of the experience of the ordinary soldier in the Great War. At the Somme in 1916, up to 40 per cent of casualties were apparently suffering from shell shock. But what was it? Myers's original article suggests it had a direct origin in the explosion of a shell or shells nearby, but as the war went on some of the same physical symptoms and perceptual deficits, as well as heightened and unpredictable emotional states, began to be observed among soldiers who had had no such proximity to bursting shells. And so a controversy developed, continuing into the years after the war, about whether shell shock was caused by a physiological reaction to the battlefield or some kind of neurosis or even psychosis, with origins perhaps pre-dating the war. In some respects it suited the military to believe the latter, for if shell-shocked men were not physically ill they might be sent back to the front. Belief in the physical nature of the illness persisted, however, and it intersected in ambiguous ways with earlier types of battlefield sickness, and with research throughout the war into the physiological effects of explosions. Meanwhile, such was the generalized use of the term 'shell shock' that many physicians and military commanders, often for competing reasons, rejected the category of shock entirely.

In the first weeks of 1916, the *British Medical Journal* was host to a controversy concerning the physical and mental effects of exposure to high explosives. On the 22nd of January, Alexander Morison had referred to a phenomenon known as 'the soldier's heart' that was then affecting many British troops in the field. On the 29th James Goodhart responded that the so-called soldier's heart was nothing but a generalized strain on the whole system, the result of a deficit of nervous energy. Morison, given right of reply in the same issue, stated that his remarks had been misreported in the original article: the phenomenon was indeed a generalized one, and one might as well speak of a 'soldier's brain' or 'soldier's spine' as attempt to isolate the problem as a coronary disorder. But he departed from Goodhart's claim that it was caused by nervous exhaustion.

The culprit, rather, eight times out of ten, was a prior infection that had weakened the soldier's constitution.

Among the remaining cases were many, Morison remarked, who had been exposed to, but not necessarily injured by, the detonation of high explosives. But the 'soldier's heart' may be found beating uncertainly too in the breast of 'the overworked civilian, harassed by anxiety'. Recovery, Morison wrote, 'depends a good deal on the man himself' – those who recover fastest and fullest are 'men of some mental force'; by contrast, 'the neurasthenic who becomes introspective and critical of his state is lost'. Morison, who had seen strong men reduced to a condition of 'exaggerated sensibility', noted finally that treatment must consist of reassurance and complete rest, followed gradually by 'increasing physical exertion and mental change'. He doubted, he said, that such patients were improved by each other's company, as at a sanatorium – better they lay alongside a man who had lost a leg than another like oneself who sighed and clutched at his chest.

What exactly did the *BMJ* correspondents mean by the phrase 'the soldier's heart'? The term pre-dates both the First World War and the use of high explosives on the battlefield. It appears the phenomenon first presented itself during the American Civil War, when soldiers began en masse to complain of chest pains, breathlessness, palpitations, dizziness, faintness and fatigue. In 1863 Dr Henry Hartshorne of the Union army delivered a lecture to the College of Physicians in Philadelphia, where several hospitals had been set up or expanded to treat casualties. 'Among the chronic affections of soldiers, which are best studied in hospitals remote from the field,' he said, 'is one which does not seem to have met, as yet, with full appreciation by medical officers, inspectors and pension surgeons . . . The affection to which I allude may be designated as muscular exhaustion of the heart.' Hartshorne allowed that he was not the first to have come across the phenomenon: four months earlier, a Dr Alfred Stillé had addressed the Philadelphia County Medical Society on the subject of palpitations apparently caused by exhaustion; these men exhibited shortness of breath after only moderate exertion and rapid pulse consequent on the slightest effort. And yet on examination they appeared quite well: neither Stillé nor Hartshorne could diagnose a heart murmur nor any other cause for the symptoms in question. Before the assembled college, Hartshorne ventured that the 'soldier's heart' was caused by prolonged exertion in the most unfavourable conditions: lack of rest, deficient food, bad water and malaria.

In the January 1871 issue of the *Journal of Medical Sciences*, Dr Jacob M. Da Costa, something of a prodigy among Philadelphia doctors and already president, in his thirties, of the city's College of Physicians, published his report on 'the irritable heart' and its origins. The condition frequently followed a period of hard service in the field, a bout of fever (with or without accompanying diarrhoea), affliction with scurvy or a wound sustained in battle. Da Costa rehearsed the now familiar symptoms – palpitations, chest pain, breathlessness, all apparently unrelated to effort or exertion – and added to them the common appearance of digestive complaints. On examination, there seemed to be no signs of illness apart from a rapid pulse. Da Costa recommended complete rest and a prescription of digitalis. A few men thus treated would recover fully and might be expected to return to their duties; most would have to be retired from service.

Some of the men seen by Da Costa and his precursors were

very likely suffering from acute or chronic heart disease, and many from malaria, typhoid, gastroenteritis, scurvy, malnutrition or fatigue. The idea persisted, however, that there was a distinct disorder that affected soldiers, though it was unclear whether it was of organic or emotional origin. The First World War did not settle the matter for good, but it provided an extraordinary number of cases. In 1919 the American researcher Alfred E. Cohn reported that as of the 31st of August 1918, 41,699 men had been discharged from the British army because of heart disease — 'most of them', Cohn claimed, were suffering from Da Costa's syndrome, as it had become known. (It was more commonly called 'the soldier's heart' by those who seemed to have suffered from it, and it was not only Allied soldiers who complained: it seems the German army had encountered the same problem.) By 1915, research was under way at University College Hospital in London; early the following year, 250 beds were set aside for the treatment and study of the condition at Mount Vernon Hospital in Hampstead. Here doctors recorded the patients' reactions to sudden visual stimulus followed by the 'unexpected discharge of a blank cartridge under the examining couch'. It was found, unsurprisingly, that men thus stimulated developed a faster pulse and breathing rate. It is hard to see how the result of the experiment might have been put to use, but in 1917 the study was expanded, and 700 beds at a hospital in Colchester, Essex, were earmarked for heart patients.

In 1919 Thomas Lewis of the University College Hospital published a monograph reporting what had been learned about the condition during the war. *The Soldier's Heart and the Effort Syndrome* presents 'derangements, real or supposed, of the cardio-vascular system'. The patients, he found, could be divided into six categories: those with incipient but so far unrecognized heart disease; men who had been gassed; men who were suffering from an undiagnosed infection; those not yet fully recovered from rheumatic fever, influenza, pneumonia, pleurisy, dysentery, trench fever or tonsillitis; those 'played out' by continuous labour, disturbed sleep, exposure and 'the constant strain and jar to the body and nervous system which work in the front brings'; and finally the large fraternity of the constitutionally weak, whether their debility be 'nervous or physical or both'. Into this last group Lewis places the under-sized, the flat-chested, men with a family history of insanity, and also 'those who in childhood were nervous weaklings, bed-wetters, somnambulists, etc.'. To a modern ear this last categorization may sound harsh and imprecise. Lewis, however, was not the epitome of Edwardian severity that we might imagine from these judgements; he writes with some feeling about the effects of war on the bodies and minds of a generation:

When the young manhood of a whole nation is placed suddenly under arms, its whole habit of life, its housing, dietary and clothing, its times of rest and of work, the nature of its employment changed, when with little or no preparation it is submitted by such a war as this to enforced training of a strenuous kind, when subsequently it is sent to meet wholly unusual and unnatural conditions, which stretch each muscle fibre and vibrate each nerve cell and nerve fibre of the body to the full, then the manhood is submitted to a most drastic test. Who then can affect surprise if many men fail when so tested?

But however widely he may have reflected on the mental and physical health of the British soldier, Lewis's conclusion in the case of the 'soldier's heart' was quite specific: he thought the disorder arose most commonly among men recovering from an infection.

Alfred Cohn published his findings regarding the condition in the same year as Lewis, drawing on his experience at Colchester and the hospitals of the American Expeditionary Force. Cohn concluded that 'the heart in convalescence after acute infectious disease and the Irritable Heart are probably not the same thing'. The soldier's heart was 'essentially a neurosis, depending upon anxiety and fear; it is removed by the disappearance of the inciting cause and . . . cured by measures designed to influence the neurotic state'. Cohn's American colleague Paul White, who in 1917 had travelled from Boston to work under Lewis at Hampstead and Colchester, later expanded on this view, asserting in 1920 that in the space of six to eight weeks he had seen twelve young patients with the same disorder, all of them civilians and most of them women. White and Cohn added to the list of symptoms: their patients were given to heavy sighs and flushing of the face and neck, or felt that they might suffocate in the midst of crowds. In time White, who published his last paper on the subject in 1972, came to the conclusion that there were two forms of what had once been called the soldier's heart: first, a real but mild disorder called neurocirculatory asthenia; second, a more severe illness with many symptoms – among them fatigue, breathing difficulties and problems with the heart – and which in fact was a form of manic-depressive disease.

And so an affliction that had first been diagnosed in the Civil War hospitals of Philadelphia, and regarding which so much had been observed, recorded, conjectured and written up, an illness that nobody could quite locate in mind or body, or

definitively ascribe to a temporary infection or chronic disease
of the heart, separated itself out, in the minds of physicians
in the middle of the twentieth century, into minor heart
trouble on the one hand and a violently oscillating psychiatric
disorder on the other. In 1941, while White was at work on
the subject, Paul Wood delivered three lectures to the Royal
College of Physicians; he declared that Da Costa's syndrome
ought finally to be considered a type of neurosis: 'The symptoms and signs of Da Costa's syndrome more closely resemble
those of emotion, especially fear, than those of effort in the
normal subject. The mechanism of somatic manifestations
depends on central stimulation, not upon hypersensitivity of
the peripheral automatic "gear". This central stimulus is emotional, and is commonly the result of fear.' Patients were apt to
misinterpret emotional symptoms as physical ones, to become
convinced by a 'vicious circular pattern' of thought and feeling
that the heart is to blame, to the point of a morbid fear of
death should they exert themselves. It was a question in the
end of 'hysteria'.

Psychic upsets

In an issue dated the 1st of January 1924, the *American Journal
of Physiology* carried an article by one D. R. Hooker entitled
'The Physiological Effects of Air Concussion'. Hooker's immediate subject was a series of experiments carried out at the
Sandy Hook Proving Ground in New Jersey, but he began with
some general remarks on the topic of shock. He dispensed at
once with the broad category of 'shell shock'; it had been
shown, Hooker wrote, that cases of shock 'unrelated to obvious

traumatism' were in fact examples of psychosis or 'psychic upset' to which the detonation of high explosives, or the report of a nearby large-calibre gun, 'contributed only incidentally'. Hooker conceded, however, that once the inaccurate applications of the term had been set aside, there remained cases of shock, seemingly caused by air concussion, in which some physiological damage had been done though there were no external signs of injury. Such examples of 'primary shock', he asserted, 'are undoubtedly analogous to the experimental cases considered in this paper'.

According to Hooker, the experiments in question took place in the winter of 1918–19, though the dates noted later in his article suggest the programme was under way in the spring of 1918. The task at Sandy Hook – a spit of land on the Atlantic shore that had been used by the US military since the 1870s to test weapons – was to discover the physiological effects of proximate exposure to the report of a large gun or mortar, and secondarily to study what happened to bodies in the vicinity of high-explosive detonations.

Here is an early example of the kind of experiment that Hooker described. On the 14th of January 1918, a live cat was bundled into a wooden crate or cage, and placed twenty-two feet from a twelve-inch mortar. The mortar was fired, but had no effect on the cat. The crate was moved closer, fifteen feet away, the mortar fired again, and the crate opened. The army researchers made detailed notes on the condition of the animal: 'Out of crate. Badly shaken but walks naturally; seems stupid. Hair slightly singed on back. Sight and hearing good.' Forty-five minutes later: 'Acts ill. Climbed out of box and settled near warm fire.' And after three hours: 'Condition much the same. Comes when called. Hair ruffled and looks sick. Phlegmatic.

Does not move when lightly pushed in head with foot.' The following morning the cat was briefly active and alert, then became lethargic and began to cough. On the 16th, it was found dead.

This unfortunate creature, closely watched and nudged in the head as it lay dying, was one of numerous animals – a few cats and rabbits, Hooker tells us, and 'a considerable number' of dogs and frogs – tested at Sandy Hook. The first experiments were carried out without anaesthesia, and established that the pressure of a gun blast produced a condition 'analogous to shock'. Hooker writes:

In unanaesthetized cats and dogs the most striking effect of exposure to the gun blast was the sudden onset of extreme fatigue. An animal previously alert, active and normal in every way was promptly changed into an exhausted, lethargic animal which roused when spoken to or when touched; it would move about heavily for a few moments at a time and then settle down again in stupefied quiescence. Such animals neither ate nor drank; they could see and hear, exhibited no signs of external or internal injury other than the exhaustion just described.

Later, except in the case of frogs, the animals were anaesthetized with morphia; the wooden containers were replaced with strong cloth bags, attached to the gun carriage with heavy wire. The bags were then placed close enough to the gun for their drugged contents to be affected by both the initial concussion of air and the sound wave. The results, Hooker admits, were varied, and the process involved 'much labour and waste of effort'. Certain dogs seemed quite unaffected by proximity to the blast of a twelve-inch gun; small differences in distance or direction appeared to be crucial to the outcome, and Hooker wondered whether the degree of blast pressure was merely one of the factors in play, alongside duration and oscillation.

Alongside these experiments with gun blasts, Hooker described an ancillary series of tests with high explosives. These proved a deal harder to carry out, let alone interpret. Hooker was at first vague or evasive on the subject: 'It developed that the results obtained were unlike those which resulted from exposure to the gun blast and did not simulate the shock conditions. The use of high explosives was therefore abandoned.' It seems, however, that there had been another and more fundamental problem with these tests: it was extraordinarily difficult to place the animal subject close enough to the detonation to suffer easily studied effects of air pressure, without killing the creature stone dead and even blowing it to pieces. Take for instance the case of 'Dog 12', exposed on the 7th of March 1918. This large male animal was given 'one grain morphia hypodermically. Dog exposed 2 feet from 2 pounds T.N.T. Instant death. Thrown 20 feet. Hind limbs shattered and abdominal wall ruptured. Skin burned. Lungs brightly hemorrhagic. Huge blood-clot in thoracic cavity. No specimens preserved.'

The dogs that lived were all subsequently 'sacrificed' by bleeding, then dissected. On the 14th of March, 'Dog 19' was placed forty-one inches away from four pounds of TNT: 'Animal placed back to charge. Snout wrapped in towel and pushed into 3 inch shell.' This last was presumably meant to ensure the dog could breathe after the blast, for it was the lungs that especially interested the Sandy Hook researchers in these cases. Dogs 13, 17 and 18 were similarly dispatched after exposure to high explosives, and it was found that 'the method was inadequate for the production of shock'. It did, however, yield some instructive effects on the lungs, as tissues were extensively lacerated and haemorrhage was widespread. 'It was very evident that the destruction of lung tissue was much greater than in animals exposed to gun blast,' Hooker writes. The phenomenon was not readily explained, though Hooker conjectures that it might be due to the relative suddenness with which pressure increases in the case of high explosives. Whatever the precise distinction to be made, it was clear to Hooker that there was a difference between gun blasts and TNT explosions: the latter 'in no case' produced typical symptoms of shock, and the experiments 'indicate further that extensive lacerations and destruction of lung tissue does not release a toxic substance, i.e. histamine, into the circulation in sufficient quantities to produce a physiological reaction'.

As Hooker notes, the Sandy Hook researchers were not alone, around the end of the war, in their attention to the physiological effects of high explosives. In 1919, in the *Revue neurologique*, Albert Mairet and G. Durante published the results of several experiments with rabbits and different amounts of explosive. The results were varied, as Hooker recounts: 'Those lightly affected appeared slightly stunned with a rapid respiration, while of those severely affected, some were greatly depressed and died within the hour and others showed a stage of excitement and subsequent recovery. The animals which did not die in the first twenty-four hours recovered without the subsequent development of symptoms indicative of central nervous system injury.' In the rabbits that died, Mairet and Durante discovered lesions in the spinal and cranial nerves that led them to conclude that 'it is the commotion which is responsible for the injury'; that is, the initial blast wave. But Hooker was once more uncertain. There were other factors to take into account, such as the sudden change in pressure: the explosion involved a short wave of positive pressure followed by a longer negative. The change was neither uniform nor predictable in degree: its 'billowing' nature may also have played a part in the type of injury found in these rabbits. At Sandy Hook, the maximum pressure caused by each detonation had been measured by baroscope, but not its duration or probable oscillations. In the matter of the physiological effects of explosions on nearby bodies, it seemed there was still a moment of uncertainty for which neither ballistics nor physiology, nor the staff of either the Ordnance or the Medical Corps, could exactly account.

Copies can always be had

Young Syd Twist had heard the first explosion and 'by the vibration knew it was a large one' – locals had grown used to judging the severity of the sounds and the shocks that came from the factories. His brother Percy had taken Syd's bicycle and set out for the marsh; the second explosion knocked him off and into a field, and the third blast soon followed. Recalling all of this in 1977, Syd gave a brief account of the efforts to put out the original fire, the magazines filled with TNT, the workers watching without much anxiety at first: all of which he was told about later, having left the plant at noon. In the morning he went to see the wreckage, though the factories were closed to all but those charged with searching for more dead. The cycle shed was filled with bodies, laid out on wattle gates, and there were more in the tile works near the entrance to the plant.

At dinner time I walked over to the [Explosives Loading Company]: where the stores had stood was a huge crater at least 100 ft across and about 10 to 20 ft deep. The boiler house had disappeared, one boiler lying on its side and the other lying where the other two buildings were, with unexploded brass primer cases scattered all about. The offices had been burned out and all the other buildings damaged or destroyed . . . Those killed numbered over 100, I believe 107.

Syd Twist is not quite right about the number of dead, but he is not alone: the published accounts, whether in newspapers in 1916, later press stories printed around the time of anniversaries, or the first versions of the event put together by local historians, differ frequently as to the exact number. The last death occurred on Tuesday the 4th, at the Mount Hospital. A coroner's inquest commenced the following day and took eight days to reach its verdict of 'accidental death caused by shock and injuries received in an explosion due to an accidental fire, cause unknown'. Major Cooper-Key was one of the chief witnesses, along with Evetts. The manager declared himself at a loss to explain why the fire had started, while Cooper-Key floated his theory, on which he would elaborate in his report, regarding a spark from the nearby boiler house landing on the pile of empty bags. Any carelessness on the part of men present at the plant that morning could almost certainly be ruled out: there was no evidence that the factory had a particular problem with workers smoking inside the perimeter. Sabotage, too, seemed most unlikely; there was only one

foreign worker, a Belgian man, employed at the Explosives
Loading Company, and Evetts 'was satisfied the Belgian was a
Belgian'. The more vexing question at the inquest was whether
Evetts had acted properly in keeping his men so long at work
removing explosives from the vicinity of the fire. He main-
tained that he had, 'because there was a possibility of the whole
factory catching fire':

I admit it would have been the easier way to order the men off, but
the thought that was in my mind was if anything serious happened
the Cotton Powder Company's glycerine plant would go up and my
object was to reduce this particular thing as much as possible. I have
been told since that it was a case of touch and go with this magazine.
If I succeeded in stopping this I consider the action was justified.

On the 11th of the month the jury returned its verdict, and
attached no blame to the management. In summing up, so the
East Kent Gazette reported, the coroner had remarked 'that it
was fatally easy to be wise after the event, but it was very difficult for the man actually there when it occurred'.

Between the opening and closing of the inquest, most of the
dead men had been buried in Faversham. A mass grave had
been dug at the cemetery in Love Lane, east of the town centre,
and on the afternoon of Thursday the 6th a funeral procession
set out from the marketplace. The funeral was photographed
by a local photographer, W. Hargrave of Preston Street, whose
postcards of the event bear his name and address and the
legend 'Copies can always be had'. The procession made its
way along Whitstable Road towards the cemetery, with a military band at its head and 400 private mourners following. The
Archbishop of Canterbury, Randall Davidson, conducted an

interdenominational ceremony; ministers from all the local churches joined him at the graveside, with the mayor of Faversham and other dignitaries. In Hargrave's photographs most of the mourners are still staring into the grave from a long mound of freshly dug earth while the clergy turn and walk away at the end of the service. In the final image there are just two figures left standing on the graveside planks, leaning on a temporary fence around the huge plot. I can count sixty coffins in two rows, which means the photographer has not quite been able to find a vantage where all would fit. Sixty-nine men were buried that day, and another a week later when his body was found in a ditch near building 833. Of the seventy, only thirty-four could be identified for sure, though another five were tentatively named. Six men were buried in other plots at Faversham cemetery on the 7th and 8th of April, and the remaining dead who were found are dispersed about the county.

A year and almost five months later, a monument was raised above the seventy dead. On the 29th of September 1917, the

Faversham and North East Kent News reported that the cost of the memorial had been borne by the Explosives Loading Company, which had also made arrangements for the maintenance of the grave. A Celtic cross of Cornish granite, ten feet tall and weighing four tons, was erected at the midpoint of the 108-foot-long grave. A granite kerb around the grave was interrupted at intervals by ornamental terminals; there were steps at either end, flanked by vases. On the kerb were the names of all those buried in the mass grave, rising to seventy-three now that some confusion regarding the bodies and body parts interred in April of the previous year had been cleared up. A separate slab in front of the cross listed the names of the men buried elsewhere. Forty-four of them had ages appended in parentheses; the youngest was seventeen and the oldest sixty-one.

I have to report

Telephone or telegraph wires are visible in many of the photographs that accompany Cooper-Key's report, and in the postcard images of Faversham on the day of the funeral, and news of the fire and the explosion was swiftly transmitted. Among the Cabinet papers held at the National Archives is an almost minute-by-minute account of information received from the scene and passed between the army, the Admiralty and the Home Office. The details are frequently wrong – it is assumed at first that the explosion took place at the larger Cotton Powder Company, not the Explosives Loading Company – but the paper gives a striking impression of the way information travelled at high levels. At 12.55: 'Eastern

Command report that the Cotton Powder Factory at Faversham is on fire in the TNT and Bond Store; am afraid that it is not possible to get it under.' Within minutes, the timeline attests, the Home Secretary and the Admiralty had been informed. At 1.40: 'Eastern Command reports that the Cotton Powder Factory at Faversham blew up at 1.25 p.m.' Reports of the subsequent explosions soon follow. Fire engines and troops are on their way from Canterbury and Sittingbourne; the local hospitals are being readied, doctors and nurses dispatched. It is obvious there have been many casualties, but numbers are not yet certain. Shortly after three o'clock it is reported that a 'very large' explosion is expected soon: fire brigades are at the scene but cannot put out the fires. At 5.53 the navy at Sheerness conveys news from the anti-aircraft battery at Faversham: the fires are under control, and 'the large explosion expected will not now take place'. Half an hour later the first reports of casualty numbers appear: 117 dead and between 150 and 200 injured. There was apparently no communication then until 7.40 in the evening, when it is noted that the *Daily Chronicle* has 'full details' of the accident, conveyed from the newspaper's local office in Sittingbourne. The paper has been asked to pass on all their reporter has seen or gleaned from witnesses and locals.

A degree of wartime secrecy surrounded the factories on the marshes, but an event such as the explosion of the 2nd of April could not simply be kept quiet. News of course spread quickly in the county and beyond, and with it rumours and anxieties about sabotage; government silence would only fuel such fears. Some minimum of information would have to be released, an acknowledgement of the tragedy that was sufficiently vague so as not to compromise the site or threaten morale. Accordingly, a couple of days after the event newspapers across the country published a short, precise but evasive statement:

The Minister of Munitions reports with great regret that during the week-end a serious fire broke out in a powder factory in Kent, which led to a series of explosions in the works. The fire, which was purely accidental, was discovered at mid-day, and the last of the explosions took place shortly after two in the afternoon. The approximate number of casualties is 200.

It was common in such cases to speak generally of 'casualties' rather than specify the numbers of dead and injured. *The Times* noted the same number on Wednesday the 5th, in a six-line report, halfway down a column of brief and mostly minor stories. Towards the end of the month, the paper carried a brief statement by the Home Secretary, Herbert Samuel:

The number of casualties on this occasion, although large, was happily not so great as the first estimate. One hundred and six men were killed and 66 injured. No women were killed or injured. With the exception of five men belonging to the military guard, all the killed were employed in the works affected by the explosions. The majority of them were rendering assistance when they were killed, and the rest were present as spectators. No one was killed or injured while engaged in his ordinary work. Those who were present as spectators were warned to leave, and would have had ample time to do so. Steps will be taken as speedily as possible to bring the essential conclusions and recommendations resulting from the inquiry to the notice of all firms engaged in the manufacture of similar explosives.

Circumstances attending

Cooper-Key's report to the Home Secretary is dated the 17th
of April, and so we may assume Samuel based his statement
either on the full text or on the ten-page summary with which
the Inspector's document begins. Cooper-Key outlines first
the circumstances of the most disastrous event in the history of
his department: the establishment of the Explosives Loading
Company to the west of the Cotton Powder Company plant in
1912, the addition of amatol to the range of substances with
which the factory worked, and the dangers attendant on storing TNT and ammonium nitrate in the same or adjacent
buildings. George Evetts is at the centre of the narrative
Cooper-Key briefly outlines: his efforts to have the initial fire
put out, the moment he realized it was impossible, and his
decision to concentrate his own efforts and those of his men
on removing as much explosive material as possible from the
vicinity of 833. There is little doubt in Cooper-Key's mind that
the fire began with a spark from the neighbouring boiler house
falling on the pile of empty TNT bags. Some alternatives are
'possible of course': a workman may have been smoking and

. . . thrown a cigarette end or a glowing match on to the bags which
impregnated as they were with TNT dust, would easily ignite, but
having regard to the time at which the fire was first noticed, viz. just
before the dinner hour, and to the strict regulations against matches
and smoking which had only recently been emphasized by prosecution and fine, it is extremely unlikely that any employee even if he
had so far infringed the rules as to smoke on the premises would

have failed to take the precaution of completely extinguishing his match or cigarette before throwing it away.

Spontaneous ignition is also unlikely, though as the bags lay there for about three months it cannot be discounted. And it seems implausible that a 'mischievous person' could have put a match to them: any such saboteur could not have reliably foreseen that the fire would catch hold of 833 and cause such destruction.

There is then the matter of storing TNT and ammonium nitrate in the same building, in contravention of the factory's licence, the quantities present constituting, he says, 'the makings of at least 75 tons of high explosive'. The management cannot be completely exonerated, but Cooper-Key, who had of course inspected the factory just days before the disaster, is not prepared to apportion much blame:

. . . at the present time rapidity of output is of the first importance, and from this point of view it is extremely difficult, if not impossible, strictly to adhere to the exact letter of a licence. Changes are called for almost daily and have to be met in the way that appears best at the time with due regard to the essential matter of output. This particular combination of ingredients even when intimately mixed to form Amatol, an explosive now commonly used for the bursting charges of shells and bombs, is regarded more as a fire-risk than as an explosion risk, and it may well be that the responsible officials failed to appreciate the danger they were running in keeping these ingredients in the same building or that appreciating the risk they considered it justified by the urgency of the national requirements.

If there are more serious questions remaining for Cooper-Key, they have to do with the behaviour of Evetts and his men in the interim between the discovery of the fire and the first explosion. Ought Evetts, once he realized the fire at 833 could not be got under control, have ordered all the workers present to leave at once? The Inspector acknowledges that many or all of the men killed might indeed have been saved, but the danger outside the immediate vicinity would surely have been greater had the TNT lying around not been removed. There was also the matter of what Evetts dutifully considered a greater good, and whether this was the continued supply of munitions to the forces at the front. Evetts acted, says Cooper-Key:

. . . not hastily but with full appreciation of his responsibility, that in view of the proximity of the Cotton Powder Company's Cordite Works and of the importance of these to the nation the proper course was to make every effort to limit the destructive effect of an explosion to the smallest possible area by removing to a safe distance all the TNT that could be handled by the men at his disposal. In this he was, I understand, loyally supported by his men, and although the loss of life is most deplorable it may truly be said that those who thus died at their posts gave their lives for their country in the fullest sense.

That is to say, as Evetts and others attested, most of the men who died were at work removing explosives and making safe the surrounding buildings. But what of the others, and Herbert Samuel's comment about 'spectators', who had ample time to escape but failed to leave the scene? Cooper-Key mentions 'the presence of a certain number merely as spectators', saying that they may not have known the danger they were in. In fact there is some confusion about whether any workers at all were 'spectators'; two of the statements appended to the report state explicitly that all the men present were working when the first explosion happened, and none of them merely watching.

Samuel's statement on the subject of spectators did not go unnoticed in Kent, and on the 9th of May the Faversham branch of the Workers' Union wrote to the Labour MP Charles Duncan (founder of the Union and Member for Barrow-in-Furness), complaining that the comment amounted to slander. The letter was passed to the Home Office, and Cooper-Key was asked for his observations. On the 19th, his handwritten memo stated that the Union's interpretation of Samuel's remark was 'very inaccurate'. He points out that the Home Secretary noted that the majority were rendering assistance, and goes on to say:

I cannot see that there is anything in this reply to hurt the most sensitive feelings. Mr Evetts, the manager, distinctly stated to me that he had warned off those workpeople who were not engaged in rendering assistance but that no notice was taken of his warning, – but I fail to see that there is anything to be ashamed of in this, &, although in the circumstances it is impossible to be certain, it is probable that few, if any, mere spectators would be near enough to be killed or seriously injured.

On hearing from the Home Office, Duncan wrote to this effect to the union, adding that the fact of their being spectators at the scene 'does not of course imply any reflection whatever on the men in question'. There is, however, a disconcerting note neatly written towards the end of Cooper-Key's memo, in another hand that it is hard to identify among the many initials and dates by which the document has been signed off at the Home Office. It reads: 'It is possible that the question of compensation is what they are really troubled about.'

In fact, the official records show that the trade unions were most concerned with the appalling loss of life and possible future danger to workers at the plant, and not with compensation, which was seen to by the Explosives Loading Company itself. On the 27th of May the Chatham and District Trades and Labour Council wrote to the Home Secretary asking for an explanation of what seemed 'a futile effort to save the buildings and material' when lives might have been saved by sending away the men gathered around the burning building. This letter speaks too of 'the most primitive arrangements' in the way of precaution against disaster.

In the final pages of his report, Cooper-Key returns to the conspicuous bravery of certain workers, chief among them the managers, Evetts and Bethell. In the end eight men were awarded the Edward Medal, having been recommended by the proprietors of the two companies and vouched for once more by the Inspector. Alongside Evetts and Bethell were Urbane Charles Beech, John Harrison and John Sears of the Cotton Powder Company's fire brigade, Explosives Loading Company workmen William Wallace and George Gilham, and finally a private soldier, William James Wiltshire. The eight had been chosen as representative of the eighty or ninety survivors who had rendered assistance at the scene and might as easily have been recognized. A year later a ceremony was arranged to present them all with 'a silver token commemorative of the occasion'.

In the repercussing air

The postcard was printed in Amiens in 1919, in black and white, which has faded to green and grey, or perhaps was always meant to be that way, tinted so as to recall the landscape it depicts. A landscape of which, by the looks of things, there is not much left. If it were not for the detailed legend at the top, and a thin lateral strip of trees and sky that occupies perhaps one-tenth of the image, you would be hard pressed to determine just what this postcard shows. An aerial view perhaps, though at what scale it is impossible to say. Maybe we are looking at a single ravaged field, traversed by chalky paths and scattered here and there with clumps of weeds. Or it could be a scene that stretches for hundreds of miles, from mountain peaks via forested and bouldered escarpments to placid lowlands at the upper edge of the photograph. It might equally represent a cross section through flesh or bone, with nerves and vessels descending from the dermis, bunched in the interior, at the bottom, in junctions and ganglia.

The title at the top reads: 'LA BOISSELLE (Somme). – Trou de la grande Mine (300 m de circonférence, 40 m. de profondeur, 420 000 m c.).' There seems to be a network of footpaths worn into the soil and chalk, over on the right. There are no human figures to provide scale, at least none that I can make out among the rubble. We can be sure, however, that there are bodies beneath that debris – hundreds, perhaps thousands of them. Because what we are looking at is one of a pair of craters produced at precisely twenty-eight minutes past seven on the morning of the 1st of July 1916, either side of the village of La Boisselle, by two of the vast mine explosions that signalled the beginning of the Battle of the Somme. Perhaps there is another postcard showing the devastation on the far side of La Boisselle, or the view from the other side of the crater. In fact, I have in my possession – bought online while writing – a stereoscopic view, or rather a pair of views, of the same vast hole, captioned: 'Looking into the depths of the enormous crater of our mine fired at La Boiselle [*sic*] on the Somme.' (The pair of photographs was produced by the firm Realistic Travels – founded in 1908 by the Canadian photographer Charles Hilton DeWitt Girdwood – and was part of an album of 600 images published after the war.) From this angle the edge of the crater is swollen and uneven, the paths to the centre worn deeper and whiter into the chalk, and halfway down on the left-hand side is clearly visible the tunnel by which the explosive was delivered, along which British sappers had scurried back beneath their own lines.

For months these engineers had been at work beneath the countryside, tunnelling their way slowly (and quietly, lest German tunnellers hear them) and ferrying, in the case of La

Looking into the depths of the tremendous crater of our mine fired at La Boiselle, on the Somme

Boisselle, some twenty-four tons of ammonal – a mixture of ammonium nitrate and aluminium – under the German fortifications. The explosive charge to the south of the village, known as the Lochnagar mine, caused very likely the loudest man-made sound on Earth to that date. The explosion was seen by Second-Lieutenant Cecil Arthur Lewis:

The whole earth heaved and flashed, a tremendous and magnificent column rose up in the sky. There was an ear-splitting roar drowning all the guns, flinging the machine sideways in the repercussing air. The earth column rose higher and higher to almost 4,000 feet. There it hung, or seemed to hang, for a moment in the air, like the silhouette of some great cypress tree, then fell away in a widening cone of dust and debris.

The aftermath was described by Corporal Reginald Leonard Haine of the 1st Battalion, Honourable Artillery Company: 'I saw the effect of the mines. I saw the crater at La Boisselle. It really petrified me. I mean, it was as big as a cathedral.'

The most vivid account of a mine explosion on that morning of the 1st of July 1916 – providing also some inkling of just what workers saw at Uplees on the morning of the 2nd of April – comes from Lieutenant Geoffrey H. Malins, a pioneering film-maker responsible for much of the extant footage of the First World War. In his book *How I Filmed the War: A Record of the Extraordinary Experiences of the Man who Filmed the Great Somme Battles Etc.*, published in 1920, Malins recalled that shortly after seven o'clock he and his hand-cranked camera were installed in a trench, the apparatus poking just a little above a row of sandbags. (They are visible in a series of images

taken from close to the film-maker's position by the still photographer Ernest Brooks.) He had a clear view of the Hawthorn
Redoubt, a massive German fortification at Beaumont Hamel.

Time: 7.19 a.m. My hand grasped the handle of the camera. I set
my teeth. My whole mind was concentrated upon my work. Another
thirty seconds passed. I started turning the handle, two revolutions
per second, no more, no less. I noticed how regular I was turning.
(My object in exposing half a minute beforehand was to get the
mine from the moment it broke ground.) I fixed my eyes on the
Redoubt. Any second now. Surely it was time. It seemed to me as if
I had been turning for hours. Great heavens! Surely it had not misfired? Why doesn't it go up?

Malins now began to shake and to sweat: he had used a thousand feet of film already, and was suddenly afraid of running
out before the planned detonation occurred.

Another 250 feet exposed. I had to keep on. Then it happened. The
ground where I stood gave a mighty convulsion. It rocked and
swayed. I gripped hold of my tripod to steady myself. Then, for all
the world like a giant sponge, the earth rose in the air to the height
of hundreds of feet. Higher and higher it rose, and with a horrible
grinding roar the earth fell back upon itself, leaving in its place a
mountain of smoke. The earth was down. I swung my camera round
on to our own parapets. The engineers were swarming over the top,
and streaming along the sky-line. Our guns redoubled their fire.

How I Filmed the War reproduces many stills from Malins's
films, but the start of the Battle of the Somme is the instance
for which he prints a sequence of images – not quite adjacent

frames, but near enough to give a sense of unfolding action. There are eight of them, arrayed in two columns but meant to be viewed from the top left to bottom, then up again on the other side. The first frame shows a featureless sky, either packed with pale cloud or washed out by the inadequacies of the film. The horizon slopes down a little to the left; it's not clear if it's the earth or Malins's camera that is not quite level. There is a ridge or slope on the left, with a battered wooden fence running along it, down to an expanse of mud in the fore-ground. Midway to the horizon there is a narrow stand of vegetation, at which I have stared for some time, trying to work out its scale, but I still cannot tell if these are thin shrubs or tall weeds. (I want the plant to be rosebay willowherb, col-onist of blasted landscapes and seasonal companion to my explorations at Faversham – but F, who knows her flora far better than I, is sure it is not that.) In this first picture there is barely a disturbance of the horizon, a tiny swelling perhaps. In the second it is as if a small hillock has appeared, with a cross-hatched object like a ruined house at its summit. In the third a defined hill, like a fin emerging from the earth. It then becomes a great rounded oblong thing, smooth-edged then rugged, till in the final two frames it declines, as though collapsing under its own weight, and slumps towards the ground. It finally looks like smoke but is still made of soil and chalk; in other photographs of the scene, the smoke comes later, rising in three huge plumes and one smaller. Nothing else in the scene has changed at all: the sandbags, the fence, the plants in the middle distance, these are all precisely in place throughout. It looks as if the catastrophic event on the horizon is entirely isolated in space and time, having no effect on its environs. It is said that in the immediate aftermath of the explosion, in advance of which bombardment had ceased, the British guns, due to some failure of communication, did not begin firing again, and silence prevailed in the minutes before the trenches were emptied towards the horizon, towards the still ascending pall of smoke above Beaumont Hamel.

An overcharge

On the afternoon of the 25th of October 1916, there were seventeen women at work in building number 110 at the Marsh Works, a short walk to the east of the woods and ponds of the Oare factory and less than a mile from the devastation at Uplees. The works occupied a site on the right bank of the creek where it began to widen out. Gunpowder manufacture had begun there in the 1780s, under direct government control; in 1832 the site was let to John Hall and Sons, and they bought it outright in 1854. By the end of the century the factory had been absorbed by Curtis and Harvey, who specialized there in the preparation and pressing of blasting powders. During the war, machinery and infrastructure were adapted to produce charges for high-explosive shells; after the war the industry continued here, as at most sites in the Faversham explosives archipelago, until the relocation of production to Ardeer in Scotland in 1936.

In 1916, as at Uplees, the Marsh Works were operating at or beyond capacity and the plant's managers had had to accept at least a certain habituation to risks that would not have been countenanced in peacetime. This almost certainly accounts for the events of the 25th of October. The women had returned from dinner, so the Ministry of Munitions report tells us, at about two o'clock. Building 110 was a pre-war pressing house, and in fact had been in constant and it seems entirely uneventful production for thirty-five years. It was a brick building measuring forty feet by twenty-five, divided longitudinally in two by a passageway three-and-a-half feet wide. On each side of this corridor there were three compartments, also with brick walls intervening but fronted only in wood; the whole interior was timbered and painted. At one end of the building was a cloakroom, and beyond that an engine house containing a steam engine, from which a shaft ran down the middle, beneath the floor. A wooden platform surrounded the building and gave access to others neighbouring. The building was lit by electric lights, enclosed for safety purposes in bulkhead fittings, and heated by steam pipes.

At the start of the war, the pressing house had been adapted for the preparation of charges of TNT and amatol, to be used in high-explosive shells – though gunpowder pressing also continued in the same building and at the same time. On the 25th of October five of the twelve presses were working with TNT and amatol – it would usually have been six, but one was out of action – and the rest with powder. No matter the material being worked, the process was broadly the same, though with certain small and essential differences. Each compartment housed two cam presses, linked to the central shaft by a belt drive. One woman was assigned to each press; she stood flanked by a spindle that emerged upwards from the enclosed machinery and pressed the charge into a mould, and another that did likewise to force the charge out of the mould again. Between the two was a third, rotating, spindle that held six moulds, and above this a powder hopper by which the charge could be measured and funnelled into these moulds. In the case of high explosive, there were just three moulds, and as the substances would not flow like powder, they could not easily be measured in the hopper but had to be transferred by hand; a degree of estimation was necessary each time.

In the report submitted to the Ministry of Munitions, there is no doubt that the fire began in compartment number 1: 'Esther Gardner who was working with her two sisters in No. 1 stated that smoke was seen by her sister Bertha rising from the box cover of the driving belt. She immediately called to the others to run and herself got out unhurt, but the others were injured.' In a very few seconds, says the report, the whole building was involved. Esther Foyles, who was working with amatol in number 4, told the inquiry that she heard a rumble, and almost immediately the place was in flames: the fire had seemed to advance down the central passage. She got out quickly and safely. In number 3, Jenny Farthing heard nothing before she saw the flames and smoke – again, she and her companion at the machine ran from the building at once, and were unhurt.

James Burton was in charge of the Marsh Works on the 25th of October. With his colleague Chambers he had been approaching the building in question when they heard two explosions, neither very loud. They saw Edith Gardner emerge from the central corridor: 'This unfortunate girl must have lost her head on running out of No. 1 Compartment where she was at work and instead of running straight away, ran round the platform and into the entrance of the passage way. Here a piece of timber or brickwork fell upon her and pinned her down and she was extricated with great difficulty, terribly burned, by Chambers.' The second woman Burton recognized was Ethel Broadhurst, aged thirty-one and married; she was standing just outside the entrance, apparently so transfixed by fear that she could go no further. 'How she came there was not clear as apparently she was in the Cloak Room and could have escaped in the opposite direction with safety.' Burton and Chambers had no time to reach her before a large piece of masonry fell on top of her and pinned her to the platform. The two men tried hard to get her out, but the flames were now too fierce and the masonry too heavy.

Inside the building, the body of Ethel May Shrubshall, aged twenty-four, was discovered in a corner: she had been blown there, most likely already insensible, by the explosion of her gunpowder hopper. Mrs Broadhurst had meanwhile died at the scene; Edith Gardner succumbed to her injuries on the 2nd of November; and a fourth woman, Norah Jemmett, died after the official report was written: there is a note appended to the effect that she expired from the combination of her injuries and pneumonia. The jury at the inquest had returned a verdict of accidental death, and now reconvened to reach the same conclusion in the case of Miss Jemmett.

Under the heading 'Causes of the Accident', the report concludes that it was 'beyond reasonable doubt' there had been an overcharge of a mould with TNT or amatol. When this happened, the press would stop but the drive shaft would continue to spin, causing friction and heat as the belt slipped on its rollers. The building had been in use for over three decades, and in that time the machinery, its wooden housing and the timbers that lined number 110 had become impregnated with gunpowder dust. 'There is little doubt, therefore, that the ignition was caused by explosive dust on one of the pulleys being ignited by the heat generated by the belt slipping.' Once the initial fire had taken hold there was no chance of saving compartment number 1: the high explosive erupted, and the rest of the building was doomed. None of the women working with gunpowder escaped death or serious injury, but the remaining TNT and amatol did not detonate, merely burning away until nothing was left of the building but its brick walls. It seems, as the report asserts in its final section on the 'Question of Blame and General Remarks', that it was the combination of gunpowder and high explosive that sealed the fate of the women who died. Under normal circumstances, neither traditional nor new explosives were thought especially dangerous when properly dealt with, and in fact subsequent tests on samples of the high explosives in use at the Marsh Works found them in no way more likely to explode than was usually the case. The report records certain recommendations made at the inquest: 'In future none of the old gunpowder buildings will be used for pressing Amatol or T.N.T. blocks; only new buildings which have been erected for this purpose since the commencement of the war, and all the compartments of a building will be devoted to the same work, either gunpowder, or T.N.T. and Amatol.' Each compartment would also be fitted with two doors, so that in the event of an accident the workers might quickly exit and avoid, in their panic, finding themselves trapped on the platform by falling debris, or frozen in terror, staring out in their last moments through smoke and flames, at the marshes dotted with buildings and the figures rushing towards them in hope.

A waste of black desolation

I have not seen the monument in Silvertown, in the East End of London, to the seventy-three people killed there by an explosion in 1917. The writer Patrick Langley, who has written a fascinating account of the post-industrial allure of the place, says that it is easy to miss: tucked under a bridge, beside a bin. Silvertown is known today for not much more than waste and destruction; it is a district of London's Docklands that has so far resisted regeneration, never mind gentrification. There is, or was, no silver in Silvertown; it takes its name from Samuel Silver, who in 1852 opened a factory there producing rubber goods: gutta-percha for use in waterproof clothing and electrical insulation; belts for machinery; and vulcanite, or ebonite – a combination of rubber and sulphur, hardened by exposure to intense heat. Silver's factory was the main British producer of housings for telegraph cables, and was responsible for lines that crossed the Mediterranean from Marseilles to Algiers, and from Galveston, Texas, to Valparaiso in Chile. By the end of the century the company had laid 40,000 miles of ocean cable.

But the town that Silver built was just one especially thriving enterprise in an exurban landscape increasingly littered, in the latter half of the nineteenth century, with infamously noxious industries. In 1857, in the pages of *Household Words*, Dickens wrote that the area had become 'quite a refuge for offensive trade establishments turned out of town; those of oil-boilers, gut-spinners, varnish-makers, printer's ink-makers, and the like'. Products included creosote, naphtha, nitrates, phosphates and superphosphates derived from the carcasses of diseased cattle. The combined stench of these manufactures melded with the constant output of coal dust and smoke, and the tidal river twice a day revealed a scurf of organic waste, including animal bones and human faeces. Even the emanations of the Tate and Lyle sugar factory, which might have been expected to smell more pleasant, were sickly sweet and hard to bear. Fires and explosions were frequent in the last decade of the century: stores of oil and gas ignited, and late in the summer of 1897 a labourer named Joseph Gardiner was roasted to death in molten sulphur when a boiler erupted at Silver's factory.

Among the later additions to this landscape of fervid production and its foetid collateral was the Brunner Mond chemical works, established in 1893 for the manufacture mainly of caustic soda. The factory was located on the north bank of the Thames, just south of a tidal basin containing the Royal Victoria Dock. The North Woolwich Road ran laterally between Brunner Mond and the docks; to the east and west were scores of tiny streets and hundreds of terraced houses. Dotted around the complex were a plywood factory, twin flour mills adjoining the docks and the vast oil tanks of the Silvertown Lubricant Works. In 1912 Brunner Mond shut up the factory, and it stood idle for three years. But in 1915 the 'shell crisis' led Lord Moulton, who was in charge of production, to ask the company to reopen its works for the purification of TNT. There were obvious risks attached to siting such a facility in a densely populated area, but the view of the newly constituted Ministry of Works prevailed, and production began in September 1915. Dr F. A. Freeth, a Brunner Mond chemist, would later recall: 'It worked, but was manifestly very dangerous. At the end of every month we used to write to Silvertown to say that their plant would go up sooner or later, and we were told that it was worth the risk to get the T.N.T.'

The evening of Friday the 19th of January 1917 was already starlit and cold when the men and women working the day shift began to leave the factory and their colleagues started arriving for the night shift. Some of the day workers stayed on for an evening's overtime, and several children arrived at the factory to deliver their parents' evening meals. The fire must have started around a quarter to seven, in a building that housed the melting pot; here, impure TNT was poured from barrels into a hopper and thence made its way into a vessel below, where it was heated, foreign matter removed, and the molten explosive repoured into moulds. For expediency's sake around fifty tons of TNT had also been stored in the same building.

We have several accounts of the events of that evening, among them the detailed reminiscence of one J. J. Betts, a young fireman stationed nearby. He saw the bright orange flames shoot high into the air above the Brunner Mond works. Immediately, one of the factory's men rushed into the station, shouting: 'Brunner Mond's alight!' Betts yelled at his wife in their quarters behind the station, 'Get out of it, Polly, for

God's sake! We're all going up in a minute!' Out in the street, people were running away from the factory while others stood and stared; all of them knew that a fire meant an explosion might happen at any moment. Some of the fleeing workers and local residents, Betts recalled, threw themselves face down on the pavement, or flattened themselves against walls and prayed. In the seconds or scant minutes after first catching sight of the flames, Betts recognized one of the hurrying figures; it was the factory's timekeeper, who shouted, 'Run for it, mon, we'll be gone in a minute!' They did not have a minute.

Betts woke up 200 feet away, amid the roar of flames, the bells of ambulances and fire alarms, and the screams and groans of the wounded. The Scottish timekeeper had not survived. The Brunner Mond works was reduced to smoking rubble; nine other factories and mills had caught fire as burning fragments, including glowing iron girders, so it was reported, rained down on the surrounding area. Boilers were discovered several streets from the factory, and parts of a fire engine found a quarter of a mile away. It was, said Betts, as though a giant pestle had descended from the heavens and pounded those streets to powder. Clouds of smoke towered above the district, lit (as was much of the city, for several hours) by the fires below. The flour mills provided the most extraordinary spectacle; millions of tiny sparks flew from the ruins like a hailstorm turned incandescent – each one was a single grain of wheat, sent burning into the night air by currents of heat from the burning buildings.

An army of helpers, so Betts attested, was already at work digging survivors out of the rubble. One man, he said, dragged four badly injured children from the ruins of a house; it was only after they were clear of the wreckage, and this man sank to the ground unconscious, that those around him realized he had lost a foot. Betts's own wife, Polly, survived, but had been deafened by the blast. All around them, people were still fleeing: 'One woman was putting her babies to bed when the explosion occurred. She rushed out with them, and in her terror ran on until she was taken in by some kindly people, at whose house she stayed. A number became mentally unhinged by the shock.'

On the 27th of the month, the *Stratford Express* newspaper carried a description of the event, and 'A Tour of the Stricken Area'. The explosion, the paper reported, had been heard not only in London and the Home Counties but in Cambridgeshire and Norfolk. But for reasons of security the district in which the disaster occurred was not named, and so the vividness of the report is oddly undermined by its geographical vagueness – not that anybody in the East End itself could have been unaware.

As often with descriptions of such scenes – we might think of *Household Words* in 1852 – the journalist finds it impossible not to reach for lofty, even classical, metaphors and certain grand personifications:

Titan, armed with a mighty club, seemed to have struck indiscriminate blows in his attempt to batter the houses without wholly destroying them. Roofs had been lifted bodily from their positions and deposited in queer positions upon the side walls. Some had been ripped off entirely like the lid of a tin; others were blown to pieces, and flung away to alight where the attraction of Mother Earth overcame their borrowed power.

At street level, lace curtains still hid a few of the interiors from sight, but for the most part the skeletons of the houses had been laid bare: walls stripped of plaster and paper, back to their laths, the stairs canted over at an angle. It was reported – one of those inexplicable details that stick in the mind a century later – that the most fragile objects in some of these houses had mysteriously survived, so that many of those still fleeing the area were to be seen clutching glass vases and other ornaments as they hurried through the cordon now flung about the site by police and army.

The writer finally attains the seat of the disaster, a 'ghastly' place:

Apart from the knowledge of the appalling tragedy involved, the sight was physically nauseating. Acre upon acre of devastated buildings, shapeless, confused and hopeless. One vast heap of ruins, gruesome witnesses of the terrible power, followed by the man's best friend, but his worst enemy. In the middle of this horrible heap was a big hole, marking the exact spot where the explosion occurred. Hundreds of tons of earth had been forced out, to fall like a mantle of death upon the surrounding debris. The water that filled the cavity was still and sombre.

Nearby stood the flour mill, built of reinforced concrete that had been considered fireproof; the contents, of course, had not been. A fire engine was still pouring water into the ruins – 'and as if the depressing desolation of the picture needed a touch of Nature to complete it, festoons of icicles hung from the coping stones. The ground was deeply covered with sodden flour, whose virgin whiteness was stained to a sickly yellow.'

A number of inquests were carried out in the weeks that

followed, a report prepared for the Home Secretary, and some desperate or foolish souls arraigned for crimes committed in the aftermath. At the first inquest, a labourer who lived close to the factory said that he had identified the body of his son, aged eight. Another recounted how he had discovered the body of his 21-year-old daughter outside his house; he had already lost her older sister, aged twenty-three. A third labourer confirmed the bodies of his son and two daughters. The remains of a Liverpool plumber, aged thirty, were identified by his landlady. A mill hand told how he had been taken to a mortuary to verify the corpse of his wife, then to another where he recognized his son, aged thirteen; in the ruins of his house, finally, he found the body of his daughter, aged ten. At the coroner's inquest there were more detailed accounts of some of the deaths: 'Dr Brews told the coroner that he had examined a charred body, which was headless and without arms or legs. It was the body of a young female under 23 years of age.' Some of course had survived the blast, only to die later; Catherine Smith, aged sixteen, had been 'burned practically all over the body. She lived until 8 a.m. on the 22nd, and then died from shock following the burns.'

Seventy-three lives had been lost either immediately or in the days that followed, and about a thousand people injured – a hundred of those seriously. A dozen residents from the surrounding streets had simply vanished, no trace of their bodies being recovered. There were stories, however, of narrow escape. A small mission church in which local children were gathered had partially collapsed in the blast, and the women in charge of the group had had to hold up what remained of the roof until the children had all escaped. Many children had of course been injured, orphaned or made homeless; a local committee was swiftly formed to house them, and many were sent to Park Wood, a convalescent home near Swanley in Kent, where they were attended by doctors and supplied with clothes and boots. The newspapers reported that the children were surrounded by woods and flowers. Back in Silvertown, however, there were also tales of unheroic and uncharitable behaviour. One John Podesta, a bus conductor aged twenty-seven, was sentenced to three months' hard labour for having looted a shop of cigarettes, soap, boot polish, a purse and a pair of bloodstained spectacles belonging to the injured husband of the shop's owner, Ann McCready. 'Prisoner appeared staggered by the sentence,' noted the local court reporter.

On the 23rd of January the Home Secretary, Sir George Cave, appointed three members and a secretary to a committee tasked with discovering the cause of the explosion 'and the circumstances connected therewith'. The group included Sir Ernley Blackwell, Assistant Under-Secretary of State, and Major Cooper-Key, who remained in the post of His Majesty's Inspector of Explosives. Their report commenced with a description of the factory: its rectangular site, the railway and river to north and south, the factories, mills and oil depot nearby. The committee had suborned Lord Moulton to explain the choice of the Brunner Mond works for the task of purifying TNT, and he had responded that it was the only facility that could easily be converted to the method considered most expedient: a process by which the explosive was washed in hot alcohol. Before long the plant had been producing ten tons of purified high explosive a day, and working seven days a week. It was hard to know, said Moulton, how much TNT would be needed by artillerists in the months to come, and so he 'never felt safe in discontinuing Silvertown which was doing its work very well, and I believed and still believe was in very good hands'.

The fire had begun in the factory's melting-pot room: a purpose-built structure of corrugated iron, erected on top of the former caustic soda plant. Crude TNT was conveyed in bags to this room by a hoist, then emptied into a lead-lined funnel, leading to the steam-heated melting pot below. From here, molten explosive was run off to be dissolved in alcohol, subjected to vacuum treatment and spun in centrifuges, then cooled so that it solidified into 'flake'TNT and could be bagged up again and sealed in boxes with brass screws. The melting pot itself was made of iron, and held five or six tons of TNT; it was entirely enclosed but for an opening, a foot and a half across, where the funnel entered from the floor above it and continued inside the pot for another twelve inches. In the room over the pot, workers cut the bags open using pocket knives and emptied the crude explosive into the wooden hopper on the floor that formed the entrance to the funnel. A simple plan that accompanies the report shows how concentrated on this one activity the room in question was: there is just the hopper, a staircase, the trap in the floor where the hoist carried crude explosive to the melting-pot floor, and a couple of hand-inscribed crosses where electric lights were installed.

The committee considered – and for the most part ruled out – various possibilities: that the fire had been deliberately set, started by a stray match or cigarette end, by a spark from a chimney or locomotive, or caused by the spontaneous ignition of one of several materials. Records of an inspection carried out at the end of 1916 revealed that insufficient attention had been paid to the danger of using metal vessels and implements, and to the prevalence of grit on or around such equipment. Brunner Mond had taken 'prompt steps to eliminate glaring evils in this category', and in fact on the night before the accident iron tools had been replaced by brass, which did not produce sparks. It seemed, however, that this process was incomplete – the possibility of a spark from the striking or scraping of metal tools could not be set aside. It was possible too that no matter the vigilance towards tools and machinery and transportation of explosive, a simple and unstoppable process might have been started by a humble hobnail:

As has been stated, a certain amount of T.N.T. was allowed to accumulate on the floor in the neighbourhood of the mouth of the hopper, and a detonation spark from the nails of a worker's boot and grit or metallic foreign bodies in the T.N.T. might have conceivably ignited this material. Any attempt on the part of the workman to extinguish the fire by knocking it out with his cap, as has been done, would probably lead to the projection of burning T.N.T. through the hopper into the melting pot, when a very rapid conflagration would have ensued.

The Narrows

On Thursday the 6th of December 1917, there were about forty ships and boats in the waters off the port city of Halifax, Nova Scotia. They included schooners, patrol boats, ferries, tugboats and minesweepers – the harbour was alive, in other words, with normal maritime business as well as military. This was not unusual: Halifax had been a naval base as well as a commercial port since the eighteenth century, when it was settled by the British after a protracted struggle with France for control of the surrounding territory. The dockyards and factories were overlooked, as the city's steep thoroughfares are still, by the solid edifice of Fort Needham. But the number and variety of vessels on the day in question – a profusion we can also blame in part for the catastrophe to come – was a direct result of the war, Halifax having become crucial to the transport of troops, munitions, horses, food and other supplies bound for Europe. The larger ships that docked there included many from the United States (which had joined the war on the 6th of April 1917), and they typically set out in slow-moving convoy, risking by their conspicuousness attack from German submarines, but protected too by US and Canadian naval craft.

Such had been the scrum of maritime traffic on the late afternoon of Wednesday the 5th that it had become clear certain vessels must be delayed till the next day in their progress into or out of the harbour. At sunset, shortly after half past four, two anti-submarine barriers – vast nets of steel mesh weighted with concrete and buoyed on the surface by spherical floats – had been dragged as usual across the harbour, cutting off all exit and ingress for shipping. Among the vessels held up was one that had been built in England and launched in 1899, but whose stern now advertised her home port as Marseille. *Mont-Blanc* was a 320-foot freighter, with a crew of forty, which under the captaincy of one Aimé Le Médec had left New York on the first of the month, aiming to join a convoy at Halifax. Like all French merchant ships at this point in the war, she was under the control of the Admiralty, and had already made several journeys across the Atlantic. The iron walls of the ship's four holds were lined with wood, secured with copper nails to reduce the risk of sparks; *Mont-Blanc* was thus safe, or as safe as such things got, to carry explosive cargoes of armaments and chemicals. At New York, she had been loaded with a million pounds of coal for the Atlantic crossing, and the holds filled with 2,925 tons of diverse explosive materials: picric acid, TNT and guncotton. On the deck, metal drums stacked three or four high contained highly flammable benzene. As Sally M. Walker, a historian who has recounted the horrible course of events that ensued, has put it, by the time she left New York *Mont-Blanc* was a monstrous floating bomb.

On the 3rd of December, the Norwegian-registered cargo liner *Imo* – at 430 feet, considerably longer than *Mont-Blanc* – had anchored at Bedford Basin, the innermost part of the harbour. The ship was owned by the South Pacific Whaling Company and chartered or leased to the Belgian Relief Commission: large red letters on each side of its white hull spelled 'BELGIAN RELIEF'. *Imo* had a crew of thirty-nine and was captained by a Norwegian, Haakon From. It was scheduled to sail to New York, where it would take on relief supplies. On the 5th of the month, as the sun went down, the ship was still being loaded with coal, and by the time it had taken on sufficient fuel for the trip it was half past five – the harbour barriers had been closed for the best part of an hour and *Imo* would have to wait out the night at anchor.

At half past seven the next morning Francis Mackey, the local pilot assigned to *Mont-Blanc*, received a signal to proceed through the submarine gate and into the harbour, heading eventually for Bedford Basin. Shortly afterwards, *Imo* began to steam out of the basin, passing through the Narrows, a strait that separated Halifax from the smaller town of Dartmouth across the way. Her empty hull was high in the water but the propeller sufficiently submerged for forward movement. Regulations stated that ships navigating such a narrow channel should hug the shoreline to starboard, so *Imo* steered close to the Halifax side, and *Mont-Blanc* to the Dartmouth shoreline. The harbour was already busy with other boats, including, as *Imo* headed into the Narrows, a ship named *Clara* which appeared to be ignoring harbour rules and steaming towards *Imo* along the Halifax shore. At the same time *Imo*'s pilot, William Hayes, spotted a tugboat, *Stella Maris*, towing a barge into the harbour from the Halifax docks. Captain From and Pilot Hayes now decided to move out of the way of *Clara*, and signalled to that effect with the ship's whistle. *Mont-Blanc*, meanwhile, was approaching the Narrows; Le Médec and Mackey could tell that on its present course *Imo* would soon collide with their smaller ship.

As both vessels now entered the Narrows they signalled to each other to move aside, but neither seems to have understood the other's messages. Mackey, alarmed, turned *Mont-Blanc* hard to port, towards Halifax. Hayes ordered *Imo* into reverse, but such was the height of the propeller in the water that the ship hardly slowed. *Imo*'s bow now swung towards *Mont-Blanc* and smashed through her hull at the waterline, ripping the freighter open to its rail, twenty feet above, and penetrating nine feet into the starboard hold. Barrels of benzene tumbled loose and burst on the deck. *Imo*'s engines and propeller engaged and the ship reversed. Small fires started by the crushing on impact of explosives in *Mont-Blanc*'s hull ignited the benzene vapour, causing flames and smoke to pour from the deck of the freighter. Fire quickly took hold too below decks, and clouds of steam came from the hole in the ship's side as seawater flooding in was vaporized straight away. The flames on deck had made it impossible to reach the ship's fire hose; Le Médec knew that the cargo would soon explode, and he ordered his forty men to abandon ship. As they rowed the two lifeboats towards the Dartmouth shore, Mackey waved and shouted to the ships around them, but nobody noticed let alone heeded his warnings.

As the bow of *Imo* had disengaged from the gaping hull of *Mont-Blanc*, it caused the stricken ship to turn towards the Halifax shoreline, in which direction she now continued without a soul on board. Eventually she struck Pier 6 at the Richmond docks, igniting the pier's timbers. Fire engines were soon called out. People ran into the sloping streets below Fort Needham to stare. In the harbour, the captain of the tugboat *Stella Maris* tried to reach the burning ship with a fire hose, but the flames were too intense; he then ordered a hawser to be attached to *Mont-Blanc*, hoping to tow her away from the docks. Around this time, the ship's crew landed at Tuft's Cove on the northern side; looking south towards the burning pier and their intact vessel, which they knew must explode at any moment, they called to onlookers on the eastern shore to run for cover.

It was nearly nine o'clock when the barrels of benzene on the deck began to explode, sending red streaks of metal arcing through the black smoke above the pier. At four minutes past the hour, the main cargo followed suit. In a short-lived crucible of fire and force, the ship itself vanished: inside the explosion – if such a sudden outrush of energy may be said to have an inside – the temperature was later estimated to have reached over 9,000 degrees Fahrenheit. The resulting shock wave travelled at 5,000 feet per second: that is, almost five times faster than the speed of sound. (The sound of the explosion itself was heard twice by those in the city, across the harbour and for scores if not hundreds of miles around: once as the shock wave travelled through earth and rock, and again as it arrived through the air.) In Halifax, the shoreside neighbourhood of Richmond took the full force of the blast: wooden houses and brick-built factories alike were flattened. Several schools in the area were destroyed, including the Halifax School for the Deaf, with its 400 windowpanes; across the city, and on both sides of the harbour, many people were killed, lacerated or blinded by what Sally Walker calls a blizzard of glass. Hundreds had been atomized at once by the heat and force of the first unthinkably swift eruption. A second, or rather an implosion of sorts, followed. In the first fragments of a second the blast had created a central vacuum that the evicted air now rushed to fill again: the result was a wall of energy, weaker but still lethal, that tore at the buildings still standing as it sped towards the place where the ship and Pier 6 had been.

About fifteen or twenty seconds after the explosion, a photograph was taken of the vast pall of smoke and debris that rose above Halifax. The name has not survived of the photographer who trained his apparatus, with impressive presence of mind and steadiness of hand, towards the aftermath. The picture seems to have been taken from Bedford Basin, where *Mont-Blanc* had been headed. The sea is flat, barely rippled in the foreground; the light from the east picks out a row of trees above the dark shoreline on the left, and seems to pierce the grey sky and illuminate the horizon on the right-hand side. A boat or ship with two masts and a single funnel, loaded fore and aft with cargo or fuel, sits on the horizon nearly midway across the image, between darkness and light. And above it

towers the cloud of grey smoke: vague and already drifting westwards at the bottom but rising to a well-defined and monstrously organic-looking roil and thrust at the top. A Captain W. M. A. Campbell, of the Canadian merchant ship *Acadian*, then eighteen miles away, recorded with his sextant the height of this cloud at two and a quarter miles. (Sailors aboard the USS *Tacoma*, fifty miles away at sea, also observed the cloud and, grasping at once what it meant, began to steam towards Halifax.) About a third of the way up it in the photograph, a darker mass hovers laterally, ragged and seeming not to mingle with the pale smoke. We may surmise that it has something to do with the black rain that is reported to have fallen for ten minutes following the explosion: a thick, oily precipitation composed of benzene residue and one can only guess what dust, ash and organic matter. Perhaps in that black cloud too, as it appears in the photograph, are fragments of the city still suspended and about to fall: in the seconds and minutes after the blast, boulders, building materials, gun barrels and chunks of metal from *Mont-Blanc* rained down on Halifax. The ship's anchor, weighing over a thousand pounds, landed two and a half miles away.

A tsunami over forty feet high now rose and spread from the place by the dock where *Mont-Blanc* had grounded herself. The explosion had forced so much water into the air that for an instant, witnesses later said, the floor of the harbour was exposed; this water now crashed to earth. Among the many vessels lifted and transported by the wave was *Imo*, swept across the harbour and grounded on the Dartmouth shore. In Halifax, many more died as the tsunami swamped the ruins created just seconds before, water now dispatching those whom fire and air had not yet killed.

Pass for devastated area

The explosion at Halifax on the 6th of December 1917 was the largest man-made explosion in history to that point, and remained so until the first atomic bomb was dropped twenty-eight years later. (The largest planned detonation before 1945 occurred on the 7th of June 1917, when the British Second Army began the Battle of Messines in Flanders by exploding nineteen mines deep beneath enemy lines, killing or injuring 10,000 German troops.) The final death toll at Halifax is estimated at over 2,000. Thousands more were injured, among them the hundreds whose eyes were damaged, many having watched the portside fire from the windows of their homes, workplaces or schools: of these, thirty-five were left permanently blind after the panes shattered. Among the several stories of individual heroism later recounted was that of Vincent Coleman, telegraph operator at the Halifax railway office, seated that morning about 750 yards from Pier 6. Fully aware of the nature of *Mont-Blanc*'s cargo and the likely explosive outcome, Coleman remained at his desk and watched as the ship burned, long enough to send a message to the station at Rockingham, five miles distant: 'Hold up the train. Ammunition ship afire in harbor making for Pier 6 and will explode. Guess this will be my last message. Good-bye boys.' Coleman was later found dead, his telegraph key still in his hand.

The cloud above the city was visible for many miles, but it was also partly thanks to Coleman's bravery and mindfulness of his duty that news of the disaster spread quickly, and several hundred soldiers and sailors were sent to help from camps and ships in the area. Motor cars, wagons, carts and even wheelbarrows were emptied to deliver the wounded to nearby towns, Halifax's own hospitals having filled quickly. Flatbed wagons took the dead to a makeshift mortuary set up in Chebucto School: in the days that followed, during which a blizzard overtook the city and made the search for the living and the dead cruelly difficult, citizens were directed to the school to search for their loved ones. In the cold, we may assume, the corpses were preserved for longer than they might have been; but there was only so long that they could be at the school in hope of identification. It was decided that only the bodies of children would be embalmed and retained there, in case they were claimed. In the meantime, the city's coroner John Barnstead put into action a system of numbering for bodies and possessions found on the dead (by which they might be named after burial) – a system he had devised five years earlier when Halifax had received 209 of those who perished on the *Titanic*. It is thanks to Barnstead's methodical dedication to this grisly task that the Maritime Museum of the Atlantic, situated today on the Halifax waterfront, has among its holdings many of the unclaimed possessions – jewellery, children's glass marbles and pencils sharpened for school, watches stopped at five past nine – of the unclaimed dead of 1917.

Ours was the marsh country

The north of Kent, roughly from the banks of the river Medway to the shores of the Thames estuary, is what the road signs and the hopeful civic functionaries who put them there are apt to call 'Dickens Country'. Charles Dickens spent seven happy years of his childhood in the dockside town of Chatham, where his father was a clerk in the Naval Pay Office, until financial embarrassment forced the family to move to London and before long led John Dickens to the debtors' prison. Just a mile upriver from Chatham – so close that today they are both subsumed in the aggregate sprawl of the 'Medway towns' – the smaller settlement of Rochester, with its castle and cathedral, provided the brooding location (renamed 'Cloisterham') for Dickens's final and unfinished novel, *The Mystery of Edwin Drood*. About five miles to the east lies the village of Cobham, where he wrote part of *The Pickwick Papers* at the Leather Bottle inn, and where he has Pickwick discover, outside a labourer's cottage near the same establishment, an incised stone that he excitedly takes for 'a strange and curious inscription of unquestionable antiquity'. (It turns out to read, more prosaically, 'Bill Stumps, his mark'.) It was in Cobham too, near a chalk pit called Paddock Hole, that in August of 1843 the visionary painter Richard Dadd, his mind lately undone while travelling up the Nile, attacked and killed his father with a five-inch knife. Dickens, who moved back to Kent in the spring of 1856, was in the habit of leading visitors to the spot where the famous crime occurred.

At Gad's Hill Place, a house in the village of Higham which he had coveted as a boy and eventually bought for £1,790, Dickens wrote *Great Expectations*, the novel that most vividly conjures the Kent landscape of his childhood. Readers, and viewers of the many film and television adaptations, will recall that at the start of the tale we are with the young protagonist Pip in a churchyard on the desolate marshes of the south bank of the Thames, soon to meet with the escaped and desperate convict Abel Magwitch. The landscape is modelled after the Hoo Peninsula: a rough wet tongue of land, rooted around

Rochester and Higham, which thrusts twelve miles or so between the estuaries of the Thames and Medway, and almost licks the Isle of Sheppey at Sheerness. More exactly, Dickens had in mind a Thames-side portion of the peninsula to the north of the village of Cooling. The gravestones of thirteen children belonging to one family, which are still to be seen in the village churchyard, are thought to have inspired the graves of Pip's five brothers who rest alongside his parents in a bleak spot overgrown with nettles. Beyond the churchyard lies a 'dark flat wilderness . . . intersected with dykes and mounds and gates, with scattered cattle feeding on it'. And further out the 'low leaden line' of the river, and the 'distant savage lair' of the sea.

There is farmland to the north of Cooling today, and for a little way north of the adjacent village of Cliffe to the west, but it soon degenerates: first into working or flooded chalk pits and then into marsh, fit only for a few sheep on the firmer ground. A short distance out of Cliffe a sign belonging to the Royal Society for the Protection of Birds points towards the Thames and 'Magwitch viewpoint', and it is not hard to recall the cold and frightened Pip's thoughts as he watches the convict vanish into the darkling scene:

The marshes were just a long black horizontal line then, as I stopped to look after him; and the river was just another horizontal line, not nearly so broad nor yet so black; and the sky was just a row of long angry red lines and dense black lines intermixed. On the edge of the river I could faintly make out the only two black things in all the prospect that seemed to be standing upright; one of these was the beacon by which the sailors steered – like an unhooped cask upon a pole – an ugly thing when you were near it; the other, a gibbet with some chains hanging to it which had once held a pirate. The man was limping on towards this latter, as if he were the pirate come to life, and come down, and going back to hook himself up again. It gave me a terrible turn when I thought so; and as I saw the cattle lifting their heads to gaze after him, I wondered whether they thought so too. I looked all round for the horrible young man, and could see no signs of him. But now I was frightened again, and ran home without stopping.

Among the brambles that bound the green mounds

I walked out of Cliffe towards the marshes around noon on one of the wettest days of a very wet summer. By mid July it had been raining for weeks with hardly a clear day to speak of, but Canterbury had escaped the floods, and we live anyway on high ground well away from the river. During my regular trips into London the weather had not really impinged on me: in the rain the city simply feels more like itself. This Saturday morning, then, had been my introduction proper to the dismal reality of the season. The rain had come down some way out of Faversham, where the high-speed train picks up its pace for a while before slowing again among the Medway towns, then racing towards London. Through the carriage window I watched three small figures descending diagonally the slope of a cornfield, three dots smeared against the glass as the torrent started and the hikers ran towards shelter under trees at the lowest corner. Seconds later a pigeon, disoriented perhaps by the swiftness of the downpour and the gathering dark, misjudging the substance and speed of the blue streak ahead of it, flew directly at the window a few seats in front of me, and abruptly expired in a cloud of purple-grey feathers.

I had come to Cliffe and the marshes beyond in the hope of expanding my knowledge of explosives factories at the start of the twentieth century. In the woods at Oare the partially restored ruins can feel more instructive than resonant; the well-tended walkways and detailed signs threaten to neutralize the imagination. At Uplees, among the ditches and the sheep, observing only the occasional low structure or its foundational ghost in the grass, I have to work much harder to imagine how the place operated, even to grasp the scale and atmosphere of a busy factory rather than a heritage amenity or nature reserve. Cliffe seemed, from what I had read, to answer this problem: here, the remains of a factory dating from the late nineteenth century were more intact, and the landscape wilder and less attended. Somebody still owned the site – a local shoot, I'd heard, though surely neither hunters nor birdwatchers were likely to be skulking or squelching across it today. Old and new maps showed black lozenges where the buildings were, and earthworks denoted by circles or horseshoes of tiny pointed marks; aerial photographs I found on the Internet confirmed that many of the ruins were still sufficiently extant as to cast shadows, even if the precise condition of the buildings could not be made out.

The village itself is ancient, seeming to have been settled since Anglo-Saxon times. It is said that the Magna Carta was drafted there in 1215, before the document was conveyed to Runnymede, twenty miles up the Thames from modern London, to be signed by King John. By the fourteenth century Cliffe was a thriving agricultural centre of 3,000 souls, owned at that time by the monks of Christ's Church, Canterbury. A slow decline set in following a fire in 1520, and by the nineteenth century the population had fallen to 900. In 1826 the opening of a canal between Higham and Strood, to the north-west of Rochester, brought labourers to the area; the canal soon failed as a business venture, but the route was later used for a railway line which by the 1880s extended as far as Cliffe. (The railway is of course long gone; I detrained at Chatham and took a bus to the village.) Late in the century the main industry at this northern extremity of the peninsula was a cement works that is still operating; to get to the explosives site I would have to edge around the lakes it has gouged in the land. In 1892 the firm of Hay, Merricks and Co. established a factory to carry out specialized finishing procedures, notably the blending, dusting and packing of gunpowder. A jetty was built and fourteen buildings planned, though it appears only two were finished. In 1898 the site was bought by Curtis and Harvey, a firm with a controlling interest in half of Britain's gunpowder manufacture. Three years later the company's licence was extended to produce cordite, gelatin and dynamite. As may be expected, the factory grew during the First World War, and it closed not long after, in 1921. The parish register at St Helen's church in Cliffe records the deaths of fifteen workers, three women among them, in six explosions that occurred at the works between 1902 and 1917.

The road out of Cliffe hardly deserved the name – I had walked north for less than five minutes when it became a flooded track veined just sufficiently with isthmuses of gravel for me to make my way slowly and soggily along it. To my amazement a big estate car lurched towards me half a mile from the village: birdwatchers thinking better of it. A middle-aged man in black weatherproof jacket, walking boots and rain-blinded spectacles – thus, in the rain and gloom, my doppelgänger – nodded a greeting as he too retreated from the marsh. I would see nobody else for the next four hours. When he had vanished I stopped beside a stand of rushes to record a curious gurgling, quavering, almost quacking noise that I could not ascribe to any creature I knew, avian or amphibian. Later, trawling the website of the RSPB, I decided it was a Savi's warbler – an amazing encounter if true: there are likely less than half a dozen pairs in the UK each summer – before realizing that in the recording I was listening to, I'd ignored the high-pitched noise in the foreground for the guttural one in the background, which must have been a frog after all.

Knowing I had soon to turn west and then north again around the largest of the flooded pits, I tried to orient myself in the wider landscape. To my left, a chalk cliff from which the village takes its name had begun to rise behind me, sheltering the cement works and quarries to the west. (It is in that direction too that the ruins of Cliffe Fort, dating from the 1860s, are to be found – it is not the 'old Battery' to which Pip is made to bring Magwitch his 'wittles', but might well be the successor to an older gun emplacement, of the Napoleonic period, that Dickens had in mind.) To my right and ahead: a mile or two of pasture and marsh, topped by a dark sea wall (I thought of Pip's tangle of black lines), so that the river was invisible. In fact I would not see the Thames all afternoon, and the first of the visual disorientations of the day was the sight now of the bristling towers of an oil refinery across the estuary at Canvey Island, which looked at once like a distant metropolis and a stage flat planted just a couple of fields away. I had stopped to look around me, and as I set off again a red-brown cargo ship appeared slowly out of the west (that is, from London) and slid across the scene, its hull hidden by the sea wall, as if ploughing through the marsh.

After half an hour, the waterlogged track deposited me in a morass of mud and sheep shit, flanked by ditches full of black water and laced with barbed wire. Directly ahead was a steel gate, heavily chained and padlocked. An ancient wooden sign, hardly legible, declared that the site was private property; I looked around for figures in the landscape, and quickly climbed the gate. A dozen or so sheep, which had frozen and stared as I approached the gate, now blared away to the north-west along a filthy trail. I pulled out my phone, where I had saved a few aerial photographs of the place, and found I had a full signal, a reminder that no matter the weather or the appearance of remoteness, I had not actually wandered far. And it meant that on this flat land I could find my way thanks to Google Maps: the whole complex was there, photographed, judging by the shadows among the ruins, on a perfect summer's morning. To get to the largest structures, I knew I had to follow a path that curved to my right, past a short row of dense concrete cubes,

about five feet high. I stopped to photograph these and take close-ups of the shining black bricks, sharp edged and still in situ in places, where I suspect they were meant to protect from acid spills, on the cement floors nearby, or broken and scattered in the grass.

The Curtis and Harvey plant expanded eastwards during the First World War, and it was towards the latest buildings that I headed first. Nobody, it seems – not even the industrial archaeologist Wayne Cocroft, who has done most to encompass the broad history of explosives manufacture in Britain and its local manifestations in the landscape – has been able to say exactly what each structure was used for. In the scene that now presented itself to the east, it seemed the long, low, roofless and segmented buildings towards which I set out were designed to process something less stable or more violent than cordite: the concrete cells that form the buildings may have been used to handle small amounts of nitroglycerine or other high explosives. Nor is it possible to say what structures once stood in the middle of each of close on thirty square earth traverses that are off to the east a few hundred yards, though it seems most likely they protected small and flimsy storage buildings. To the south-west of the complex formed by the earthworks and the concrete cells stands a larger mound of so far indeterminate purpose or composition. By this stage I was up to my knees in soaking wet grass and didn't see till the last minute the wide ditch – too wide to jump across – that cut me off from this mound. I would have to follow it to the east and double back when I found a way across. When I got to the end I found I was among the big enclosing traverses and a series of long, deep, rectangular ponds from which the earth to build them must have been dug. I climbed up the nearest wet grassy slope and looked out over the marsh, trying to imagine the buildings intact, the land traversed by tramlines and telegraph wires, and teeming with workers, the sea wall gone and the busy river beyond. In the middle distance a dozen ragged horses, all with the same black and white colouring, came slowly from behind those long buildings and stood still in the rain, watching me.

A memorable raw afternoon

Though I was wary of the horses – they looked wild, though I suppose they must have belonged to somebody – I set out towards the largest structures in the landscape. Not wanting to alarm the animals, I headed for the far, western end of the complex of four segmented buildings. The horses doubled back to meet me, the largest coming forward as I reached what felt like an entrance, a point where the faint path in the grass ran between huge clumps of nettles flanked by twin concrete hulks. I pushed quickly through the sodden weeded narrows and started to photograph the ruined buildings. This first pair, erected in parallel and running east–west, consisted of thick central walls of brick from which on either side thin perpendiculars of reinforced concrete formed little cells, roughly the size I thought of a stable, and roofless. Originally, it seemed, they had been slantedly covered in corrugated iron; in a few places sheets of metal detached from roof level now leaned against the interior wall to form a sort of rusty bivouac or shelter, inaccessible so far as I could see, though something told me anyway that I ought not to try squeezing my way into the darkness alone. Small trees grew inside some of the cells, and I stopped to photograph an especially strange example, whose roots arched and writhed complexly above ground as if it were freeing itself from the wet black earth.

The rain had eased, and although the day was not exactly brighter as I reached the end of the first pair of buildings, the atmosphere had seemed to lighten. A skein of geese came out of the east, inscribing a loose question mark against the clouds. The remnants of a chain-link fence ran across the gap between the buildings I had just left and the next two structures with their overgrown central avenue; a fox trotted the length of the fence and turned its head in my direction without losing its footing. As I crossed the path it had taken through the long grass I thought I could smell it still, but the odour quickly sharpened – pig manure, perhaps, spread in the fields to the east.

The cells were larger on this side, and there were fewer of them: the buildings consisted simply of a concrete wall facing out to the marsh, and nine cells inside on the northern flank, eight on the southern. In most cases a portion or two of the outer wall had been knocked through to form crude apertures the size of doorways: to what end, I could not work out, because even when the buildings were intact or on their way to ruin decades ago there must have been entrances from the other side. If they were used to shelter animals it made no sense to expose them on both sides to the wind and rain. Unless of course the original doorways were too small for horses or cattle or broad-bellied sheep, and the walls had been knocked through to turn each cell into a small barn or stable. It was while trying to fathom this ruinous feature that I spotted the skull. It was lying halfway along the grassy path between the nettles, at the edge of a patch of open ground, and there

was a bright yellow metal gas canister of the domestic sort a couple of feet away. The canister and the large, long, pointed skull composed a striking arrangement on the wet grass, and I pulled out my camera and started to look for the best angle from which to photograph them. The smell on the wind was stronger now, but could not have been coming from the skull, which had been picked almost bare. I had not, oddly, thought at first what animal it belonged to; now, paying closer attention to its length and the prominence of its bunched and squarish front teeth, I realized it came from a fully grown horse. And that the rest of the animal must be nearby.

I found it soon enough. The source of the smell had been closer at hand, and only the horse's head had decayed or been scavenged down to clean bone. The rest of it was lying on its right flank inside one of the cells: headless, of course, but also missing a couple of hooves, which I spotted nearby, half sunk in a rich and stinking brown compost that surrounded the carcass and the precise composition of which was horrifically obscure. I am not, as it happens, an especially squeamish person when it comes to gore or decay; I cope quite easily with disposing of flattened cats from the busy road on which we live or half-chewed rodents and swollen frogs from the garden. But I had never been this close to so much extravagant rot. The dead thing seemed to have leached out into the earth and the air; the smell was bad enough – I felt as though it were creeping into my pores – but I was appalled too to find I had been treading for some yards already on small wet curls of black and white horsehair that were scattered around the scene. The lower jawbone was resting among the nettles. But the animal was also disturbingly intact: the flesh inside had long gone but the hide was still there, wet and matted and here and there laid bare so that it looked not so much leathery as plastic and glistening – and almost green in colour. I took a couple of quick photographs and edged carefully around to where the head had once been, the upper vertebrae more recently disarticulated and collapsed onto the ground. Here, thanks to the undisturbed skeleton inside the main part of the body, and the relative rigidity of the hide and its subtending teguments, I could stare into the interior, which was impenetrably dark and fringed at the entrance with long depending strips of rotted skin or what seemed like solidified drips of white fat, like stalactites. It was at this point that I began to feel properly sick.

I am looking about me

I walked away from the rotting horse as swiftly as I could in the long grass and the nettles, and as I went I saw to my horror that there were large bones, obviously equine, scattered in the next cell along. I had not noticed them before because this was one of those segments of the building that still had a fragment of corrugated roof attached, and the interior was in semi-darkness. But now, worried I might step in something hideous, I seemed to see bones everywhere in the grass: some of them desiccated and grey, others yellow or stained dark red so that they looked to my now somewhat delirious eye like chunks of flesh half buried among the weeds and roots. I had supposed at first that the horse had been sick and sought the shelter of the ruins, and fallen dead there some wet night earlier in the summer, before being torn at by foxes, crows and buzzards that must have come from miles around as the smell rose. Not to mention the countless smaller creatures that would have thrived on the remains. But the presence of more bones so close by must surely mean that the horse had died out on the marsh and been dragged or driven here to rot. The thought put me in mind at once of the many thousands of horses that were dying and decaying on the battlefields of Europe in 1916, and certain photographs I had seen over the years of animals lying bloated in no-man's-land or, if freshly dead, being butchered on the roadside by famished soldiers. It was some hours before I felt I had quite got the stench of the carcass out of my nostrils. As I write this I cannot recall the smell at all, but only and with extreme clarity the textures of bone and skin and filthy horsehair – the sense too of a physical seething, as if the remains of the creature were invading the soil and the air and even the wet concrete.

I had so far learned almost nothing regarding the practical workings of the explosives factory, only about its extent and the desolation that had persisted there since Dickens's time. The brief period of industrial activity in the last years of the nineteenth century, and the first decades of the twentieth, had added little to the land except reminders of the tendency of everything here to dissolve into the marsh. The place seemed oddly unreal now, my encounter with the dead horse a touch too perfectly gruesome, the whole drenched and grey mise-en-scène too exquisitely matched to the story of disaster and decay that I was pursuing at the Faversham works. I had read that during the Second World War the site at Cliffe was fitted out as a decoy airfield to distract German night-time bombers from a genuine base seven or eight miles upriver at Gravesend. On the road from Cliffe I had passed a small square brick building that is said to have been the control point for the decoy base. From here lights could be switched on and off across the complex; fires were also lit to gull enemy bomber crews, who mistook them for the results of earlier attack. Nothing else remains of this simulacrum made of light, except perhaps the extraordinary image, as one follows the faint tracery of pathways still extant, of the place almost empty and illumined, catching the eye of German aircrew as they approached the Thames estuary or, having already wrought destruction upon the city and its docks, fled into the night and took this opportunity to release the last of their bombs.

Ghost map

I seem to have been writing a story that is in part about flatness, and the way that sound and force and information – maybe also memory – travel across such level ground. If you want flatness, travel north of Faversham, past Sheppey, across the Medway to the Isle of Grain, which is flatter than flat, super-flat. Seen from above, Grain is a blunt intrusion between the mouths of the Thames and the Medway. To get there I must take a train from Canterbury to Chatham, then a bus out onto the Isle. It is, as I noted near the start, no longer an island: Yantlet Creek, which used to cut through the marshland between the two estuaries, still snakes inward from the Thames to the north, but was silted up centuries ago at its southern end. Grain Road still ducks southwards of the creek's tail, linking the isolated village to the Medway towns in the west via settlements at Allhallows, Stoke, St Mary Hoo and High Halstow. Before emerging onto Grain proper, my bus takes a contorted route through these tiny villages, so that I quickly lose all sense of which estuary I'm looking at across a mile or two of flat fields on either side. I spot half a dozen hawks, static in the air above the bus, and two pairs of concrete eagles by the roadside.

Since the nineteenth century, when a fort was erected just north of the village and a port built to the south, Grain has been a site of almost constant military, commercial and industrial activity. Airships and seaplanes were manufactured there during the First World War; the Grain Kitten, a small anti-Zeppelin fighter designed to be launched from destroyers, was prototyped but never produced, its tiny cockpit apparently suiting only undersized pilots. The first of Grain's oil storage facilities, belonging to the Medway Oil & Storage Company (later the Power Petroleum Company), was begun there shortly after the war. During the Second World War, the Isle became a depot and crucial pumping stage for PLUTO, the pipeline under the ocean that supplied petrol to Allied troops on the French coast.

The present strangeness of Grain was established in 1953, when the Anglo-Iranian Oil Company (which became BP the following year) opened a refinery that covered 750 acres of the Isle. Photographs of the facility under construction show a metropolis of gleaming pipework, buildings and towering chimneys, surrounded by scenes of desolation that look like the result of bombing or earthquake. The refinery processed 10 million tons of crude oil each year, and two decades later would become the first to receive North Sea oil, BP having discovered the vast Forties Oil Field in 1970. On Wednesday the 18th of June 1975, Tony Benn and his wife Caroline boarded a hydrofoil at Tower Pier on the Thames and were bumpily conveyed to Grain, where the Secretary of State for Energy opened a valve, held aloft a bottle of crude oil, and declared, 'I hold the future of Britain in my hand.' (In his diary, Benn recalled 'a bright, hot day [when] even the Isle of Grain, the most ravaged, desolate industrial landscape in the Medway, looked quite beautiful'.) But the advent of North Sea oil was not enough to save Grain from the effects of the 1970s oil crisis: the refinery closed in 1981; its five tallest chimneys were blown up and most of the works dismantled; 1,670 workers lost their jobs.

The signs of Britain's short-lived post-war industrial optimism sank into the marsh, but Grain did not die, which is also to say that it did not recover. Instead, even as the last vestiges of the refinery persisted in the landscape, the ruined site was overwritten with new industry. At the eastern edge lies the largest oil-fired power station in Europe. The Medway riverfront was redeveloped under the slightly misleading name Thamesport, and is now the third-largest container port in Britain. In the mid 1980s, BP opened a terminal for the importation of aviation fuel on the western end of the site, at the entrance to Colemouth Creek. In recent years a National Grid storage facility for liquid natural gas has sprung up to the north. Grain today is a landscape of the industrial living dead: a ghost territory where construction and ruin are scarcely to be distinguished. The owners of its several industries proudly advertise their commitment to the preservation of local wildlife, as though the border between artifice and nature, between the habits and habitats of man and animal, were at all clear on the Isle. In truth, Grain is a lesson in environmental indeterminacy: a zone of extreme ambiguity between nature and culture, regeneration and ruin, past and future.

The Mirror of the Sea

The bus swings off Grain High Street – a pub, convenience store, some 1970s houses and a view of St James's church at the seaward end – and into Smithfield Road, where it stops in front of a chip shop and a newsagent. I walk past a few pre-war bungalows and a crumbling community centre to get to Port Victoria Road, which divides the power station site from the seashore. The road is a sorry line of wreckage – its tarmac potholed and rutted, the vivid green of cow parsley and the purple spikes of rosebay willowherb flourishing above the rubble – which vanishes 300 feet ahead behind a curve of the grassy sea barrier to my left. In the middle distance is an unmoving white security van, marking the beginning of the station site. The scene is dominated by an 800-foot high, and surprisingly slim, chimney: pale grey but stained rust-brown in long streaks from its top. Below the chimney, and from here seemingly unattached, the anonymous hulk of the station presents no vision of appalling energies barely contained, nor much sense at all of itself as a distinct entity in the landscape: its precise shape is still unclear from this vantage.

What insists is the noise: buzzing, tearing, screeching sounds from the other side of the fence, and a muffled rhythmic clanging that will accompany me across the Isle, modulating itself in curious ways as the day advances. The driver of the white van is fast asleep at the wheel, so I peer through the dull grey metal slats of the fence at the scene of devastation within. Three huge diggers are convened like waders on the mud, about 300 feet away; one of them is dragging something slowly and noisily from

the earth, while another shunts a dark mass away from a second
hole. Fountains of sparks and noise shoot up suddenly from
masked figures, hunched on the mud, as they bear down on
smaller clumps of rusted metal: the remains of buried storage
tanks. Nearby is a pile of ragged steel so decayed it looks vegetal,
like a vast mound of rotting bracken. My map tells me that this
project of industrial archaeology is taking place at the eastern
edge of the old BP site, but there is no way of telling to which
generation of land use the tanks belong: they might be pre-war
vestiges of the first oil terminal, or prematurely aged outcrops
of the rusting power station. The stench of hot metal reaches the
fence, and I draw back gasping.

My eyes are stinging as I climb up the grassed bank for my
first glimpse across the Medway estuary. Directly opposite lies
the Isle of Sheppey and the docks at Sheerness. At the extreme
left, the low grey fort at Garrison Point provides a dark ground
to the bright yellow cranes at the water's edge, but the whole
dockland complex is no more than a sliver of activity on the
horizon. Sea and sky are the same iron grey as the fort. So too
the single point between here and Sheerness on which the eye
rests: the ruin of Grain Tower Battery, a wide stone cylinder
erected at the line of low tide in 1855, then extended during
the Second World War so that its brick accommodation block
and concrete gun emplacements form an irregular, stepped
profile, something like Bruegel's *Tower of Babel* or Vladimir
Tatlin's *Monument to the Third International*. I will not make it to
the tower today – its linking causeway is still half covered by
the tide – so I take out my camera, which I have forgotten has
no zoom; the tower is almost lost on the screen, reduced to
a small, flat, pixelated black motif stuck onto the horizon. In
The Mirror of the Sea, I remember, Joseph Conrad reflects on

the sea's feints and sleights with the sailor's sense of distance as he passes the mouth of the Medway and begins to navigate the Thames. Conrad is writing of the submerged Nore Sands:

This ideal point of the estuary, this centre of memories, is marked upon the steely grey expanse of the waters by a lightship painted red that, from a couple of miles off, looks like a cheap and bizarre little toy. I remember how, on coming up the river for the first time, I was surprised at the smallness of that vivid object – a tiny warm speck of crimson lost in an immensity of grey tones.

The tower is the first point of interest in my tour of the Isle's military ruins. I spot the second just inland ahead of me as I move roughly south along the coastal ridge. Grain Dummy

Battery is contemporary with the Victorian fort which lies behind me on the other side of the village. It was built as a secondary gun emplacement, but never finished to plan: during construction, the building started to subside and its walls to crack. By 1905, it seems it had been partially repaired, but no record exists of its having been manned in the world wars. The battery is almost entirely enclosed by a flooded ditch; to reach it, I have to leave the earth rampart and follow a path worn in the grass to the edge of a wide expanse of reeds, then double back through a patch of burned vegetation and a bizarre tangle of thick rusted cables that seems to grow from the battery's protective bank, emulating the brambles around it. In the shelter of the reeds, where the sound from the power station is suddenly muted, there sits a large, once-floral sofa, half gutted and strewn with beer cans. The building itself is hard to parse, architecturally; having none of the clear lines of sight seen, for example, in the pillboxes of the Second World War, it presents a lumpy, confusing exterior to the landward side, a grassed bank and blank walls to the sea. Its inside is burned black and strewn with debris. I climb a set of concrete steps to the roof of what seems like a more recent addition to the building: perhaps a remnant of the early-twentieth-century repairs. In the dark water of the ditch below, the shoulders of an armchair almost break the surface.

Border inspection post

From the shore, mid afternoon, the metallic noise that seemed to come from the station has begun to recede the further south I walk, and has resolved itself at length to a cleaner, higher-pitched sound, as of the rattle of rigging against a mast. By the water's edge, a group of wading birds is delicately prospecting the sand, and further out, on the last in a line of rotted pilings, a cormorant stretches its wings awkwardly against the dark water. Ahead of me on the bank, blinking intermittently in and out of sight, a pair of bright yellow dots is moving: two men in hard hats and reflective jackets, who may be holding clipboards or bulky PDAs – I cannot yet make them out. Inland, the station fence proceeds parallel to the water's edge, now regularly punctuated by successive generations of metal warning signs. There is the faded, six-pointed star of Sheriff Security (Southern) Ltd; the line-drawn profile of a figure holding a burst of yellow light that announces the presence of Powergen; the blue and white National Grid signs that simply say 'Please Keep Out'; the plain black and white of SecondSite Property which cites the Occupiers Liability Act, 1984. At least half of these signs have been peppered with holes or small indentations, probably with an air rifle. The following hazards, a row of smaller placards declares, are present in the area: underwater obstacles; sudden drop; uneven and slippery surfaces. The notices announce, more generally, that my progress is about to be blocked; up ahead is a fenced-off and razor-wired jetty and at its landward end a definitive sign: 'End of footpath. No access beyond this point.'

There is no sign of the yellow-jacketed watchers on the shore, so I duck under the jetty where it juts out over the sloping shingle and sit down to photograph its underside. Though I knew my way would be impeded at about this point on the coast – the south-eastern corner of Thamesport, whose cranes and massed containers stretch into the distance – this is not the jetty that I was hoping to reach, which lies just out of sight around the next bend of the shore. Or rather, its stumps are still visible there as the tide recedes: a parallel curving tracery of blackened wood that is all that remains of Port Victoria. Its history was almost comically short. In 1882 the owners of the South Eastern and Chatham Railway, having acquired 500 acres on the Isle of Grain, opened a line from Gravesend to the coast here, under the direction of an ostensibly independent corporation: the Hundred of Hoo Railway Company. On the 11th of September of that year, *The Times* reported that a train carrying local dignitaries and representatives of the company had travelled through 'a flat and uninteresting part of Kent' to reach the site of the new port, which it was hoped would attract considerable Atlantic and Continental (mostly German) traffic: 'the first business of the company is, so to speak, to create a traffic by building piers at which vessels of the deepest draught can load and unload their cargoes and passengers in any state of the tide, and then to construct docks for the accommodation of the largest ships afloat'.

The project was doomed: only one of the two projected piers was built, the ocean-going traffic never arrived, and rooms at the single-storey Victoria Hotel, described by *The Times* as a merely temporary structure, stayed vacant. It seems that Port Victoria (so named, says the report of 1882, by special permission of Her Majesty) only ever proved useful to one class of traveller: the Queen herself and her extended family. It was from Port Victoria that she embarked for Germany in the last years of the century, stepping from the Royal Train at the end of the pier itself, and to there that Kaiser Wilhelm II, her grandson, was conveyed on his visits to Britain before the First World War. But royal patronage did nothing for the commercial reputation of the port: declared unsafe during the war, it was finally closed and demolished in 1931, the adjoining hotel torn down as the BP refinery went up in 1952. In fact, one might say that Port Victoria hardly existed at all, such was its contingent, ramshackle and swiftly fading story. In 1906, in *The Mirror of the Sea*, recycling an impression of estuarine wilderness that is better known from the opening pages of *Heart of Darkness*, Conrad had written:

Coming in from the eastward, the bright colouring of the lightship marking the part of the river committed to the charge of an Admiral (the Commander-in-Chief at the Nore) accentuates the dreariness and the great breadth of the Thames Estuary. But soon the course of the ship opens the entrance of the Medway, with its men-of-war moored in line, and the long wooden jetty of Port Victoria, with its few low buildings like the beginning of a hasty settlement upon a wild and unexplored shore.

Dispersal point

Leaving the coast for the labyrinth of the Isle's interior, everything looks carbonized: the hedges, paths and occasional houses that abut the various fenced installations have been coated by exhaust fumes from the countless container trucks and other vehicles that ply the Grain Road without cease. I find a path around the perimeter of the power station, past the point again where many square feet of rotted steel at a time are being pulled from the soil and torn apart with blowtorches, then find myself unexpectedly at the main entrance to the station, before heading towards the main highway. From the far side of the station, the metallic sound I have been hearing all day has begun to peal like a church bell, then is gradually drowned out by the traffic. I have to hunch every half minute or so against the turbulent wake of a truck passing less than three feet away; occasionally, two or three tear by in more rapid succession, and I'm buffeted terrifyingly on the narrow path.

In the distance on my right, I spot three dull, spalling concrete cylinders that I assume must have belonged to BP and have somehow been left to dominate the northern portion of the old refinery site. The road curves slowly towards them, past wide empty fields, hedged by blackened trees. Amazingly, a few have still managed to blossom; as I stop to photograph some tiny hawthorn flowers, a black SUV pulls up and the man in the passenger seat asks me if I need any help. No, I tell him, I know where I'm going. 'Taking photographs?' he asks. Yes, I say, entering into the spirit of the obvious: I'm photographing trees. He nods and the car moves off. I realize now how far I've strayed from the coast, the village and any normal pedestrian route across the Isle, but it is still another half-hour's walk to the open metal gates of a huge building site, from which vantage the three grey tanks reveal themselves once more. I check my map, and discover my mistake. They are not, as I had hoped, more remains of the refinery, but in fact three new storage tanks belonging to the LNG facility. Uneven and bristling with scaffolding and reinforcement, they had looked like ruins, but were merely half built.

On the outskirts of the village, at a bend in the road between green fields and a stretch of waste land dotted with the small lakes of old gravel pits, a young man is standing beside a metal tripod, atop which is affixed a large foam-covered microphone. I spotted him from the bus on the way into Grain this morning, and wondered if the Isle had begun to attract other diviners of its strange psychic and sonic energies. There is nobody else about: a few cars whip past, but we are sheltered on this stretch of road from the worst of the traffic into Thames-port. He nods at me warily, but answers my direct question without suspicion once I tell him I'm writing about the area. He is an environmental scientist who has been dispatched by the local council to test the noise levels on Grain – as a car passes, he pays attention to a small LCD device and makes a note on his clipboard. We agree that it is indeed an extraordinarily noisy place, and compare impressions of the uncanny shifts in volume and direction that we have heard today. The station, he says, is strangely silent. But has he not heard the clanging sound from the coast? He has not. I try to describe it, but find I cannot tell him from which direction it comes nor say exactly what it sounds like. It is probably something to do with the station, I tell him, or with the port. It is perhaps the noise of a construction site – a pile driver, maybe – or else the sound of demolition work. It sounds metallic but muffled, drowned or thinned out by the wind. We both shrug, then turn and look out at the fields on the other side of the road, the station chimney beyond, the oil tanks hunched behind a line of poplars, the lattices of steel that glint in the distance.

These hazards are present in this area

It is late November and I have been waiting several days now for the rain to stop so that I can cycle to Faversham and beyond, onto the marshes, to find the exact spot where the explosion occurred. But the rain will not let up. Winters are like this now: too warm and too wet a month before the end of the year, with buds on the trees and tiny shoots piercing the earth outside the shed where I do most of my writing, the occasional bumblebee idling through the open window at a time when the first frosts should be here and all this life sunk back in the land. It feels as though the landscape has gone to sleep then woken in the small hours, not knowing if it is night or day.

After a week of stalled plans the sun comes out on Monday morning and earth and sky seem newly rinsed instead of merely sodden. I leave for Faversham around ten o'clock, following the morning traffic along our rat-run of a suburban road, then turning north for a time in the direction of Whitstable, labouring uphill on my heavy steel three-speed: a machine no more advanced, nor lively on these roads, than must have been the bicycles that took some workers out to the marshes in 1916. I turn off the busy road after five minutes, heading west now through farmland with Blean Woods on my left; I could have come through there from home and cut out my encounter with the tail end of rush-hour traffic, but the woodland path would be a morass this morning. There is nobody on the road now; before long I turn again, to the right this time and down a steep hill towards the village of Dargate, thence over a dual carriageway and on to the more exposed Graveney, where I get my first glimpses of the coast as I breast certain hills. Here are Whitstable and Herne Bay off to the right, and a phalanx of wind turbines beyond; the Isle of Sheppey straight ahead with its scattered settlements by the Swale and two more turbines – I have never noticed these before – near the bridge in the west; further off in that direction the power stations of Grain, their plumes of white smoke ascending, just a waft from vertical in the near stillness of the morning. Once more the flatness of this place impresses itself upon me.

I have cycled this route many times; it takes an hour to reach the outskirts of Faversham, though today I keep stopping to photograph the land ahead and it will be well after eleven when I arrive in the centre of town. I approach Faversham from the south-east; the narrowing road meets a dedicated cycle path that runs to the creek then inland to a boatyard filled with craft in various states of renovation and decay, a few of them done up as dwellings. Before reaching the yard I turn left from the creek down a muddy track, rounding a sewage works whose stench carries a long way off even in the unmoving air. (There are signs all along an enclosing fence that warn potential intruders of anti-theft measures in place at the plant, including forensic liquids identifiable under UV light – you would think the smell might do the same job.) I have made this detour because a few hundred yards ahead is a small huddle of single-storey wooden huts, also fenced away. These make up the last working factory in Faversham's explosives archipelago. The site, not far from the location of Faversham Abbey, was opened in 1924 by the Mining Explosives Company. The Abbey Works, as it was known, now belongs to a company called Cardox: manufacturers of an explosive technology that uses liquid carbon dioxide as a blasting agent for quarrying and clearing industrial blockages in silos and the like. I have passed by here before and always found the rusting iron gates padlocked and the place apparently deserted. Nobody at Cardox has ever replied to my emails or picked up the phone when I called the numbers I have found online, and I have begun to doubt the firm's existence. But this morning the gate is open, there are two cars parked inside, and a young man in a high-vis jacket comes over as I wheel my bike towards the nearest building. I explain my interest in the factory, but he says the boss is on holiday and I will have to come back, or call, next week. May I look around in the meantime? He's not authorized to let me do that. A woman comes up the path between the huts and confirms: there is no way I will be allowed to explore the site. She ducks into a hut to ask a colleague for the manager's phone number. Afterwards I pause outside as I have done before, and when I am sure everyone has gone back to work I photograph the fragile structures arrayed in straight lines that run towards the creek. Is this what Uplees was like? A cluster of ramshackle buildings, separated by rough paths and weeds and molehills? Not in 1916. This place feels posthumous, the ghost of a fragment of what an explosives plant might have looked like during the Great War. The factories at Uplees never reached this run-down state, moving as they did so rapidly from functioning wartime and post-war sites to abandoned tracts of grazing land, nothing left but immovable concrete sinking into soft alluvial soil.

I arrive in town along an ill-planned cycle path full of potholes and pointless barriers, past the house of Thomas Arden and onto Abbey Street. Faversham is not exactly teeming this morning, but as always its traffic is chaotic and nerve-racking, with too many cars passing through medieval streets, and over a tiny bridge across the creek, as though in flight from, or towards, some scene of crisis. The traffic thins out as I turn into the road towards Oare; here there are mostly HGVs bound for a supermarket depot opposite Bysing Wood. I cross Oare Creek and am soon beyond the village, back in open countryside. This is the route that workers must have taken on their way from Faversham, if they were not on the light railway, which ran nearby; the direction too that firefighters, physicians and panicked relatives struck out on the afternoon of the explosion; and the route followed by Major Cooper-Key a few days later as he made his way towards the scene of destruction. What strikes me now is just how much of the factory would have been visible to the Inspector of Explosives at certain corners in this road: the plant stretching flat before him as the road swerved north. Today these turns are bordered by huge brown fields, above which rise pylons carrying cables that crackle and hiss: the kind of sound that gets inside the brain.

This morning I am willing to tolerate the sinister intimacy of this noise and stand with my bike for a while in a gravelly road-side stopping place, because in the field on my right, atop a telegraph pole, a huge hawk has just settled itself and is regarding the raw land below. In fact for the next half-mile or so all I notice is the birds: crows perched on every fence post or pecking in the ploughed fields; a white cloud near the horizon, below the blades of the turbines on Sheppey, that must be made of brent geese, whorling near the Swale shore and turning their white bellies towards the mainland. And out where the road dips towards Uplees, in a garden where for years a gaggle of plastic ducks and geese has always stood: here, all this ornamental birdlife has gone, except for a single dirty white goose, propped now against a woodpile, with beak and half its head smashed off and a clean, empty, plastic interior exposed.

Uneven surfaces

My plan, half formed and too long put off while I have been looking elsewhere, in the land and in the library, is to approach from the Swale-side sea wall the place where building 833 once stood. A comparison between Cooper-Key's report of 1916, a few generations of Ordnance Survey maps and the satellite view from Google Maps has convinced me it is possible. The point lies a third of a mile south of the sea wall, in a stretch of marsh scored on all the maps by the thin lines of drainage ditches or dykes. Just inland of the sea-wall path runs a much wider ditch: it is this that has made the trek inland seem impossible in the past, when I was unsure of the exact place and of the narrower channels that surround it. But here on the OS map, confirmed by Google, is a route through regularly spaced earthworks and ruins. The inland ditches roughly grid this portion of the land, but there is or appears to be a narrow strip of marsh where they do not intersect but run parallel, and it seems you could walk the pathway or ridge between and turn sharply west to the spot in question. It looks to me like a ten-minute walk, maybe longer if the footing is soft or the ground more uneven than appears. I am quite sure it can be done, so I make for the gate into the marsh, dismounting to walk between the ruts and puddles of the unsurfaced path.

There is not a soul to be seen on the straight flat route across the marsh to the shore, nor in either direction along the sea wall. A red-brown sail is moving eastwards in the Swale, the craft itself hidden from view. The path ahead is not so wet as I'd thought, so I get back on the bike and proceed slowly to the end, through another gate and past the mysterious black pool and a new sign that warns of several hazards – there are black and yellow pictures of faceless figures slipping, sliding, careering over edges – and then on to the sea wall. The Swale is full of boats, including a couple of rusted hulks. The sail belongs to a Thames sailing barge: a flat-bottomed craft of a type common a century ago. A biplane is moving overhead, and then much further away the tiny dart and swelling white trail of a fighter jet.

Look to the left and all that familiar view is there again: the bridge to Sheppey, the power stations, container port and gas storage plant on the Isle of Grain, and beyond them more plumes of smoke or steam that must denote the other side of the Thames estuary, the petrochemical hinterland of coastal Essex. The path along the sea wall is mostly grass and mud, with here and there a stretch of broken concrete or brick that has been used to fill it. I elect to walk the bike westwards rather than risk a plunge down the bank into the ditch or onto the shore, where the incoming tide is sending regular lapping arcs towards the rocks and clumps of old concrete below me. Every hundred yards or so I stop and pull my phone out of my pocket to check my position. I am not yet past the ruin of the Cotton Powder Company's acid plant, which my research has told me makes up most of the fragments just inland of the sea wall. But I am already starting to suspect that I have been stupidly optimistic: much of this land is flooded, and the concrete foundations, platforms and orphaned steps in the grass are surrounded by bodies of mirror-still water, reflecting empty blue skies.

I have walked for twenty minutes along the sea wall when I reach the place I need to be, and it is quite impossible. Yes, there is something you might call a path running from here between two long stretches of ditch; but to get to the flat area that I need then to cross, I would first have to climb or slip through a barbed-wire fence, leaving the bike behind, and set off across land whose firmness I cannot guarantee: it looks decidedly soggy from here. And besides, I seem to have forgotten since last I was here that the farmhouses and cottages of Uplees are staring straight in my direction, thus quite possibly local landowners who may not take kindly to this figure in the landscape, trudging across their field boundaries to who knows where. How did I neglect to think of my comical exposure out here? There is nothing for it but to turn back along the sea wall and consider my options as I go. Our friends at Uplees House have alerted the farmers at the end of their road that I may come out here one day looking for the seat of the explosion, but caught up among all the documents I have amassed, and distracted by other excursions, I have stupidly failed to contact them. I am cursing aloud and looking only at the mud and stones at my feet when a pair of middle-aged men come tearing towards me on mountain bikes, sweating profusely and weaving about awkwardly, oblivious to my presence on the path; I am beginning to feel invisible or extraneous as I heave my bike down the grassy slope of the sea wall and narrowly avoid emulating one of those figures on the hazard sign I passed earlier.

Beware underwater obstacles

The straight track back to Uplees is blinding now, bordered on both sides by dykes and puddles and pond-sized expanses that the winter sun has turned to silver. There are swans drifting in places where I have walked in the past, launching themselves from among the ruins or struggling noisily out of the water onto wet grass. Uplees Farm is just minutes away from the old managers' houses; two fat dogs come bounding over when I swing open the gate, and the yard is full of hens and geese that go clattering away when I wheel my bike inside. I knock on the farmhouse door but there is no answer, so I wander about the yard for a few minutes, losing heart, before a woman emerges from an outbuilding – it has been renovated as self-catering accommodation – and says that yes, she is Heather Flood, the owner. I explain that I'm a friend of her near neighbours, looking for the site of the 1916 explosion, and I pull out my phone to show her where I think it ought to be. Her husband is not here, she says; he knows more about the disaster, but she is happy to walk me up to the spot, with her dogs.

The place is a ten-minute walk north-west of the farmhouse, past bits of machinery and a stand of Christmas trees, across a field with some stunted bushes and a few tell-tale fragments of concrete. I have spotted a couple of surprisingly upright ruins on Google Maps and again from the Swale shore, and Heather confirms it: there are some with walls still standing, though who knows for how long. Not too long ago she and her husband warned a farmer who was renting this part of the farm that one of these structures would likely collapse if he let his cattle continue to rub their backs against it – but he would not listen, and sure enough one day a big reinforced slab fell and killed three cows. As Heather is talking we arrive at a lushly grassed and very wet field, bordered by dykes. In the distance is a tall structure with four intact but badly degraded walls and no roof, to the left (that is, south) of it a pile of concrete wreckage that must have fallen decades ago, and nearest to us an astonishingly pristine red-brick building, portions of whose pitched roof are still in place. For a second I picture the factory managers, Bethell and Evetts, standing on this roof, emptying buckets of water onto the burning magazine. Can I be right? I have been aware that I need to be cautious here about identifying the ruins: the destroyed buildings were quickly rebuilt in 1916, and production carried on in this part of the complex. So the damage I am looking at has nothing to do with the explosion. Or does it? I consult my phone and a paper map and before I have thought better of it I am trudging then sloshing across the field, ankle-deep in cold water, as I approach a rough circle of small fragments of concrete with two larger T-shaped chunks at its centre. I start photographing them, looking about at the near-extant structures around me, hoping to confirm that this is indeed the point where 833 once stood.

It takes me a minute or two of gawping and kicking at the concrete to realize my mistake: not only was 833 made mostly of wood, but it vanished entirely, and even if a new building had been erected on the precise spot, surely some evidence would remain of that vast crater? I walk back towards Heather, apprehensive: I am sure I do not want to drag her to another field, though she and her dogs are very patient. Where is the hole, 135 feet across and 13.5 feet deep, that was measured by Cooper-Key and appears in the album of twenty-six photographs? Heather is sure: there is no crater on her land. Perhaps it was filled in. I start photographing the ruins around us, moving vaguely back towards our entrance to the field. I think we both notice at the same time a slight elevation of the land in that direction: a low ridge arcing in the south, enclosing only grass. Could this be some remnant of the crater? It looks like nothing: a natural hump in the land, the remnants of old excavation of a dyke, a rubbish dump covered over long ago. It is only later, looking again at Cooper-Key's report, laying it over the satellite image on my laptop screen, that I realize we have paused to stare at this landscape anomaly while standing in the dead centre of the blast area, where there is nothing at all to see except wet tussocks sticking out of the black water, a place where the path has sunk away and you have to hope that your next step will be on solid ground.

Sudden drop

The light, as I cycle back into Faversham, is like nothing I have ever seen, not round here, anyway. With the sun low behind me, the light seems to rise from the land itself, the whole territory glowing. I let my hands drop from the handlebars and pedal faster without my legs feeling the slightest resistance, as if the sunset might propel me out of the marshes and into town. Outside Oare, a driver has pulled over to talk to a couple of walkers, and for a moment I think they must all have stopped in amazement at this golden emanation of the landscape. But nobody seems to have noticed; I pass schoolchildren crossing Oare Creek, lorry drivers picking up speed as they turn out of the supermarket depot and head for the dual carriageway, creaking bicycles whose riders never look up from the road ahead – all oblivious. I feel like stopping them, pointing madly to the west, directing their gaze to the deep mirrored hue of the creek and the burnished fields, then shouting in their faces: *Haven't you seen?*

Seen what, exactly? A fire in the west? The marshes ablaze? The whole view from here to the Swale and beyond newly illumined by this strange light, so that everything presses on the eye with an odd alertness or precision? Or the fact that all of this is on the point of vanishing, that we are minutes away from the catastrophe of sunset, a pall being thrown over the land again? The moon is up over Faversham, contending feebly with the still raging sun. All day there has been a plume of white smoke on the horizon to the south of the town: some refuse fire at a farm or orchard, where exactly I cannot tell. But it is fading into the background now among housing estates and streets as the town takes over. Headlights are speeding in my direction, and soon all will be lost.

I think again of Dickens's Pip, shivering on the marshes at the Magwitching hour. The landscape has one final surprise in store before darkness falls. Out past Faversham, back on the creek-side cycle path that will take me to the road home, I stop and look back at the town, burning for the last time with light from the marshes: church steeples, warehouses, boats and brewery buildings black against the blaze. It seems to start as soon as the sun goes down: from the creek itself, its muddy tributaries, all the dykes and the low-lying fields, a thick white mist begins to rise. It seethes out of every puddle, every stand of rushes or reeds. (It is a 'mystical mist', according to *Arden of Faversham*, that rises south of the Swale.) In the narrow, half-flooded back roads by which I came this morning, the mist swirls out of ditches and off the farmland, hardly distinguishable from the pale stretches of plastic sheeting under which fruit is still being harvested at this late stage in the season. Soon my way is both dark and fogged, but I am startled by faceless figures on the road ahead, then voices all around: fruit pickers coming off the orchards at close of day, wearying their way back to farmyards and caravans. Evening traffic appears as I pass through the villages, and I cycle hard on the wider country roads towards Canterbury, then duck into Blean Woods to take the short cut home: I know the paths well, and the mud will not matter now. It is pitch black all around when I turn among the trees; there are owls just beyond my bike lamp's pool of light, nobody has been here for hours, and spiders' webs clutch at my face all the way.

Note on Sources

Major Aston Cooper-Key's report to the Home Secretary is held at the National Archives in London; other references to the April 1916 accident, and related explosives-factory events, are dispersed throughout Home Office and Cabinet records. The Fleur de Lis Museum in Faversham has amassed a good deal of material related to the history of gunpowder manufacture in the town and the accident at Uplees. John Breese's detailed research into the dead of 1916, and the medals awarded to some of the survivors, may be viewed at the museum. Oare Gunpowder Works Country Park provides a fascinating introduction to the industrial and wartime history. What follows is a short list of the most essential or suggestive published sources.

Bailey, Anthony, *A View of Delft: Vermeer Then and Now* (London: Pimlico, 2002).

Bloch, Howard, and Hill, Graham, *The Silvertown Explosion, London 1917* (Stroud: Tempus, 2003).

Cocroft, Wayne, *Dangerous Energy: The Archaeology of Gunpowder and Military Explosives Manufacture* (Swindon: English Heritage, 2000).

——, *Oare Gunpowder Works* (Faversham: Faversham Society, 1994).

Conrad, Joseph, *The Mirror of the Sea* (New York: Harper & Brothers, 1906).

Crozier, Ronald D., *Guns, Gunpowder and Saltpetre* (Faversham: Faversham Society, 1998).

Donne, Charles Edward, and Giraud, Francis F., *A Visitor's Guide to Faversham* (1876; Faversham: Faversham Society, 1988).

Hoban, Russell, *Riddley Walker* (London: Bloomsbury, 2012).

Hodgetts, E. A. Brayley, *The Rise and Progress of the British Explosives Industry* (London: Whittaker & Co., 1909).

Ingleton, Roy, *Kent Disasters* (Barnsley: Wharncliffe Books, 2010).

James, Henry, *English Hours* (London: Heinemann, 1905).

MacDonald, Lyn, *Somme* (London: Penguin, 1983).

Malins, Geoffrey H., *How I Filmed the War* (London: Herbert Jenkins, 1920).

Partington, J. R., *A History of Greek Fire and Gunpowder* (Baltimore, Md: Johns Hopkins University Press, 1999).

Percival, Arthur, 'The Great Explosion at Faversham, 2 April 1916', *Archaeologia Cantiana*, 100 (1985), 425–63.

Twist, Syd, *Syd Twist Remembers* (Faversham: Faversham Society, 1977).

Walker, Sally M., *Blizzard of Glass: The Halifax Explosion of 1917* (New York: Henry Holt, 2011).

Worthington, A. M., *A Study of Splashes* (London: Longmans, Green & Co., 1908).

Picture Credits

p. 7 The marshes at Uplees (author's photograph)

p. 9 Black water at Uplees (author's photograph)

p. 13 The sound mirrors at Dungeness (author's photograph)

p. 24 The ruin of a Second World War firing range in Blean Woods, Canterbury (author's photograph)

p. 29 The gunpowder works at Oare: incorporating mills (author's photograph)

p. 31 The gunpowder works at Oare: corning house (author's photograph)

p. 44 'Remains of building 862', in the album 'Accident No. 110. 1916' (The National Archives)

p. 45 'Remains of building 844', in the album 'Accident No. 110. 1916' (The National Archives)

p. 47 'Crater of building 833', in the album 'Accident No. 110. 1916' (The National Archives)

p. 119 'Factory Plan', in the album 'Accident No. 110. 1916' (The National Archives)

p. 135 Egbert van der Poel, *A View of Delft after the Explosion of 1654*, 1654 (The National Gallery)

p. 144 Cornelis Claesz van Wieringen, *The Explosion of the Spanish Flagship during the Battle of Gibraltar, 25 April 1607*, c. 1621 (Rijksmuseum, Amsterdam)

p. 154 'Plan of Explosion Showing Craters, Debris etc.' (The National Archives)

p. 176 'Permanent splashes left when a projectile has entered an armour-plate', in A. M. Worthington, *A Study of Splashes* (London: Longmans, Green and Co., 1908)

p. 194 The mass grave at Faversham cemetery (from a postcard produced by W. Hargrave, Faversham, 1916)

p. 204 'Looking into the depths of the tremendous crater of our mine fired at La Boiselle [*sic*] on the Somme' (stereoscopic photograph produced by Realistic Travels, no date; possibly taken by Charles Hilton DeWitt Girdwood)

p. 207 The mine under German front line position at Hawthorn Redoubt is fired ten minutes before the assault at Beaumont Hamel. First day of the Battle of the Somme, 1 July 1916. By Ernest Brooks (Imperial War Museum)

p. 228 View of the column of smoke raised by the Halifax Explosion, 6 December 1917 (anonymous photographer)

p. 238 Ruins of the Curtis and Harvey plant at Cliffe (author's photograph)

p. 242 Horse skull at the Curtis and Harvey plant at Cliffe (author's photograph)

p. 250 Grain Tower Battery at high tide (author's photograph)

Acknowledgements

Catherine and Justin Richardson first led me over the marshes at Uplees, near the place where the explosion occurred in 1916, and into the woods where the Oare Works had been. I promised them this book many years ago, and it is dedicated to their three children. I first read about the explosion in Arthur Percival's article of 1985, in the journal *Archaeologia Cantiana*. I could not have begun to understand the event or its context without his work as a historian and as co-founder of the Faversham Society, and it was with great sadness, just hours after I had written my last pages, that I learned he had died in November 2014.

My initial research was made possible by a Fellowship in the Creative and Performing Arts from the Arts and Humanities Research Council, which I held at the University of Kent from 2008 to 2011. I was guided in my approach to the landscape and the central event by the work of John Breese at the Faversham Society, and by the archaeological research of Wayne Cocroft, whose writings on the history of explosives manufacture in Britain have been invaluable. Many thanks to the staff of the Fleur de Lis Heritage Centre and Chart Gunpowder Mills in Faversham, and the Visitor Centre at Oare Gunpowder Works Country Park. At Uplees Farm, where I turned up unannounced, Heather Flood was kind enough to take me to the spot where the explosion happened – or thereabouts.

Thanks also to Amy Winchester, the RSPB warden at Blean Woods, for a last-minute correction.

Portions of the book, on the 1916 disaster and on paintings of explosions, were published in *Cabinet* magazine. A version of the passage on pond skaters appeared in *The Atlas of Kent*, a volume of writings and artworks published as part of the Kent Cultural Baton, a project funded by Kent County Council and the Arts Council. A few sections, on the explosion and excursions into other parts of Kent, appeared in the *Dublin Review*. I first wrote about Marcel Duchamp's visit to Herne Bay in artist Jeremy Millar's book *Zugzwang (almost complete)*, and again in the *London Review of Books*. A version of the section on Queen Victoria and the acoustic shadow was published in *Arc*, the student magazine of the Royal College of Art. Many thanks to the editors of all those publications, and to Patrick Wright for an invitation to test some of the writing with his students and colleagues at King's College London.

Thanks to all at Penguin, and especially to my editor, Brendan Barrington, for his customary insight and exceptional patience. And to my agent, Peter Straus.

I could not have written this book, or anything at all, without the love and wisdom of Felicity Dunworth.

He just wanted a decent book to read ...

Not too much to ask, is it? It was in 1935 when Allen Lane, Managing Director of Bodley Head Publishers, stood on a platform at Exeter railway station looking for something good to read on his journey back to London. His choice was limited to popular magazines and poor-quality paperbacks – the same choice faced every day by the vast majority of readers, few of whom could afford hardbacks. Lane's disappointment and subsequent anger at the range of books generally available led him to found a company – and change the world.

'We believed in the existence in this country of a vast reading public for intelligent books at a low price, and staked everything on it'
Sir Allen Lane, 1902–1970, founder of Penguin Books

The quality paperback had arrived – and not just in bookshops. Lane was adamant that his Penguins should appear in chain stores and tobacconists, and should cost no more than a packet of cigarettes.

Reading habits (and cigarette prices) have changed since 1935, but Penguin still believes in publishing the best books for everybody to enjoy. We still believe that good design costs no more than bad design, and we still believe that quality books published passionately and responsibly make the world a better place.

So wherever you see the little bird – whether it's on a piece of prize-winning literary fiction or a celebrity autobiography, political tour de force or historical masterpiece, a serial-killer thriller, reference book, world classic or a piece of pure escapism – you can bet that it represents the very best that the genre has to offer.

Whatever you like to read – trust Penguin.